Moisture of the Earth

TITLES IN THE SERIES:

The Syntax of Class: Writing Inequality in Nineteenth-Century America
Amy Schrager Lang

Vanishing Moments: Class and American Culture
Eric Schocket

Let Me Live
Angelo Herndon

Workin' on the Chain Gang: Shaking Off the Dead Hand of History
Walter Mosley

Commerce in Color: Race, Consumer Culture, and American Literature, 1893–1933
James C. Davis

You Work Tomorrow: An Anthology of American Labor Poetry, 1929–41
Edited by John Marsh

Chicano Novels and the Politics of Form: Race, Class, and Reification
Marcial González

Moisture of the Earth: Mary Robinson, Civil Rights and Textile Union Activist
Edited by Fran Leeper Buss

Moisture of the Earth

❧ ❧ ❧   ❧ ❧ ❧

Mary Robinson

Civil Rights and Textile Union Activist

An Oral History
Compiled and Edited by
Fran Leeper Buss

The University of Michigan Press • *Ann Arbor*

Published in the United States of America by
The University of Michigan Press
Manufactured in the United States of America
♾ Printed on acid-free paper

2012   2011   2010   2009   4   3   2   1

A CIP catalog record for this book is available from the British Library.

Library of Congress Cataloging-in-Publication Data

Buss, Fran Leeper, 1942–
    Moisture of the earth : Mary Robinson, civil rights and textile
union activist : an oral history / compiled and edited by Fran
Leeper Buss.
        p.   cm.
    Includes bibliographical references.
    ISBN-13: 978-0-472-09587-2 (cloth : alk. paper)
    ISBN-10: 0-472-09587-0 (cloth : alk. paper)
    ISBN-13: 978-0-472-06587-5 (pbk. : alk. paper)
    ISBN-10: 0-472-06587-4 (pbk. : alk. paper)
    1. Robinson, Mary, 1943–   2. African American women civil rights
workers—Biography.   3. Civil rights workers—United States—
Biography.   4. Women textile workers—United States—Biography.
5. Textile workers—United States—Biography.   I. Title.
E185.97.R663B87   2009
323.092—dc22   2008033535
[B]

To our daughters,

Tracy, Lisa, and Kimberly,

and our granddaughters

Contents

Preface

I MET MARY ROBINSON in 1980 while working on an oral history collection titled *Dignity: Lower Income Women Tell of Their Lives and Struggles*. Mary was among the women whose stories are included in that collection, which shed light on issues of race, class, and gender in this country, as well as the workings of the civil rights and textile union movements to which Mary has dedicated so much of her life. Our conversations did not end with the publication of *Dignity*, however. This book, based on a fifteen-hundred-page transcript covering twenty-three years of interviews with Mary, continues that earlier work.

Oral historians must make some editing decisions. In order to tell as much of Mary's story as space allows, I reluctantly cut out much of the re-iteration that gives the story its rhythm. I also clarified pronouns and added explanatory phrases. Mary changed the names and some identifying information of many of the minor characters but kept the names of her family members, other people we hope to honor, and those individuals who are well known and easily identified. Although Mary related her life history to me over more than twenty years, in order to capture the flavor of a continuous narrative, we present her story here as if she were telling it to me in the present. This is probably the most significant violation of the original texts.

The relationship between the life and perspectives of the compiler of the oral history and the subject of the oral history is so complex, especially when the two are from different racial backgrounds, that it was only with the active assistance of Mary that I was able to write this book. In a sense the microphone at times was turned around, and Mary interviewed me. The entire work is a shared construction. For example, the transcripts refer seventy-eight times to Mary's mother's work when Mary was a child, and I tried to choose among these references and weave them into some sort of chronological narrative. Likewise, in the transcripts Mary refers seventeen times to the murders of black prisoners by white sheriffs. The choices for inclusion here were somewhat intuitive, depending on the emotion with which Mary relayed the story to me, the frequency with which she referred to it, and its location in the center or the periphery of each account.

Finally, to keep the book at a workable length, I eliminated most of the questions I put to Mary over the years. Because of all of these interventions, I have tried to give a sense of our working style in the introduction and epilogue. The transcripts from the 1980 interviews are in the Schlesinger Library on the History of Women at the Radcliffe Institute for Advanced Study. The more recent ones are in my personal library in Tucson, Arizona, but are available to scholars, so they can review the data directly.[1]

This book is many things. It is an edited oral history based on audiotapes of my conversations with Mary, including those from our first collaboration in 1980. It is also a story about location and place, meaning and community, violence and morality, struggles for the land that people work, and an ultimate refusal to accept dispossession. To quote the historian Anne McClintock: "It is a device against oblivion, a strategy for survival."[2] As the Pulitzer prize–winning writer Toni Morrison wrote in Beloved, it is about the battle not only to love small (the mist, a woodpecker, a blade of grass) but also to love large (a partner, a child, one's work, the land).[3] Mary's experiences tell a story of the unyielding moral universe that gave the uneducated and dispossessed women in her community the courage and stamina to become the backbone of the Montgomery bus boycott in 1955. This sense of unwavering moral strength, as Mary describes it, sustained these women as they became key actors in insurgent Southern labor movements. Finally, Mary shares with us a life guided by a profound religious vision, based on the moral landscape of her childhood—a vision that places her in a long tradition of other African American, Christian activist-mystics.[4]

Acknowledgments

CREATING THIS WORK has been one of the most profound experiences of our lives. We thank the Coordinating Council on Women in History— Catherine Prelinger Scholarship Prize for their first inaugural award in 1998 that gave basic financial support for our book. We also want to thank the Amazon Foundation for Women for their funding as well as the Southwest Research Institute for Research on Women at the University of Arizona for its ongoing institutional support.

Our editor at the University of Michigan Press, LeAnn Fields, has believed in this work for many years and has expertly guided its progress. She has also been a good friend. The members of Fran's writing group— Marge Pellegrino, Gerald Barton, Kay Sather, and Lynne Weinberg— have been enthusiastic colleagues. Penny Waterstone and Karen Anderson gave us intellectual assistance. We thank Maria Elena Lucas for her inspiration.

Although we dedicate this book to our daughters and granddaughters, we also want to acknowledge our sons and grandsons. Watching them become compassionate, loving men and boys has been a joy for each of us. The love of Fran's husband, David, has been a constant presence through the years. We cannot imagine this book having been created without him. There are also many people we need to thank in Alabama. Mary's relatives and neighbors took Fran into their lives. Civil rights workers, textile mill workers, and union crusaders opened their doors to us. Strangers answered our questions when they learned of our search. We thank all of those people.

Prologue

*We has a right to the land where we are located. For why? I
tell you. Our wives, our children, our husbands, has been sold
over and over again to purchase the lands we now locates
upon; for that reason we have a divine right to the land.*

—Freedman Bayley Wyat

MARY ROBINSON AND I sat on a stuffed couch, while her aunt, ninety-
year-old Rebecca Freeman, rested in a nearby rocking chair. We had
gathered on the country porch of Mary's sister, Ann Lois. Ann Lois, still
lovely despite being disabled by arthritis, rocked back and forth in
rhythm to Mary's speech. A fan barely moved the air that felt dense with
coming rain, while an aged brown dog panted on the cement floor. In a
corner an old pop machine groaned. Mary talked while Mrs. Freeman
and Ann Lois listened, nodding their heads: "Oh yes, yes she did. Lord
have mercy."

"I go back now and I look at the land—Aunt Becky's place, the sixty-
three acres Daddy used to farm, the hills, the trees," Mary said. "New
owners came, then swooped our past off the earth. They tore down our
house, wiped up our poor little childhood, and threw it away. Now they
got two three-hundred-thousand-dollar houses sitting where we loved
and worked and bled."

"Yes, that's what happened," the others echoed.

"The new owners say, 'Anytime y'all ever want to come and look
around, you're welcome,' but nothing looks familiar no more. The barn,

the smokehouse, our place has vanished. Even the dust has gone from beneath our feet. But I remember way, way back. I remember the dirt of our yard, our little house, and Mama."

Ann Lois rocked and listened.

"One time when I was real little," Mary continued, "we heard that five women prisoners broke out from a women's prison about thirty miles from where we was living. The sun was almost down that night, but we could still discern things, and when I looked outside the house, I saw the women prisoners walking up our road. They was white womens, wearing gray-looking prison dresses."

"Yes, they was. They was coming."

"Back then, all black folkses kept their yard as smooth dirt, with no grass. The womens swept it with a broom once a week. Mama was sweeping when she looked up and saw the prisoners. The womens walked on up to our yard and over to Mama. Mama nodded her head at them. Us six kids stood in the doorway of our little house on stilts and stared. One of the womens said, 'We need some food and some clothes. Do y'all have any? We've traveled a long way.'

"Mama answered, 'I ain't got no clothes, the only thing I got is some peas, but you're welcome to them. Let me finish sweeping this spot, then come on in.' That's what happened." Mary paused and swatted at a fly with her hand. The wind with the smell of rain blew in the trees surrounding the porch.

"So Mama finished sweeping, set the broom against the house, and led them prisoners inside. 'Y'all sit down now, and I'll have the peas warm in just a minute.' Then she fed them, just as good as we had.

"All at once my daddy's shadow stood in the door, and he stepped inside. He knowed exactly who they was. They was sitting there, eating. Them prisoners looked at Daddy.

"'Sarah!' Daddy said.

"'What?'

"'What you doing?'

"'What do it *look* like I'm doing?'

"'Do you know who they is?'

"'Yeah, I know who they is. They them prisoners that broke loose.' She said it just like it was an everyday thing. My daddy was short and bald headed, and he just stood in the doorway staring at them like he didn't know what to do."

Ann Lois and Mrs. Freeman chuckled. "Yes, he stood there."

"It was getting dark," Mary continued, "and we didn't have nothing but a lamp light, so the lamp was making shadows outside the doorway. One of the womens spoke to Daddy. 'We not gonna hurt y'all. We're not gonna do nothing. We just want something to eat.'

"So Daddy said, 'Ain't they looking for y'all?'

" 'Yeah.' So they finished eating, and Mama gave them what was left. 'We sure thank you,' they said and hurried up the road.

"About an hour later, we heard tracking dogs, sheriff's dogs, in the distance. They was following the women's smell. Lester Holley, the sheriff, was chasing them. Young as I was, I already knowed about Lester Holley's violence."

"Yes, he be vicious," Mrs. Freeman added.

" 'What you feed them prisoners for?' Daddy asked Mama. 'Now the sheriff'll know they was here.' The sheriff had a little truck with a cage on the back of it where they'd haul the tracking dogs and where'd they throw prisoners when they finally got them. Whenever you saw this truck, you knowed some prisoners was out somewhere, running. Now the dogs ran in front of the truck, barking, and they ran up our doorstep, snarling and baring their teeth and scaring me to death. Out past the dogs, this little old truck pulled over, and these white mens got out. The sheriff be tall and skinny, with a wide-brimmed hat.

"He asked Daddy and Mama, 'You see white womens pass by here?'

"Daddy said, 'Yeah.' You couldn't lie to Lester Holley. Black folkses believed he might beat you to death. 'Yeah, we seen them.'

" 'Where'd they go?'

" 'On up the road.'

" 'What they want?'

"Mama answered. 'They was hungry, so I fed them.'

"The sheriff looked around our cabin, nodded, and left. Afterwards, Daddy said to Mama, 'You shouldn't have given them food.'

"Mama answered real firm, 'They was hungry.'

"Sheriff Holley caught the womens, but what happened shows the type of person my mama was. And Aunt Rebecca too. She was just like Mama. I used to watch them all the time. Mama was constantly trying to give somebody something else, as if she was a maid of Howard Hughes. If you gave her opposition to it, she'd just say, 'If God blessed you, then you ought to try to bless somebody else. God let me grow them peas.'

"See, that earth out there held Mama and her peas; the boards of our house had her handprints all about them; and her feet left imprints in front of the stove. None of it, none, was no stranger's to take."

Introduction

Around us the history of the land has centered for thrice a
hundred years. . . . Actively we have woven ourselves with the
very warp and woof of this nation. . . . Would America have
been America without her Negro people?
    —W. E. B. Du Bois, *The Souls of Black Folk,* 1903

OVER TWENTY-THREE YEARS Mary Robinson has told the stories that
have become this book. Often in front of an audience—her sisters,
cousins, children, and friends—and sometimes with me as a listener. Her
storytelling took on features of a call-and-response, a basic style of the
African American oral tradition. Mary's storytelling has been inter-
mingled with our responses, exclamations, laughter, and nods of ap-
proval or empathy. Often these interactions took on the rhythm of a ser-
mon, ending with a moral interpretation by Mary of its contents.[1]

Born on November 26, 1943, Mary was a child of African American
sharecroppers in rural east-central Alabama, on the edge of what geog-
raphers have called the "plantation counties." The sharecropping system
was an exploitative form of farming in which poorer black families did
the work for wealthier white farmers for a share of the crop in return. A
middle child in a loving family with eight surviving children, Mary
worked long hours in the cotton fields alongside her parents and siblings, beginning at age three. Throughout her childhood, she carefully
observed the injustices and eccentricities of her rural neighborhood.
Her parents' generation of black southerners had learned that survival

depended on outward compliance within the larger white power structure and subtle subversion, lessons they tried to teach their children.
Mary suspects that her own father had worked in secret with the National
Association for the Advancement of Colored People (NAACP), but to
protect his family, he locked these records away in a trunk that was never
opened.

But for Mary's generation it was different. A new wave of social and
political protest was growing among young African Americans. In 1955,
at age twelve, Mary and other curious classmates traveled to Montgomery to witness the historic bus boycott, intended to oppose the city's
policy of segregation on its public transit system. After high school graduation, at sixteen, she left the fields to marry a soldier, James Robinson.
She went on to join the largest Selma to Montgomery march in 1965, to
campaign for the rights of black voters, and to integrate a rural restaurant. Mary's inner strength and innate sense of justice sustained her
throughout her tumultuous marriage, as she raised four children while
enduring spousal abuse. For years she wrestled with the ideals of patriar-
chal obedience that she had been taught as a child; ultimately the marriage ended.

Mary's most active and personally fulfilling work in the civil rights
movement began when in 1966 she helped to integrate the textile mills
in nearby Montgomery. She was one of the first mill workers to join the
Amalgamated Clothing and Textile Workers Union (ACTWU) when it
began to organize throughout the South. Beginning in 1976, Mary
worked relentlessly to recruit members; she bravely testified during trials
and court hearings; and she campaigned tirelessly, both on her own and
in the media, for support of the consumer boycott of the textile company J. P. Stevens. Her efforts helped to expose the oppressive conditions
throughout Stevens's textile plants, forcing corporate and financial institutions to acknowledge their complicity and demand that the company accept public responsibility.

Today Mary continues to struggle for the rights of women and other
poor people of all ages and ethnicities, especially those who feel silenced
by fear and discrimination. As a community activist, she continues to research the history of her people; she organizes her fellow school bus
drivers; and she spreads her message of enthusiasm, hope, and sacred
expectation. Mary believes that God has put her on earth "for the underdog, for the people that can't fight for themselves. God gives me the
ability." She has said: "He knows I'm not one of those who will sit by and

let somebody else be run over. So I raise all kinds of hell and cause all kinds of problems."

Mary's story helps expand our understanding of African American resistance movements throughout the twentieth century.[2] In a description of her childhood community, Mary makes a claim to the space where poor black people toiled with no legal rights to the land. In chapters 1 through 9 she then maps out a neighborhood in which nature itself recorded the moral struggle between good and evil, maintaining its own history and system of justice—a belief system that was ultimately transplanted to the religious and moral convictions that underlay the civil rights and subsequent social and political resistance movements. The story of her early involvement with the civil rights movement is told in chapter 10. Next, in chapters 11 through 14, Mary carries forward the belief in the righteousness of the struggle for social justice to her participation in the textile union movement. She adds a redemptive religious vision that locates a final claim for the poor and the meek that supersedes earthly claims on space. This final story, revealed in chapter 16, is told in metaphor, squarely locating Mary in the tradition of other African American, Christian activist-mystics, such as Sojourner Truth and Fannie Lou Hamer.[3]

All of these experiences provide a document of resistance. In this introduction, with Mary's help, I have situated her story in its geographical and historical location, describing the existing economic, racial, and gender structures. I also provide a brief history of African American religious traditions and their relationship to resistance. Equally important is the story of African American women's involvement in the civil rights and textile union movements. The main body of this book—the story of Mary's life in her own words—includes the stories of resistance of many other women and of the community in which she has lived.

The epilogue tells the story of our joint research on the area surrounding Elmore County, Alabama. Here we place Mary's record in the long history of insurgency that began before she was born and will continue long after her residence there. Mary believes she would not have survived to narrate her story if those who had come before her had not fought for their lives, for the lives of their children, and for their personal dignity. Mary, in turn, hopes to pass the movement on to those who follow. Thus this story of resistance is part of an ongoing stream in history.[4]

In this final section Mary and I explore several questions: How do individual lives fit within overall movements of protest? Why do people respond to the call to join in social justice campaigns differently at different times in their lives? What possibilities lie dormant within individuals, waiting for the right challenge to inspire action? Why did Mary and her generation, while they were growing up, not hear stories of radical acts of rebellion that had taken place in or near their home community? Finally, when adults in the community did relate stories of resistance, why did they so often phrase them as parables?[5]

Mary's story provides a female perspective to that of the influential book *All God's Dangers: The Life of Nate Shaw,* compiled and edited by Theodore Rosengarten in 1974. *All God's Dangers* went on to win the National Book Award and to influence both oral history methodology and an understanding of the sharecropping South. Nate Shaw, a contemporary of Mary's grandmother, Salena Damous, has since been identified as Ned Cobb. Born in March 1885 to parents who had been slaves in a county neighboring that of Mary's childhood, Cobb and his family toiled as sharecroppers. Cobb himself fought briefly for the Share Croppers Union during the Great Depression. He was consequently imprisoned for twelve years. Part of that prison time was spent in Mary's community, also the base of the white posse that was eventually sent to hunt down his fellow union members. In the epilogue Mary and I uncover additional information about Cobb's union.

On the afternoon of Rebecca Freeman's ninetieth birthday, Mary, Mrs. Freeman, and I entered the gates of the historically white-only cemetery that overlooks the cotton fields in which Mary's family labored. Most of the white southerners who had been buried there decades before would have never considered lying forever in a resting place that included African Americans.[6] As far as Mary and I know, the small cemeteries for Mary's parents' generation are still kept separate. But the people buried in this cemetery had not reckoned on Mary. At the time many whites had felt so sure about the inferiority of African Americans that they would have barely noticed Mary as a child. Who was she but a shadow to their world? Someone to help with the chores or make jokes about.

On that hot afternoon at the cemetery with its one tree, birds singing, and grasshoppers jumping in front of our feet, I held a tape recorder as we walked from grave to grave. Mrs. Freeman served as a chorus full of laughter that began in her face and moved down her body. Mary acted out the story of each deceased person's life as she had viewed it as a child. We wrote down dates of births and deaths, which we would later use as the basis of elaborate family trees within which Mary anchored her memories. To be sure, Mary's sharp recollections of her childhood observations represent the inherent dangers a ruling class faces when it conceives of a whole category of people as invisible.[7]

We had a wonderful day. Mrs. Freeman and I laughed at Mary's performance until we could barely stand. Following our visit to the white cemetery, we went to the two cemeteries serving African Americans. Again, Mary walked from grave to grave, telling stories. I became confused by names and nicknames and half cousins. We developed complex genealogies and then began to map out the cabins and houses of Mary's childhood. We stopped for some time over the grave of Mary's mother, Sarah Freeman, with its gray marker and plastic flowers. Later, Mary and I physically charted specific locations in the approximately one and a half square miles of rural Elmore County, where she had grown to young adulthood. The once vibrant, rural African American community, with its surrounding natural features that had nurtured Mary so well as a child, was known to its residents by the names of its two black churches: Good Hope and New Style. However, the community was not recorded on any official road map and was thus erased by the dominant white establishment.

Long ago, slave labor had cleared the original pineland forest in Elmore County, but stands of long- and short-needled pine, interspersed with oak, gum, chestnut, poplar, maple, and a thick undergrowth, still stand or have regrown as less land was used to grow cotton. When Mary was a girl, most of this cleared land was still used for the principal crop of the Southland: cotton. The nearest large plantation, somewhat of the style imagined in *Gone with the Wind*, was located to the south and west of Wetumpka, the county seat.

Mary's neighborhood, a few miles north of Wetumpka, consisted of farms owned, with a few exceptions, by white landlord farmers. During the beginning of the twentieth century, this land was worked by black sharecropping families, but because of mass migration of African Americans to the North and to southern cities and the simultaneous mechanization of the cotton industry during the 1920s to the 1940s, Elmore County's traditional cotton economy and social system was breathing its last gasps by Mary's childhood in the 1940s and 1950s.[8] Still, the white farmers—many so poor themselves they used outhouses—had several even more impoverished black families working for them. These African

American families lived in little two- or three-room shotgun-style cabins that were owned by the white farmers and scattered the equivalent of perhaps two or three city blocks from each other.

The remnants of the unpainted cabins stand isolated in the fields today. They serve now as homes to birds, vines, and insects as the earth takes the refuge for which the sharecroppers paid so dearly. Often only stone chimneys, a broken dish, a child's shoe, a pear tree, a few flowers, or a piece of cherished linoleum remain. At best, the cabins had provided the large, hardworking families a partial independence from the white owners. Unlike slave quarters, these cabins were not designed to keep humans under the master's constant view. Also still standing today are a number of the more substantial homes that served white owners, lived in by the elderly whites or rented to tenants. These houses have often benefited by modern siding and remodeling and have plaster figurines, flowers, vegetable gardens, and porch swings. Most of the land is now used by upper-middle-class white commuters or white retirees who have luxury houses on several acres. Many of these property owners have bulldozed hills and dammed creeks for fish ponds.

Two small country stores—one owned by the white sheriff, the other by another white man—served Mary's community during her childhood. Typically the white farm owner decided which store should get the black sharecropper's business. Sometime in 1945 or 1946, without any assistance from the state, the African American community, desperately desiring education for their elementary-age children, constructed a small, cement-block, blacks-only school. Before that black children in this section of the county received no schooling, a policy deliberately designed by the white power structure to keep African Americans as an illiterate, cheap labor source.[9] Mary's own mother had been unable to sign her wedding license, and she never learned to read.

The small city of Wetumpka, where Mary's family bought school clothes and Mary went to high school, still serves as the county seat of Elmore County. It runs along the brown, slow-moving Coosa River, near its juncture with the Tallapoosa River in east-central Alabama. The oldest of the downtown buildings were built before 1855, and the irregular streets wind through the usually quiet old southern town and around the low bluffs that indicate the slight beginnings of the Appalachian foothills.[10] When Mary was a girl, Wetumpka's handful of adjacent African American businesses included a café, a barber shop, a beauty shop, and two funeral parlors. The largest black church in town, the First Baptist, was situated near the black high school. Despite the African American community's pride in the high school, white city fathers called it the Elmore County Training School in an effort to associate it with vocational training—in contrast to the white high school's supposedly superior emphasis on academics.

Mary described a vivid image from her childhood. In this memory her mother is standing outside, perhaps hanging up clothes, and looking across the creek to the next sharecropper dwelling, where a single woman, Miss Velchie, lives with her children and works in her yard. The women pause for a moment in their continuous labor, and Mary's mother calls across the cotton fields and the creek, setting off an echo: "Hey, Velchie, how ya doin'?" The echo replies: "Hey, Velchie, how ya doin'?" Mary sees her mother, perhaps with a baby on her hip, talking to Miss Velchie. The broom with which Mary's mother had been sweeping the dirt yard rests against the cabin for a few brief moments, and then, as Mary watches, the women pick up again with their hard, unpaid, reproductive labor—domestic toil that ensures the subsistence survival of another generation of workers.[11]

The never-ending work of Mary's mother and other women of this era has a long history. As early as 1619, slave traders first ripped Africans from the continent of their birth and brought them to North America, to provide the plantation labor that contributed to the industrial wealth that eventually spread throughout the United States and Europe. At first these slaves worked the East Coast, but gradually southern coastal regions lost their soil fertility, and European Americans, with dreams of becoming wealthy planters, drove American Indians from a region of fertile prairie soil that expanded across central Alabama from Georgia to Mississippi. Then white would-be planters marched chains of slaves into the area. Mary believes some of her ancestors came to Alabama from the Carolinas in a similar way.

At the end of the Civil War newly emancipated slave families dreamed of small farms of their own, where they could live in peace, but white planters starved and terrorized these freed black workers, attempting to coerce them into slavelike work gangs and to compel them to live near the planters in former slave quarters. Some African American families, sacrificing and struggling for their independent farms, succeeded for a while, but most were eventually "driven from their land by intimidation, violence, and even murder." In an eighteen-month investigation culminating in 2001, the Associated Press documented the stealing of that black-owned land, which is now overwhelmingly "owned by whites or corporations."[12] Still, these ex-slaves continued to resist, and they eventually compelled white owners to enter a compromise—sharecropping: the social structure into which Mary was born.[13]

In the sharecropping system African American families gained the right to live in cabins away from the owners and to work together as a family group, thus offering each other a measure of protection from white physical and sexual violence. But these farm laborers paid a heavy price. Landlords forced sharecroppers to borrow money, materials, and the use of a cabin at high interest at the beginning of each season. The entire African American family worked from sunup to sundown in the fields, only to receive a "share," often a third or a half, of the harvest at the end of the season. Frequently the landlords declared that the family had earned no profit during the year and thus claimed the family to be further in debt than when the year had begun. Often the sharecropping family gained nothing but bare subsistence for their year's labor and was further bound to a system of unpaid labor.[14] Many times this resulted in white landlords profiting from violence perpetrated against children. Mary's beloved sister Shane, for example, hated working in the cotton fields, but her father felt compelled by the system to force her to do a long day's labor. Although the other children could be talked into working in the fields, Mary's father whipped Shane into compliance.

Black women played a pivotal role in ensuring family survival under this system: laboring in a home without running water, working in the fields alongside their husbands and children, taking on additional work for whites, and giving birth regularly so the family had enough workers. Women also embodied the complex system of neighboring: they cared for or adopted orphaned children, they tended the sick and the pregnant, and they taught new mothers necessary skills. Women also worked in an informal economy: bartering household goods, sharing their scraps of cloth to create new quilts, and organizing fish fries to raise money.[15] While doing all this work, African American women struggled to teach their own children the rules of the complex racial caste system. Mistakes could prove deadly.[16]

Single black women were vulnerable in a family economy that relied on a husband's or a son's contribution, especially in farming. Farm owners expected to negotiate with men; more than one adult was needed for heavy farm labor; and it was difficult to perform outdoor farm chores and inside domestic labor simultaneously, especially with young children in tow who were in constant danger. Cynthia Williams, an African American midwife in Georgia who was born in 1921, described the overwhelming labor her widowed mother undertook to raise her six children alone on the edge of town. According to Mrs. Williams, her mother "worked herself almost crazy." She worked five days on a farm; cooked in a tearoom on the weekends; and did many loads of laundry each week for white families, carrying buckets of water and washing outside. In the summers she took the family out to do daily farm labor, picking cotton or shaking peas. The children were always under her supervision, because she did not like most of the work children would get doing errands and babysitting. She felt these jobs put the children under the direct command of whites who might whip them. "We came up pretty [hard]," Cynthia recalled. "But we came up with a mother that really wanted her children."

One of her brothers had convulsions and could not work on the farm, however, even under his mother's direction. Cynthia remembers: "So, one man she was picking cotton for, he told her, he says, 'I ain't gonna haul that boy [to the fields] because he doesn't do anything no way, and you don't make him do anything.' He said, 'So I ain't gonna hire him.' My mother was doing so much more work than the others that he was hiring. She says, 'Well, okay, if you can't carry him, you can't carry me. Because I have to see about him.' When he [the farmer] finally found out he wasn't getting much work done, he [told] her he didn't care how little work he [her son] did. 'You just come on back, 'cause you doing twice as much as another person anyway.'" Her mother's life goal, Cynthia says, was for no one to whip her children.[17]

Before World War I, large numbers of black workers were forced to continue toiling away on these poor-paying, labor-intensive plantations, despite their deep desire for better conditions.[18] Among the reasons for this were southern paternalism (the idea that wealthy whites knew what was best for poor whites and blacks), white planters' threats of inducing starvation among their black workers, widespread "violence and social warfare" inflicted upon many African American males (especially lynching), and a lack of alternative employment for African Americans. When European immigration to the northern United States ceased during World War I, however, some employment opportunities opened for African Americans.[19] Many of Mary's relatives joined the enthusiastic outmigration from the South to the North at this time.[20]

The coming of World War II, about a year before Mary was born, brought dramatic changes to the plantation region, as many black workers flocked to new opportunities in the military, so-called war work, or to jobs that had been vacated by whites. "By 1945," according to political scientist and historian Daniel Kryder, "one million African Americans had joined the armed forces and another million had moved from the southern countryside into cities across the nation." Thus the number working in agriculture and domestic service "dropped dramatically," and those remaining could negotiate higher wages.[21] In turn, white planters and landlords finally invested in labor-saving machinery and shifted away from cotton production. Eventually they ejected the remaining blacks from white-owned land. Many African Americans enthusiastically left or escaped the sharecropping system, but others were too illiterate or too old to find other work.[22] Clinging to the margins of economic life, they lived as a dispossessed people on the outskirts of southern cities or in rural neighborhoods like that of Elmore County.

> I was big enough and old enough to stretch my eyes at conditions
> and abominate what I seed.
>
> —Nate Shaw [Ned Cobb], 1974

In the racially segregated Jim Crow South, whites and blacks coexisted within fiercely enforced, racially based caste-like, hierarchical categories—categories so rigid that nearly every square foot was fraught with racial, sexual, and economic meaning and involved spatial rules of conduct.[23] When African American and white children played together at a white-owned house, for example, the black children had to go to the back door before they could meet up with the white children inside. African Americans who went to movies had to sit in the balconies.

Mrs. Williams described to me the humiliation of her younger sister when Mrs. Williams had taken her to a local dime store: "We were in the store on Saturday, no work that day, and she held my hand. She said she wanted to pee-pee, so 'Oh Lord, don't ask me that. I don't know where to take you today.' And it was going all down her little legs before I could get to the car. . . . I didn't want their [her younger siblings] feelings hurt by things like that. . . . But I know a little boy, maybe he didn't read, and he didn't know 'Black' and 'White.' He was up drinking water here, and one of the store clerks just had a fit on it. 'You know better than to be drinking that! Don't you see that sign says "White," and that says "Black"? You can drink water over there.' And he, well, when she stopped him, he just didn't drink anymore . . . he just didn't drink. . . . He said, 'I don't want none.'"[24]

There are more fatal examples of these racial lines being crossed, to be sure. Mary and her sisters remember one incident when outraged friends of a white woman threatened an African American woman who had had sex, probably coerced, with the white woman's husband. The African American woman fled the county by nightfall and never returned to her family. American studies scholar Stephen J. Whitfield has speculated that in August 1955, in nearby Mississippi, black Chicago-bred Emmett Till was lynched primarily because of how he had spoken to a white woman but partially because his wallet had contained a picture of a white girl.[25]

Institutions also were segregated by race. For example, the community maintained separate schools, churches, hospitals, restaurants, and burial grounds for both its white citizens and its black citizens. The inequality and separation included neighborhoods, types of jobs, and levels of social welfare. When African Americans got telephones in Elmore County, for example, they were assigned separate party lines from those of European Americans (these were telephone lines shared by three or four families).[26] When nearby Montgomery was forced to integrate its swimming pools as a result of the victories of the civil rights movement, town leaders paved the pools over with cement, rather than allow blacks to use them.

Despite these often vicious restrictions made on blacks' freedom of movement, I believe the African American residents of Mary's childhood community claimed the land on a moral level—an interesting claim, given that few of them owned the land they worked. Many blacks endowed the natural features in their landscape with spiritual meaning. That is, elements of the land they loved served as symbols for the body and the divine, for morality and remembrance. Symbols of history and justice, these places stood rooted in God's nature itself. As the leaves changed colors on the trees, Mary explained, so would ultimate control over the earth. Innocent blood spilled on the earth would rise to the surface in the rain, many of these African Americans believed. And some crimes against humanity were so irredeemable that creation itself remembered. For example, when whites lynched and burned a black man, they believed that the tree would die; all the life around it would die; then finally the town and the lynchers themselves would die. In witness, the leafless tree would still stand.

In the process of telling her many stories over the years to me, Mary has claimed repeatedly that places have meaning and that meaning is formed by labor and the hard struggle to love, to raise a family, and to form a just community under conditions of bare subsistence and deep oppression. She believes that although modern property rights have legally severed relations to those places and appear to give no place to go outside of property for meaning, traces of an alternative value system are still alive; these traces are ultimately revealed by a sacred history itself.[27]

> It is a question with an answer cruel enough to stop the blood.
> —Alice Walker, *In Search of Our Mothers' Gardens*

The ideological and institutional framework of this unbreakable racial-class system was reinforced by terror. Members of the Ku Klux Klan dressed as night riders in white robes and masks, targeting African American families, especially community leaders and anyone who violated the strictly defined racial categories. During the decades of lynchings between the end of the Civil War and 1968, white vigilantes tortured and murdered five thousand black men, women, and children.[28] Although the majority of these lynchings were against black men, black women were not safe from this threat.

Many African Americans fought back against this form of violence. In the 1880s, under the leadership of women's rights activist Ida B. Wells-Barnett, African Americans created the Anti-Lynching Bureau, which campaigned tirelessly against such terror. The National Association of Colored Women, especially under the leadership of Josephine Ruffin and Mary Church Terrell, also fought segregation and lynching and pushed for women's suffrage.[29] Black women in the NAACP promoted the Dyer Anti-Lynching Bill from 1918 to 1923, the first anti-lynching bill to be voted on by the Senate.[30]

But violence against African Americans continued. One example from the 1940s concerns the family of activist Fannie Lou Hamer. Just when her parents had finally owned a few animals, fixed up their house, and started to get ahead, someone (presumably a white man) stirred poison into the animals' food at night. Hamer recalled of the incident: "That poisoning knocked us right back down flat. We never did get back up again. That white man did it just because we were getting somewhere."[31]

Often the local (white) sheriff, rather than being a protective force for an entire community, was deeply involved in the violence routinely carried out against African Americans. Eventually the tide turned, however, and the general public (black and white alike) rejected the Klan's flagrant actions and passed anti-Klan laws throughout the South. Segregated schools were declared illegal in the mid-1950s, as a result of the

Supreme Court decision established in *Brown v. Board of Education of Topeka, Kansas*. After this landmark decision, recalls Mary, the White Citizens Council took over much of the public anti–civil rights activity in Wetumpka, Alabama. Mary's father minced no words about the organization: "Same dirty dogs as the Ku Klux."

In 1965, when fifteen African American children finally entered the white school system in Wetumpka, white vigilantes firebombed two of the children's homes in retaliation.[32] Following the growing successes of the civil rights movement, organized groups such as the White Citizens Council gradually died out, but small groups of white vigilantes continued their hate campaigns in Elmore County throughout the 1960s.[33] In more recent times, unfortunately, especially with the advent of the Internet, the Klan has become a public presence again.[34]

> She had to lay down for him [the white man], poor woman; didn't, no tellin what would happen. She belonged to him but he wanted to keep his doins outside his wife.
>
> —Nate Shaw [Ned Cobb], 1974

As historian Jacquelyn Dowd Hall has explained, among the many racial assumptions that were used to anchor the system of segregation and violence was the belief that all African American men desired white women and were unable to control their lustful impulses. All that protected white women from the terrible consequences of such animal craving, this belief system held, were the structure of racial segregation and white supremacy and the chivalry and power of white fathers, brothers, and husbands. As payment for this protection, white women were expected to be submissive to "their men."[35]

In fact, this belief system often reflected an inversion of reality. More frequently it was white men who claimed sexual rights to African American women. This sense of white male entitlement can be directly traced back to the circumstances of slavery, when the master and his male relatives, whether married or not, had sexual access to all slaves.[36] This attitude was still common in 1948, when a white mother wrote to Governor James Folsom in Alabama regarding her son, who was imprisoned for what appears to be group rape of a black woman. Asking for her son's release, the mother wrote: "If the girl had been a white girl, it would have been different."[37] In Mary's own family she recalls that as soon as her beloved older sister Shane reached adolescence, white men she knew well started accosting her. This situation was so common to black girls Shane's age that it was almost unremarkable, except, of course, to the girl herself and her family.

Like lynching, severe sexual violence was used to send powerful messages to African Americans about the dangers of resistance.[38] For example, the sexual assault and near lynching of the activist Annie Mae Meriwether, recorded in NAACP records, was graphic. Meriwether had recently joined the biracial and radical Share Croppers Union. Her assault appears to have been made in retribution for that action. Taken in Montgomery sometime between 1927 and 1936, Meriwether's testimony states:

> Vaughn Ryles [the leader of the mob] started doubling the rope and told me to pull off all my clothes. He said, "Lay down across the chair, I want naked meat this morning."
>
> I lay down across the chair and Ralph McGuire held my head for Ryles to beat me. He beat me about 20 minutes. He was beating me from my hips on down. and [sic] he hit me across the head.[39]

Oral histories from a variety of southern locations attest to sexual pressure being exerted on African American women by white men. Many of these actions appear to be in response to such women's resistance to the existing power structure. For example, Josephine Hunter, a contemporary of Mary's mother, described a situation to me in which the husband of the woman she worked for pressured her for sex. One time "he stood outside my house and called me and said he was gonna pay me, but he wanted to get in the house. I had the screen door locked between us, but he jerked the door loose. He came in and I fought him. Then I grabbed my rolling pin and hit him over the head with it and broke the rolling pin."[40] The man ultimately left. Later his wife contacted Josephine. She knew all about her husband's infidelities and assaults, she said, her voice filled with disgust toward her husband.

There was violence in Mary's marriage as well, often reflected in her husband's accusations of her infidelity. Mary experienced a degree of protection as long as her parents were living, but with their deaths in 1967 and 1974, her system of defense was gone. Eventually, Mary had to find the internal resources to fight back on her own. She asserted her independence from her husband in 1967, when she organized for the union, and the marriage ultimately ended. Today, although she main-

tains close relationships with her three sons, she lives relatively independent of men.

For both white and black women daily life in the segregated rural
South, and Elmore County in particular, reflected the costs of being female, as opposed to the "wages" automatically due men, black and white
alike. Among the advantages granted to black men were the following: if
food was scarce, they were fed first; they took nights out, often with no
questions asked; and they preached in the church, although almost
everyone agreed that the women were the religious mainstay. As for
white men, they benefited from the opportunity to hold public office.[41]
Men, not necessarily their wives or girlfriends, expected to get sexual
pleasure and could demand whatever it required. Unlike women, they
did not have to fear sexual harassment or resort to self-induced abortion.

White men could write editorials and make political speeches. All
men kept their original names, while women lost their birth names, even
in cemeteries. Men from both races did not have to do housework or to
carefully hide any clues of menstruation. Men received higher wages and
inherited greater portions. They imitated the male heroes of mytholo-
gies and television shows, while there were no female counterparts for
women and girls to look toward. Finally, they heard the deity spoken of
with a male pronoun.

The cruelty of the complex and vicious structures of race, class, and
gender in the segregated South was often smoothed over by an extrava-
gant politeness expressed between the social groups. Symbols of respect
and even affection sometimes cushioned the male/female and black/
white relationships that were simultaneously intimate yet profoundly su-
perficial and unfair. For example, men talked about the women they exploited as their "better half." For years Mary's aunt, Rebecca Freeman,
cared for an elderly white couple on whose land she and her family had
worked most of their lives. She fed them and changed their linen, even
when they had lost all bodily controls. Despite this dedication and service, Rebecca was routinely excluded by the elderly couple. As a member
of the despised minority group, Rebecca learned they had actually
cheated her out of the use of the house they had promised her. All of this
happened even though the old couple had treated Rebecca with warmth
and politeness to her face.

In another example, the son of the white man who supposedly lit the
match for the legendary lynching that took place when Mary was a child
always tipped his hat to Mary's father when he passed by the family home

in his car. In this community, Mary explained, most black men treated their wives with deference and referred to white girls as little ladies. "Whatever they did [to women], they did it behind closed doors," she recalls. Yet one of the touching details Mary discovered as we worked on this book concerns her beloved white friend, Miss Abby (we'll learn more about her in Mary's story). Mary told me that her stepgrandma, Miss Lula, hid in the cornfields when Mary's grandfather was drinking and threatening her. After Miss Abby's death her nephew told Mary that during Miss Abby's first marriage, she, like Miss Lula, had also hid in the cornfields during her first husband's drinking and ensuing violence. Perhaps the two women had hid not far from each other.

In the racial hierarchy of the segregated American South, all African Americans were subordinate to all whites, but class hierarchies did exist between various groups of African Americans. Mary makes these distinctions clear in her story. She recalls that African Americans of the countryside were considered lower class than the more middle-class blacks who lived in Wetumpka. On the bottom of the rural workers were the poor, non-farm-owning farm workers like Cynthia Williams's mother, who worked as day-wage laborers, assisting during times of labor shortages and eking out a living as best they could. Next were sharecroppers, like Mary's family, who lived on a landlord's farm and generally used his stock and equipment in exchange for part of the year's profit. Above them were the tenant farmers, who usually owned their own stock and equipment and rented the farm. At the top were black farmers who actually owned their land, a condition often made precarious by white hostility and resentment.[42]

Poor whites also lived hard lives throughout the post–Civil War period. The Civil War had devastated the South, which then functioned almost as an economic colony of the North. Few banks, little investment, and a weak consumer base limited its growth. Its unskilled and uneducated labor force worked on farms or produced cheap manufactured goods, like textiles, cigarettes, and lumber products, and as long as conditions remained desperate for both poor whites and blacks, they often competed for jobs on the bottom. Southern industrial development also lagged behind that of the North partly because of white planters' reluctance to encourage any attractive alternative to lure away its impoverished workforce. As the geographer Charles Aiken has noted, many planters also opposed manufacturing because they feared such industry would bring in new leaders with alternative ideas and political visions.

"Not only were the newcomers usually better educated than members of the indigenous white power structure," observes Aiken, "but they had economic, political, and social connections beyond the small provincial worlds of planters."[43]

Nevertheless, large textile mills, the first major industry in the United States, moved south from New England after the 1890s in search of low wages, a labor force unlikely to unionize, and "one hundred-percent Anglo-Saxon cheap, contented labor."[44] Along the red-clay hills and on the outskirts of southern cities, they built mill towns, owned and operated entirely by the company. These towns—composed of the plant, an elegant house for an owner or manager, small company houses rented to workers, a company doctor, a company church, and a company store in which workers quickly went into debt—encompassed the workers' lives.

White families who had lost their farms and white widows with children moved to these factory towns. The entire family, including children, would work for the mill. There they frequently acquired byssinosis, commonly known as brown lung—a fatal disease caused by breathing cotton dust twelve hours a day. As the workers' lungs filled, slowly drowning them, company doctors tried to ease their symptoms. Company preachers performed their funerals, burying the victims in company graves. Despite the mills' policies of paternalism, many of them paid textile workers nearly the lowest wage for industrial work in the United States. They also gave workers few fringe benefits and allowed them to suffer frequent accidents.[45]

Still, these white workers earned more than the African American sharecroppers did in the countryside. Generally, until the 1960s African Americans only worked in these mills as janitors or in the most dangerous jobs. The larger class issues of the era affected all workers: whites in the cities often labeled white textile workers as trash, but those white textile workers could take their vengeance out on all African Americans. In this way the textile industry continued several traditions of the segregated South: it separated the races—factories were for whites, plantations for blacks—and all blacks were considered subordinate to all whites.[46]

> For the oppression of the poor, for the sighing of the needy, now will I arise, saith the Lord.
>
> —Psalm 12:5

The question of whether to baptize slaves as Christians was debated among some white Americans for two hundred years. Opponents of the idea were fearful that no matter how carefully they couched their teachings, slaves would seize the instruction and come to believe that they were equal to their masters in the spirit and that God cared personally for them. But a deeper fear of these whites, which ultimately came to pass, was that the slaves would hold their masters' unchristian behaviors up to higher judgment.[47] Slaves knew the cruel and unjust slaveholders were going to hell. They created an alternative vision of a moral universe with their own sacred history, a different story from that of the European Americans, both Christians and Jews. To the slaves, a living God revealed himself most clearly in the Old Testament story of the liberation of the oppressed, a story where Moses led the slaves of Israel—a chosen people—out of Egypt to the Promised Land. To the slaves, Jesus became almost an "Old Testament warrior" who fought for the lost and enslaved. In this view God was thus on the side of those who suffered.[48]

Slaves met covertly in the swamps or woods to dance in circles, sing out the pain they suffered, proclaim their knowledge that God would deliver them someday, and declare this world to be a moral battleground in which the earth participated with the slaves in their struggle for justice. Theirs was not a passive belief. Historian Lawrence Levine has quoted white interpretations of the accent with which slaves sang about their faith: "Gwine to argue wid de Father and chatter wid de son," "Did yo' ever, Stan' on the mountun, Wash yo' han's In a cloud," and "We all got a right to de tree ob life."[49] The slaves believed that they, like the ancient Israelites, would one day be set free: "Go down Moses, way down in Egypt's Land; Tell old Pharaoh, let my people go."[50]

Even after the slaves were emancipated, when, according to Levine, the ex-slaves' religion became more otherworldly and less overtly political, many of the earlier primary worship techniques continued, including "the ecstasy, the spirit possession, the shouts, the chanted sermons, the sacred sense of time and space, the immediacy, the feeling of familiarity with God and the ancient heroes, the communal setting in which songs were created and re-created."[51] But in the newer form of the religion now Jesus, not the Hebrew liberation story, was emphasized. Jesus was less a warrior figure and more a "benevolent spirit who promised His children rest and peace and justice in the hereafter."[52] African American religion thus continued its potentially revolutionary force. In this view God made no distinctions and judged behavior in the so-called public sphere as well as the private, and the meek would literally inherit the earth.

Throughout this period the church also served as the African American community's dominant self-help institution. In rural communities the church functioned as a center for worship, recreation, teenage flirtation, and social and spiritual mutual aid, as well as public participation and leadership. In larger communities the black church established schools, colleges, hospitals, newspapers, and complex social services.[53] Many black churchwomen organized social welfare institutions, and they also struggled against lynching and campaigned for voting rights. As historian Evelyn Brooks Higginbotham has claimed, these women also developed a form of feminist theology. For example, Mary Cook, born a slave in 1862, taught about women's public responsibility to spread the gospel. Virginia Broughton, raised as a free black, declared to her husband: "I belong to God first, and you next."[54] In all of these ways the black church gave its believers a sense of sacred meaning to their struggle for political and social justice.[55]

But Higginbotham has also criticized the African American church. Analyzing the black Baptist church from 1880 to 1920, she states that although black women provided the most energy in its press for social and political change, the church members often copied the white culture when it "sought to provide men with full manhood rights, while offering women a separate and unequal status."[56] Mary describes this phenomenon as well, evident throughout her story. Time and again she recounts the deep spirituality and religious dedication of African American women, but she acknowledges that the church structure of her childhood seemingly endorsed women's submission and male leadership. She believes this was done partly to compensate black men for their low status in the larger (that is, white) world.

To many of the poor African Americans of Mary's childhood, the world itself acted out God's moral purpose. God's will will eventually be done, they believed, regardless of human behavior. God's sacred history will be recorded, in the earth itself if necessary. Over the years Mary frequently repeated the story to me about the community lynching, always mentioning the subsequent suffering of the lynchers themselves. "God don't like ugly," Mary's mother warned her again and again. Fannie Lou Hamer, the sharecropper-activist, gave a similar theological message to the jailers who had imprisoned and tortured her in Mississippi in 1964. She told the wife of the jailer to read Proverbs 26:26: "Whoso diggeth a pit shall fall therein: and he that rolleth a stone, it will return to him."[57]

The cruel and unjust will pay in God's time, these believers maintained. The land will alternately beget or withhold fruit according to the goodness of those who plant the crops. Spirits will haunt the man who struck the match and burned another alive. Innocent blood will rise up in the earth each time it rains, bearing continued witness. The death agony in the hospital of the racist white sheriff will be watched by expanding circles of his black victims, who whisper each unfolding detail from person to person. "When you dig a grave for another person," Mary's mother warned, "you must dig one for yourself as well." Goodness and evil thus have real consequences.

During times of great repression, like in the Jim Crow South, the strong moral vision of these African Americans could simply serve as a promise of future redemption—not at all a small pledge to a suffering people. But when the social circumstances made it possible, that sense of absolute moral righteousness could be tapped for other purposes. For example, along with the rural despair in these parts during the Great Depression in the 1920s and 1930s, pressure for fundamental economic change built throughout the country. As white sheriffs foreclosed on cherished stock, equipment, and land, landlords evicted sharecroppers from land they depended on for food as well as employment. Many African Americans who found themselves in these dire circumstances forged new techniques of collective action and protest, such as the Southern Tenant Farmers Union (STFU) and the Share Croppers Union (based, at times, in Elmore County, Mary's home community). In these unions black and some white farmers joined together to negotiate and even strike for better joint contracts.[58]

Religion was a significant part of this union movement.[59] Some of the organizers were preachers, and meetings were often held in churches. These black churches, which were beloved, primary institutions to the country poor, blessed the unions in a sense and gave them political legitimacy.[60] Joseph North, a white writer for the *Daily Worker*, traveled during this period with a black communist as his escort. He wrote that the escort "had reached his destination—the tumbledown shack of a 'sharecropper comrade' [who] . . . was an elder in the Zion [A.] M.E. Church, who 'trusts God but keeps his powder dry'; reads his Bible every night, can quote from the Book of Daniel and the Book of Job . . . and he's been studying the Stalin book on the nation question."[61]

Black women played key roles in these unions. In Tallapoosa County, just east of Mary's childhood home, a young African American schoolteacher named Estelle Milner put black leaders in touch with socialist or communist organizers in Birmingham, Alabama. They then offered sharecroppers strategic assistance.[62] The resulting organism, the homegrown Alabama Share Croppers Union, reached across both racial

and gender divides. In 1931, for example, several white landlords announced that they were withholding all cash and food advances in order
to force sharecroppers to work in a sawmill. In reaction, eight hundred
sharecroppers, primarily African American, met in secret groups in
homes and churches. Under the leadership of two brothers, Tommy and
Ralph Gray, they demanded seven basic concessions, including the con-
tinuation of food advancements and nine months of school for their
children.

The first confrontation occurred near Camp Hill, Alabama, as eighty
sharecroppers met in an abandoned house. Tipped off by an informant,
the white sheriff deputized vigilantes, raided the house, and viciously
beat the participating (mostly African American) men and women. The
sharecroppers met again the next evening in a house guarded by sen-
tries. This time Ralph Gray was wounded in an exchange of fire and
stumbled to his home. There, in front of his family, a member of the
white posse forced a pistol into his mouth and shot down his throat.
Then, after mutilating Gray's body, the posse "waged genocidal attacks
on the black community that left dozens wounded or dead."[63] Still, the
sharecroppers did not give up, and Ralph Gray's niece, nineteen-year-old
Eula Gray, went on to lead the movement. Mary and I take up this story
in the epilogue to this book.

Because a coalition of poor blacks and whites could significantly challenge landlord and planter power, the planters and the public authori-
ties struck back with a reign of terror—with beatings, shootings, and
lynchings. Despite this harassment, however, the STFU organized a five-
state cotton strike in 1936, relying primarily on the organizing of African
American tenants and sharecroppers. Union activist Annie May Meriwether described the violence with which planters maintained their economic power. They shot, tortured, and then lynched her husband;
hanged her until she passed out, revived her, and questioned her again;
and then threatened her seven-year-old daughter. Finally, Meriwether
and the child escaped.[64] The events she talks about took place in
Lowndes County, Alabama, on August 22, 1935.[65]

Eventually, the farmers unions were crushed but not totally forgotten.
Nearly seventy years later Mary and I interviewed Grady Canada, a deeply
religious old man with dark circles under his eyes, who talked with enthusiasm to us about these long-ago actions. He chuckled as he remembered his vibrant younger sister, Eula May. She had taken on the role after her uncle had been killed and her father was in danger. Canada
stated again that God was on the side of the poor.[66]

This sense of absolute moral righteousness could be tapped for other mighty purposes as well. Take the Montgomery bus boycott of 1955, when the women and men of the small rural and urban black churches shook the world. On the Thursday evening of December 1, shortly after Mary had turned twelve, a tired African American seamstress named Rosa Parks refused to give up her bus seat to a white man. When news of Parks's arrest for her so-called crime became known, other African Americans, primarily women from the Women's Political Council, such as Jo Ann Robinson and Mary Fair Burks, unleashed their preplanned strategy of resistance.[67] By the following Monday morning, one of the most significant mass actions of the century had begun, as thousands of African American women, most of whom were dispossessed rural women who had moved to the city and become domestic servants, refused to ride the buses to the white homes in which they were employed. Thus they added hours of walking to a ten- to twelve-hour workday.

This was not merely a spontaneous action. Rather, the act resulted from nearly five years of "nonconfrontational grassroots leadership, especially persistent organizing by the Women's Political Council," involving thousands of daily organizational decisions.[68] One such organizer was Catherine McGowen, a young woman laboring to raise two small sons at the time, who worked as a hospital cleaning woman when the boycott began. She became a friend of Mary and mine throughout the course of my interviews. She showed me her first voting card, for which she had risked her life. The only daughter of tenant farmers from "Bloody Lowndes County," Mrs. McGowen had moved to Montgomery for more opportunity with the demise of the sharecropping system.[69]

Mrs. McGowen attended the first mass meeting on December 5, 1955, when Dr. Martin Luther King Jr. called on people to fight "until justice runs down like water and righteousness like a mighty stream."[70] She boycotted the buses and sang freedom songs at church rallies. One night white vigilantes trapped her and others inside the First Baptist Church on North Ripley for the entire night.[71] An estimated twenty thousand people took part in the boycott, the majority of which were black working-class women. Historian Stewart Burns has stated that three levels of leadership developed in the yearlong action: "Charismatic Baptist and African Methodist Episcopal (AME) preachers were mobilizers. . . . several dozen others, mostly women, comprised the organizers, including a score of ministers. As many as several thousand activists led at the micro level of extended family, neighborhood, church, and workplace."[72]

Religion scholar Theophus H. Smith has written that "religious vision and political struggle were twin energies in [such] social transformation."[73] Contradictory religious visions revealed themselves at times throughout the thirteen months of the boycott and in other civil rights events. I have heard contradictory visions of these events reflected in Mary's voice over the years. On the one hand, she and other activists saw God as all-powerful, omniscient, totally in control; on the other hand, God seemed to them unable or unwilling to prevent human suffering. Mary asks, if God is all-powerful and all-good, why does God allow the suffering of innocents? Why do young men hang from trees? Why do faith-filled women grow old prematurely from exhaustion? And if such suffering occurs because God is circumscribed in some way by the forces of evil, how can goodness be reclaimed?

These questions examine the problem of evil directly. Many African Americans during these tumultuous years dealt intimately with evil and knew firsthand what cruelty humans could inflict upon each other. On the one hand, many held a bedrock belief that God and goodness would prevail, regardless of human behavior, a belief affirmed even in the face of a lynch mob. On the other hand, others believed that God was in some way limited in the face of a very real Satan or a similar evil, and in order to have the victory of goodness, God's people must actively participate in the struggle against that powerful evil. Even Martin Luther King Jr. hesitated in his affirmation of the predestined outcome of the struggle: "It is a conflict between justice and injustice, between the forces of light and the forces of darkness, and *if there is a victory—and there will be a victory*—that victory will not be merely for the Negro citizens . . . [but] for justice."[74]

Mary expressed this same ambivalence in 1963, when she cried out to God, questioning his goodness and power, when white racists killed four little girls attending Sunday school in Birmingham, Alabama. King and others declared that African Americans could not just sit and wait for justice to happen. Instead, in a messianic mission as mighty as a whirlwind, he believed, they must join with God in a rigorous life-and-death struggle against the world's evils and create a commanding form of righteous action that was physical as well as moral. In a sense this returned many African Americans to the theology of the slaves that had been expressed in the spirituals: aided by a Moses, they would be led into the Promised Land. Now, however, God required them to be his agents of justice.

This revised theology was born of a synthesis of African American religion, with its potentially revolutionary undercurrent, and the nonvio-

lent resistance taught by Mohandas Gandhi, the leader of the postcolo-
nial independence movement in modern India. The combination resulted in a mass movement of nonviolent power made of "moral ab-
solutes, certitudes, and commandments. Such a force was fueled by
powerful faith [and] tempered and bounded by compassion, understanding, and humility."[75] It required repeated inspiration and rigorous
training in personal and group control as participants took part in mass
direct action and did not strike back when attacked. Thus this theology
sustained an oppressed people, giving them the fervent conviction necessary to survive and to judge the behavior of their oppressors and draw-
ing on an underground tradition of resistance. This theology of civil
rights theorists propelled those people forward.

In turn, the civil rights movement inspired other movements throughout the United States and the rest of the world, including second-stage
feminism, the Chicano movement, parts of the labor movement, gay liberation, and other insurgencies.[76] "The movement of the fifties and sixties was carried largely by women, since it came out of the church
groups," stated Ella Baker, an early African American activist. "It's true
that the number of women who carried the movement is much larger
than that of the men."[77] Certainly, the existence of that relationship between the morality of many African American women, the activism of
many black churchwomen, and subsequent liberation movements suggests that African American feminism has deep roots. It also points to the
multiple histories of the women's movement beyond that of white main-
stream feminism.

> And as you are trying your very Best to get our textile trouble ended,
> at the H.ville Manuf. Co which we do need your help very bad As
> they are really trying hard to burst our union and make slaves out of
> us.
>
> —Letter to Governor James Folsom, May 12, 1955

A combination of grassroots agitation and the early successes of the civil
rights movement allowed poor African American workers to begin to
force open spaces for themselves as laborers inside the textile mills. Using Title VII of the Civil Rights Act of 1964, the African American freedom movement encouraged black workers to enter the textile plants, a
story Mary tells with enthusiasm.[78] Three mills operated relatively close
to Wetumpka when Mary was young, including the West Bolyston textile
mill on the outskirts of northern Montgomery, about twenty-five miles

south. Two of Mary's white neighbors commuted there, and eventually Mary worked there as well. United Elastic purchased the West Bolyston mill sometime in the 1960s, and then in about 1968 J. P. Stevens, the second largest textile company in the South, purchased United Elastic.[79]

The West Boylston/J. P. Stevens factory still stands today, although it has closed down. Its founders had built a huge plant and added a nearby company store; small frame houses that it rented to workers; and, for its owner, a gracious mansion set back along a curving drive in an almost private park. The textile mill resembled a plantation in several ways. Its elite owner/manager almost functioned like a feudal lord. The mill had centralized buildings, and its large workforce of fairly desperate laborers was isolated from the broader community. It certainly was not a world of skilled, middle-class workers.[80]

Workers in various textile plants struggled to unionize at different times in their history, and the planters, professionals, and business owners often joined in the debate, claiming that workers must be denied access to labor unions for their "own good." For example, in an editorial on January 2, 1964, in the *Wetumpka Herald* conservative activist Thurman Sensing stated: "Where right-to-work laws are not enforced, the working man is without adequate protection. He must in effect pay tribute to a union in order to hold down a job. This is an outrageous situation."[81]

Indeed, the southern textile industry, employing 45,800 people in 1976, was the last major industry largely without union organization in the country, when in 1963, with strong backing from the AFL-CIO, the Textile Workers Union of America (TWUA) began organizing J. P. Stevens. The TWUA subsequently merged with Amalgamated Clothing in 1976 and called themselves the Amalgamated Clothing and Textile Workers Union.[82] In 1976 someone in the West Boylston plant contacted the national union and asked that an organizer be sent to the plant. The evening that organizer showed up at the plant door, Mary's life was changed forever.

The ACTWU developed four components in its strategy to pressure Stevens into negotiating with its workers. First, they campaigned to organize the workers; second, they undertook a legal struggle designed to demonstrate that Stevens engaged in unfair labor practices; third, they initiated a consumer product boycott; and fourth, they engaged in a campaign aimed against Stevens's power base, a "base made up of other corporate and financial institutions."[83] Over the years Mary fought for the union on all of these fronts. She worked constantly to organize the workers; she testified during a trial; she campaigned personally and in the media about the consumer boycott of Stevens production; and she testified to corporate and financial institutions about the oppressive conditions in the plants.

J. P. Stevens was known throughout the nation for its defiance of the National Labor Relations Act, signed into law in 1935. In 1977 the Court of Appeals for the Second Circuit stated: "J. P. Stevens, in particular, has acquired 'a reputation as the most notorious recidivist in the field of labor law.'" These unfair practices included illegal firing because of union activity; sexual harassment; racial discrimination; illegal surveillance; refusal to post union notices where employees could see them; and lack of worker safety, especially by using dangerous equipment, having such loud noise the workers' hearing was injured, and generating so much cotton dust the workers developed byssinosis. In fact, administrative law judge Robert A. Giannaski found the company guilty of "massive unfair labor practices" in the West Boylston plant, where Mary worked. There, a majority of 457 workers signed cards authorizing the union to represent them, "a solid 57.3 percent, which, in the parlance of political election results, would have been a landslide."[84]

Over the years Montgomery has grown north, and it now encloses the West Bolyston/J. P. Stevens plant and mill town. The empty plant seems to be crumbling into the earth, its work now being sent to third world countries. Tall trees line the street in front of the plant, and huge garbage trucks pull under the shade trees in front of it during the noon hour. There, the garbage collectors eat their lunches as they let their loud engines continue to run. The company store next door has been converted to a butcher shop, and small wooden dwellings still indicate the outline of company housing.

Late one afternoon in November 1998, as Mary drove her school bus across town, she glanced up at the sky and saw a city where there had been clouds before. It was a city built of old buildings that reached up to the heavens, buildings with countless windows. She thought of a Bible passage: "In my father's house, there are many rooms. If it were not so, I would have told you" (John 14:2). The city remained in her sight for a number of minutes. A few days later she awoke spiritually changed, in a sense reborn. Mary had always been intensely religious, but now a new sense of awe and purpose overtook her. Nevertheless, this transformation was deeply rooted in her religion.

After this vision fellow Christians in Mary's family and community in-

terpreted it to represent the New Jerusalem, as described in the last book
of the New Testament, Revelation. Revelation, in highly symbolic language, describes the end of the world, when God will destroy the oppressive imperial city of Babylon and raise up a New Jerusalem, a site of
justice and salvation. In the New Jerusalem:

> the tabernacle of God is with men,
> and he will dwell with them,
> and they shall be his people.
> And God himself shall be with them,
> and be their God.
> And God shall wipe away all tears
> from their eyes; and there shall be no
> more death, neither sorrow or crying,
> neither shall there be any more pain
> for the former things are passed away.
> —Revelation 21:3–4

According to religious scholar Elisabeth Schüssler Fiorenza, the vision of a New Jerusalem described in Revelation can offer the political
"promise of justice and salvation to the poor and to the oppressed or
[serve as a] challenge [to] the complacency and security of the relatively
well-to-do."[85] Furthermore, she states that Martin Luther King Jr.'s "Letter from a Birmingham Jail" contains a "glimpse of the New Jerusalem,"
an image echoed in his "I Have a Dream" speech.[86] In this way the content of Mary's vision can be related to key ideas of the civil rights movement. Since her revelation, Mary has become personally less judgmental
toward those she believes to have sinned against her people. God will
judge, not her, she believes.[87]

To be with Mary is a remarkable experience, as her kindness flows out
to all. But although her faith is based on a belief that God manifests
mercy to those who truly repent, she also expects a fierce judgment, especially for those who mistreat the earth. We will pay, she says, for the
ecological destruction we have wrought. In a sense this theology is fer-
vently anticapitalist: no one owns the earth, Mary repeats; property rights
sever relationships; and material benefits are meant to be shared.

Mary's spiritualism reminds me of other African American activists
before her. Like Sojourner Truth and Fannie Lou Hamer, Mary grew up
surrounded by a pantheon of biblical characters and stories that she in-
terwove with her perception of the surrounding events. Like Truth and

Hamer, she experienced a form of Protestant mysticism in which God was utterly present in her life. Mary too undertook a mission, answering a direct call to a specific political action. All three women believed they lived in a sacred time, when battles between good and evil bristled with energy, and all three rotated periods of activism and contemplation throughout their lives. Each woman believed in a God who manifested both mercy and a fierce judgment; each felt that God had given her the gift of discernment; and from descriptions of witnesses, all three activists reflected a radiance of spirit, a personal incandescence that drew others to their message.

Mary's story presented in this book is a celebration of community, an explanatory tale, and a warning. She describes the oppression of a community of people as well as the love, belief, and inspiration that enabled them to survive. She warns of the spiritual, social, and ecological destruction to come unless the larger community heeds God's warnings. The necessary changes Mary presents include mutual support, especially for the old; a rigorous love for the young, including responsibility for their moral development; the creation of loving and forgiving hearts; profound ecological changes; and a vision of justice that links a community with its God.

Today, after decades of activism, Mary no longer talks a great deal about either the civil rights or the labor movement. African Americans still suffer deeply, she believes, and the labor movement has repeatedly let her down after all her years of service. Instead, Mary shines with a sense of joy that feeds all who touch her life. She lives a simple life filled with nonjudgmental kindness and service.

Mary Robinson's Story

⊰ one ⊱

For, while the tale of how we suffer, and how we are delighted,
and how we may triumph is never new, it always must be
heard. There isn't any other tale to tell, it's the only light we've
got in all this darkness.

—James Baldwin, "Sonny's Blues"

I was born on November 24, 1943. There was eight of us kids, and my father was a tenant farmer, a sharecropper. That meant that our big family—black, of course—lived on this white farmer's land. We did the farming, all the work, and, in exchange, we was supposed to get a third or half the profits. But black families never did.

I thought it was so hard for us. I kept saying, "How much poorer can you be in this world?" After the crops was in and my father had settled his debts with the white man he sharecropped for, we'd go to town and buy a pair of shoes for the whole year. We never got in school until around the last of October, so then we was always behind the other kids. Then around April, we'd have to come out of school again to start working in the fields again.

Still, we was a happy family, and I wouldn't change my childhood for nothing. Sometimes, when I'm up there at the land where I was raised, even though I know the soil that's there has been turned over and that somebody else's footprints is being put on it now, I realize that the footprints of our lives is still imbedded in that soil. There's things that we will carry to our graves that the place left on us: the scar on my sister Shane's knee, the scar on my ankle. My older brother Tom took his sawed-off finger to his grave: he lost part of it cutting wood, right there, on that piece of soil.

When we was kids we loved to watch whirlwinds moving across the earth, leaving a clean path, and, today, it's like there came a whirlwind across the home we loved. That's what it feels like to me; when the rich whites came in, they took the land poor blacks had worked all their lives. It was like they took a whirlwind across the earth and sheared off the land. But even a whirlwind couldn't erase what was underneath that soil. That was still a part of us.

My sister Shane, who was just a little older than me, and my younger brother Jack, they like thrived on doing things to Daddy. When we was grown, Jack'd get so tickled remembering, he couldn't even tell the stories about what they did, and Shane'd be laughing so hard she'd cry. Shane and Daddy was always fussing at each other; they was always fighting.

When Shane comes down to visit, if my sisters and my kids and my nieces and nephews are here, she'll start telling stories. "Y'all know how I loved to eat, but when I was a kid, as soon as I'd sit down at that table for supper, Daddy'd send me off to get something. We drank buttermilk all the time. We'd mix cornbread in with it, and that's what we'd eat. I sit on one end of the table and Daddy sit on the other, and to keep Daddy from noticing me, I push that old buttermilk jug between us. Then I be eating and eating, but all at once Daddy'd peep out at me from behind that jug and say, 'Shane, go down yonder and get me an onion.'

"I would be so mad. So I'd stomp to the garden, pull up that [damn onion], and start up the hill. But I had to pass right by the chicken coop and the water, where the chickens'd drink. Dog, that water be dirty, full of chicken shit. Then I'd get me an idea. I'd get back in the house and give the onion to Daddy. 'Here's the onion, Daddy. I washed it for you.' Then I'd sit down real nice and think of the fact that I washed his onion in the chicken trough."

I was real close to Shane, and she was always getting herself and me in all kinds of trouble. We used to have this old cow named Pet that we milked. Pet had a little bull, and one day Shane says, "I bet you can't milk that bull." So she gets by his head and feeds him some corn shucks, and I get on back behind him and I mashes his balls. My sister laughed her head off, and I have a scar on my lip where he kicked me. Mama come running 'cause I started hollering at the top of my voice, and Mama grabbed my sister and tore her up, saying, "I'll teach you to do these things." [laughs] You could whop Shane and whop her, but it didn't change her.

Still, it didn't always be funny. We had to learn our so-called place in terms of white people. I remember us all working out in the field, being so tired, and looking back up at the house of them white folks that we worked for. We could see them out there, swinging on the porch swing while we worked in the fields.

I had a little white friend named Joy that I loved. My first remembrance of having a playmate was her. She lived in town, and we lived out in the country, but Old Lady Bernice, on whose place we lived, was Joy's granddaddy's sister, so she was Joy's great-aunt. If Joy was going to her grandparents, she'd always say, "Let me go down to Aunt Bernice's so I can play with Shane and Jim." That's what they called me, my full name is Mary Jimmie.

We played with her dolls and had babies. We was so naive. We'd say, "It's your time to have a baby." Then we hid the doll and the other one had to find it. After we found it, we'd rock the baby and talk and talk and talk to each other.

My first inkling about race happened when I started realizing that even though Joy was nothing but a child, she was younger than me, she could call Mama by her first name. She called Mama "Sarah" and she called Daddy "J.D.," but Mama had to call the white people we worked for "Miss Bernice" and "Mr. Paul."

Me and Joy dressed up and played in Miss Bernice's chicken house and cleaned the outside toilet, but Joy always gave the orders. She knowed about black maids, and I had to be the maid and she be the person I was supposed to take care of.

We also figured picking cotton was a job for blacks. When Joy showed up and Shane, me, and the rest of the family was going out to work in the fields, Joy pleaded with Miss Bernice. "Mama Bernice," she'd plead, "can I go with Shane and Jim?"

"No, you can't. They going to the field. They gonna pick cotton and you can't go." A couple of times we heard Miss Bernice stammer, "You're not supposed to pick cotton. You're white. That's what they're supposed to do."

Up there in the country, we wasn't around many places that said "Colored Only." Of course, we lived different rules for blacks and whites. But when we went to Wetumpka to a movie, we blacks had to climb up rickety, outside stairs and sit up in the balcony instead of down in the front with the whites. And the courthouse water fountains said "Colored Only" or "White Only." And the white bathroom be right inside the front door and it be the big one. The ten-cent store also had separate drinking fountains for white and colored. The water fountain for the colored was way in the back, so I asked Mama and Daddy, "Is it different water? What could a drinking fountain do?"

Daddy said, "It just be the way things is," and Mama kept silent.

African Americans still got lynched back then, and the Klan'd still sentence blacks who they thought were causing trouble. Blacks be taught as kids that kids didn't interfere in grown people's conversations. It was dangerous. And kids was taught that if you did hear something, you better not repeat it to nobody because you'd get your behind whopped. Adults'd say, "What was you doing in there? I'll teach you to eavesdrop."

I think that was because they was afraid that if you overheard something, the child might say something detrimental, especially to whites, and blacks'd end up being killed. When it came to something serious, the kids had to go outside.

There wasn't nothing that none of the blacks could do 'cause the sheriff was the worst of all when it came to violence. Even the sight of the sheriff's car coming down the road, its tall old antenna swaying from side to side, be putting fear in us childrens. 'Cause we knowed the stories, the things that he did to African American people.

And African American adults couldn't vote. You didn't have no way of getting nobody out of office when that person be doing all this low-down stuff. All people could do was believe and trust in God. Old folkses would say, "You don't have to do nothing, just give God time. God'll balance it out. Don't worry, God don't like ugly. Those low-down sapsuckers'll pay a price."

Nine times out of ten, the old black folkses be right. Over the years, you hear about this low-down night rider or that one falling ill. Somebody'd say, "I heard old so-and-so's in real bad shape. He just laying there, out of his mind." And the first thing that would cross our mind was, "He's settling up with God for some dirty deed he done."

But it be very confusing when you be young and you see bad things. I used to wonder, "Why don't blacks fight back? Why is they letting things like this happen when they's big old men?" I thought Daddy be weak in a sense 'cause he couldn't provide for us or stand up to the whites. But now I understand. He did the best he could. And in many ways, he be a slave and we be slaves for him.

And my daddy was also doing dangerous stuff, at least we think so. See, my daddy was an activist. We think he belonged to the NAACP in Elmore County, Alabama—something real unsafe. I remember thinking that he kept papers he didn't want nobody to find hidden in the big old trunk in our house. And he used to go off to what he said was secret meetings on Wednesday nights.

If there was papers in the trunk, it might have been dangerous. Our house—and our lives—belonged to Mr. Paul. Miss Bernice, Mr. Paul's wife, would come down to our house and just walk inside. Nobody had no locks. She'd walk through the house ordering Mama around.

I don't remember Mr. Paul ever coming in. Instead, he'd be out there in the yard trying to holler, "J.D.," but he never would talk above a whisper.

I was the kid Daddy read the newspaper to, 'cause I be so nosy. Daddy only went to the third grade, up until after the civil rights movement, but every day Old Man Paul got a newspaper, and that evening when Daddy be walking home, Mr. Paul gives it to Daddy. After Daddy got home, even though I was just a little old bitty kid, I'd sit next to Daddy and he'd read the newspaper to me by the lamplight. Some nights, Daddy'd took the Bible and the almanac, and he'd find the place in the Bible that told our fortune. That's how I got so interested in reading.

The newspaper be only about whites, unless some black got in big old trouble, but a few years ago, I went down to the newspaper archives and read old newspapers. No African Americans got their picture in the paper, but there on the front page of February 9, 1956, my daddy stood with his back to the camera. The picture focused on white men planting trees, but of course it was Daddy that did the work. It was like Daddy came back to me for a minute.

I learned a lot from Daddy, but Mama really taught us how to love. Not a day goes by that I don't think about her. Having childrens meant so much to Mama. I never remember one time hearing her say, "I wish to God I didn't have me a one of you. Y'all getting on my nerves." I never did. She found peace and love with her kids.

Mama was my ideal person, but I know she felt real alone when she be growing 'cause she didn't have no sisters or brothers, mom or dad, or aunts or uncles on her father's side, any people that loved her. She'd been kept by her mama's peoples, her old stepaunts, but they didn't want her except to work. They always told her she was illegitimate, that her mama died when she was born.

Somehow, Mama felt like she be letting us down. She always talked about how other kids had grandmas and we didn't have none, like she be lacking us in a way. Mother's Day was the hardest. I got to the point where I wouldn't go to church with her 'cause she had to wear the white rose. If you wore a white flower, that meant your mama was dead, and if you wore a red one, she was alive. So Mama wore the white rose. It was like we all had a hole inside 'cause of Mama missing a parent's love.

Mama's hair be straight, and lots of the time she wore her hair the way some Indians wear theirs. She'd part it in the middle and plaited these two big long plaits that hung down on each side. Other times she'd have the plait up over her head, her Sunday style. "Y'all get a comb and scratch my head," she'd say. I liked to take her hair down and comb it.

I think about Mama's light skin and believe my grandmama on my mama's daddy's side must've also been part white. Now, I'm real dark, even though I know my great-grandfather on my mama's side was a white man. But then my daddy was dark. The darkness came right back in me. But my sister Magnolia's light-skinned, and my daughter Tracy's almost white. So I just believe there be white on both sides.

All of us kids had long hair, but none of us had hair like Mama's. Ours was typical black child's hair. Every one of us but Magnolia and Ludie Mae. I tell my sisters, "We went up on Daddy's side of the fence and got us some hair." [laughs] We wore our hair in plaits, but I hated mine 'cause my hair was thick. I had these big plaits on the side of my head. Big! And they'd stick straight out. So Mama and them'd try to tuck them behind my ears, and then my ears stuck out the side of my head. [laughs] And I had this big old plait up on the top of my head. It hung down on the side of my face, and if I ran, it'd pop me in the eye. We was funny-looking kids, no doubt, but none of us has a picture. No blacks owned no cameras. I guess they be just too poor.

But Mama was beautiful to me. I have a picture of her that I like 'cause she stood so tall and erect and proud. She had so much dignity and strength. She wore her hat, it was Sunday, and she dressed for church. One arm was at her side, and the other held a purse. People say I look like her, and it's true, I can look in a mirror and see Mama's face.

Mama was the most caring person I ever saw, but I think she also had a lot of anger in her about race, and it hurt so bad she couldn't talk about it. See, Mama could've passed for a white woman, and I think that in her heart Mama thought her own family rejected her 'cause she looked too white. But probably she didn't realize they was jealous of her because she be so pretty. She was tall, slender, and beautiful with long, long hair.

Mama had three pieces of clothing that I remember: a really pretty gray dress and red pump shoes and a red purse that my sister-in-law, Charlie Mae, bought her. My older brother Tom had married Charlie Mae and moved north to Albany, New York, when I be pretty young. Each year Charlie Mae got clothes for us, then her, Tom, and their kids brought them down with them when they came home to visit each Fourth of July.

It took three days to drive from Albany to our house, so Charlie Mae'd write Mama and tell them they was leaving, and we'd figure, "This is Wednesday, so Thursday, Friday, and Saturday." That Saturday night, we'd go to bed, and every time we heard a car on the road, we'd jump up, "That sound like Tom!" Finally, as soon as Tom and them came down the hill to our house, he'd start blowing, blowing, and blowing the horn, and by the time he got there, we was all out in the yard, jumping up and down. Oh, we'd be so happy. And Charlie Mae always managed to bring Mama something.

Mama was so good, but she had such a hard time when she was little. She always told us that her mama, Salena Damous, died in childbirth in 1907, when Mama was born, and that her parents wasn't married. Her mama's mama, our great-grandma, Luda Geeter, died years before Mama was born, so Mama sort of belonged to her Grandpa Lucius Damous and his second wife, the woman Mama called Grandma Sally.

'Cause her mama and grandma was dead, Mama just went from one person to another, although she always called the people "Uncle" and "Auntie." Finally, when she got old enough to work hard, then everybody wanted to keep her.

Grandma Sally and Grandpa Lucius had their own childrens, including Aunt Rudolf and Aunt Camilla, who was so hard on Mama. They really didn't treat her right at all. She told us that when she was so little that she couldn't reach up into the washtub, Grandma Sally, Aunt Camilla, and them built a little platform for her and made her climb up on it and scrub the clothes by hand. Then, when she was about thirteen or so, her family put her out to plow. One time she be plowing, and the mule leaped up and the plow hit her in the stomach. Her stomach swelled up real big, but they never did take her to a doctor. She cried when she told us those stories, and we cried with her.

I tell you, Grandpa Lucius needed his behind whopped because he neglected Mama, letting her be mistreated. Whenever Mama talked about Grandpa Lucius, she said, "He be always gone." Grandpa Lucius preached all around and had his society for public service and self-help. His name is on the cornerstone of a whole slew of buildings, but he neglected his daughter's daughter.

I don't know how Grandpa Lucius and Grandma Sally consummated their marriage. If you had met her, you'd have said, "Looord, there's no way sex is ever going to come into this woman's mind." She was like real shriveled and prim, a little old bitty, teeny, wheezily looking woman, little and afraid. She always sat drawed up. The last time I saw her alive, Grandma Sally looked like she was scared to death. Terrified looking. That was her way.

When Grandma Sally married Grandpa Lucius, they was supposed to form this sedate-like, high-class, black family, but they mistreated Mama so bad. They just kept her to work and didn't let Mama go no farther than third grade in school. They didn't tell Mama much of anything about her daddy or his family, but Mama always went by the name of Stewart, her daddy's name, so she knowed something. Mama named my oldest brother Columbus, because she heard that was her daddy's first name, but we always called my brother Tom. Mama was like this cast-off child; we figured that it was because her parents wasn't married.

I did learn that Mama was related to the Geeters through Grandma Ludie. The Geeters are a real strong black family around here, and Paul Geeter was Grandma Ludie's daddy, Mama's great-granddaddy. The Geeters have the black funeral home in Wetumpka. They take care of all our family. Sometimes when we was in Wetumpka, and Mama had something to do, she left us kids at the funeral home. If we didn't behave, Uncle Arthur would take us back and show us the dead people. Mostly, we thought it was exciting.

Bless Mama's heart, 'cause Mama had no sisters, no people really of her own; she just loved Daddy's three sisters. She took them as her own, and they worshiped the ground Mama walked on too. One of my aunties was a good cook, with a gas stove. Mama'd go up to visit her and bake a pound cake and then bring it back home. She'd say, "I sure wish I could afford me a gas stove like the one Jessie got." But the only thing we had the whole time she was living was a woodstove. Mama didn't have her people, but she had all us kids. And she loved us, and we adored her.

But something else did happen for Mama. One fall after Daddy'd done got the crop in, when I was around seven or eight, we went to Wetumpka to get school clothes. While Daddy talked to some mens that he knowed, Mama took us to the Safford's Shoe Store. We came on a man;

we didn't recognize him, but he started to walk behind us. "I wonder why that white man be following us," Mama said. We went into the store, and Mama got us some shoes. When we came back out and started back up the street, he be following us again. About halfway up the street, he said, "Hey." Mama turned around. "Hey," she said back. "What you want?"

"I think you's some of my people." Up close, we realized he be a real light-skinned black man. "Let me ask you a question," he said. "Do you know what your daddy's name was?"

"No, I don't know what his name was for sure, but I heard it was Columbus Stewart; they called him Bob."

"Yes, and your name is Sarah. My name is William, and I be your daddy's brother. I been looking for you for years, and I knowed if I ever saw you, I'd know who you was."

Mama started to cry. Then he started to tell Mama about her daddy. "Your daddy died a young man," he said. "Womens killed him."

The way I understood it later was that according to my uncle, my granddaddy just run himself to death behind women. [Laughs] Didn't get no rest, trying to satisfy every woman in town. Uncle Will also told us that he and Columbus was part white.

Mama and my uncle stood there and talked and talked. After a while, she said, "Come with me. I want y'all to meet my husband."

So Mama took him to Daddy, and they talked again. Mama could not take her eyes off him, and he kept looking at Mama. Uncle Will asked Daddy if he'd bring us to his house on Sunday, the next morning. We was so delighted. Mama had no people except those distant aunts, and now there was this uncle. He told us that he lived on a farm with a mule and a lot of chickens. Of course, we had the same thing, but these would be Uncle Will's. That made us even more excited. When we got there his wife, Aunt Carrie, cooked this wonderful meal for us, and we just had a ball.

But then Uncle Will died. Later, people said that Columbus, my granddaddy, was an absolutely magnificent-looking man, and he was really light complected 'cause his daddy was white and he had really, really, I mean extremely, straight hair.

Then years later, long after Mama was dead, I heard the most amazing story. It hurts me so bad that Mama didn't know it when she was still alive. It would have meant so much to her. I heard the story from Addie Mae Robinson. She said she heard it from another old woman who died before her. The way Addie Mae told me the story, it probably was 1907.

That was the year that Mama was born. Grandpa Lucius, my great-grandpa, was way out in the country. He was riding in his white carriage with his white horse, about sunset, and passed this woman. She carried a baby in her arms and staggered down the road. Grandpa Lucius thought the woman was drunk and passed on by. Then he got to thinking to hisself, "Maybe she's not drunk," and he turned around, and he came back and stopped and picked her up. She be his own daughter. It was Salena, my grandmama, and the baby was my mama. Salena done lost so much weight and be so sick that Grandpa Lucius didn't know her.

According to Addie Mae, Salena didn't have nothing but the clothes she was wearing and her baby, and she was trying to walk from Tallassee back to Wetumpka. That's at least twenty miles. Addie Mae said Salena was leaving her husband. They thought maybe he abused her or maybe she got no proper attention when she had the baby. But maybe she just got sick and didn't see no doctor. They figured she knowed she was dying, and she be trying to get this baby to her family, trying to walk all the way.

So after I learned this, I thought maybe now I know why they was so secretive. See, Salena and Columbus got married in the fall, and Mama was born in April of the next year, 1907, so evidently Salena was pregnant when him and her got married. Grandpa Lucius, Salena's daddy, married them in his own house, but once they was married, Salena went with Columbus over to Tallapoosa County. Then, according to the old lady who told Addie Mae everything, Grandma Ludie, Salena's mama, died and Grandpa Lucius married Grandma Sally. Maybe they was embarrassed by Salena. So, anyhow, Grandpa Lucius had found Salena walking down the road, and he took her on home, her and the baby. They got a doctor for Salena, but she be so sick, she died anyhow.

Then, it was like after Mama's mama and our Great-Grandma Sally died, nobody talked about Mama's mama to her again. My grandma was like this outcast person, and nobody ever told my mama she actually had a daddy, she was not a one-night stand. Now I realize that all those years when Mama be alive, she had all these first cousins right around her, but she growed up thinking she didn't have nobody on her daddy's side, believing that nobody ever really loved her. But that wasn't true. Her dying mama walked twenty miles to give her baby a home, but Mama never knowed it.

After I learned this I went to the Wetumpka Courthouse and looked under their "colored" files for wedding certificates, and I finally found the certificate of the marriage between Salena Damous and Columbus Steward. Grandma Salena had not been able to sign her own name, but I saw what might have been her X, and I ran my fingers over it. There it was, under September 8, 1906. That was the wedding. I think about it. Mama was my ideal woman. Somehow, in some way, I think Mama knows we have found her story, and she is grateful.

two

Dear God, . . .
. . . When I start to hurt and then my stomach start moving,
and then that little baby come out my pussy chewing on it fist
you could have knock me over with a feather.

—Alice Walker, *The Color Purple*

Daddy was born in 1909, two years after Mama. Daddy's daddy, my granddaddy, had lived and worked on Mr. Paul's farm, the white man's place where we growed up. Daddy told us that Mr. Paul took Daddy under his wings, and to a certain extent, he raised Daddy, and Daddy ended up working for him most of his life. Daddy started working at about nine, before Mr. Paul married Miss Bernice.

Daddy tolerated his father, but he didn't care for him. Because of Granddaddy, Daddy wasn't big at doing a lot of whopping of us kids when we was growing. Sometimes he'd whop Shane, but mostly he'd do a lot of talking instead. See, Granddaddy beat Daddy, and Daddy's back had this scar from when he was just a boy. Once Granddaddy got mad at Daddy, snatched a trace chain off the mule, and hit Daddy with it. The wound went from his shoulder and all the way across his back, for life.

Granddaddy had children by two sisters that lived together, but he wasn't married to either of them. Uncle Tanks was one of Daddy's full brothers. I wasn't real close to Daddy's mama, my grandmama, but she lived near us.

Granddaddy wasn't ever like a real grandfather to us, one we wanted to see, but we went up to Granddaddy's house all the time 'cause of his wife, Miss Lula. Miss Lula was so clean, and her house smelled good. I can still smell her cedarwood bucket. Her house was like ours, not sealed so that cold air could get through big cracks between the boards, but she took something like clay and whitewashed all of her house with it. It was so thick, it looked like plaster. I can still see her yard full of poppies, red and pink, and this plant called Snow on the Mountains that had green leaves with white edges. She was the most kindliest person I had ever known. My dad loved her like his mama, and I loved her to death. With her homemade syrup, she made gingerbread for us. We smelled her gingerbread about a half mile from the house, and we started running.

I can still see Miss Lula so plain. Her skin was ash color, and she had no teeth. She always wore her thin hair plaited up. She was tall, real big-boned. She tickled me so bad. Sometimes when Mama had some place to go, she'd tell me and Shane, "Y'all go up there and stay with Miss Lula 'til we come back."

"Oh, my God," Shane'd say, "I hope she ain't got no newspaper."

If she had done got one, she sat us down at the table and read the newspaper out loud to us, from front to back. She taught herself to read and sounded out each word. She said something like, "The, the, the, the, de, de, debate," and then she'd go on to the next word. Shane be rolling her eyes, she couldn't hardly stand it. But Miss Lula broke the words down to syllables so she could read. She just needed an audience, and she knew we was gonna sit there because she gave us some gingerbread or candy when she was done.

Miss Lula put up with a lot out of my grandfather 'cause he be always running in behind these women and go home and would start fussin' at Miss Lula. It could be twelve o'clock in the day or it could be twelve o'clock at night when Miss Lula'd show up at our house out of breath. Granddaddy had run her away from home again. And she always had a wet dish rag in her hand. That was the strangest thing. Then Daddy'd be real upset with Granddaddy. He'd say, "Miss Lula, you just stay here with us until the old man straightens out."

I remember Granddaddy dying. When we was little, we was scared of the sound of the owls. It and the whippoorwill were signs that somebody was going to die. The whippoorwill made this really eerie, eerie sound. When you heard it, people'd lock their fingers together against it. That was supposed to break its neck.

One year, when we was gathering crops, Granddaddy got real, real sick. We kids was working out in the field alone one day, and Mama was at home and Daddy was with Granddaddy. We was out there suckling corn, that's what they called it. When the corn comes up it has like an extra stalk that'll just sprout out from it, and you have to pull that sucker out.

Suddenly, we heard this hootin' owl. "Who, who, who." Boy, you talking about some kids flying out of the field! When we got to the house, Mama said, "What y'all doing back here?"

"Mama, we heard that thing." We be crying. Then Daddy came to the house. "Your granddaddy just died," he said.

After that, when we heard the owl, we *knowed* somebody was gonna die.

Uncle Tanks, Daddy's full brother, married Aunt Rebecca, and they had six kids and lived just down the road from us, so we was together a lot. We'd see each other out working in the fields and would holler back and forth. "We'll race y'all," and we'd take off picking, just flying. Then if the rain stopped them from working but it didn't get to us, we'd holler, "Come and help us!" And we'd sing together. Anything to make the time go by.

I'm so thankful that Aunt Rebecca's still alive. She was born in 1918 but was strong enough to have a big garden not long ago. She's a thin woman, a hard worker, and a wonderful, wonderful person. She has had a really hard life in lots of ways. Uncle Tanks was always chasing after womens, like Daddy. Neither Mama or Aunt Becky seemed to be real upset about Daddy's and Uncle Tanks's infidelities. They never let on like they was hurt. The women that Daddy and Uncle Tanks went with both liked whiskey. Aunt Rebecca never drank a thing, and Mama never drank nothing except a beer, then she'd drink a can or two. And even though Daddy was this little old womanizer, I know that Daddy really loved my mama. He was just a dog, that's all. He was just a dog, but he loved Mama.

Daddy and Uncle Tanks provided the best they could. They raised vegetables and hogs, and everybody always had a roof over their head. It wasn't the warmest roof, but we lived in a house, so it was never like anybody was outdoors. But the two of them drank white whiskey. That was their problem. Half the time, it was full of lead. So Uncle Tanks died from drinking, cirrhosis of the liver.

Aunt Becky and Uncle Tanks worked for Mr. Joe Hall and his wife, Miss Nelly, for almost their whole lives, but then I believe they got cheated out of what was due them. They sharecropped and used to have the biggest cotton crop. Wooow, it was big. Them childrens picked cotton and picked cotton and picked cotton. Then Uncle Tanks helped Mr. Joe build cement blocks in his little business, and Aunt Becky also worked for Miss Nelly.

When Mr. Joe and Miss Nelly got old, Aunt Rebecca took care of both of them until the last breath was taken out of them. She walked back and forth to their house every day, and she bathed them like they was babies and fed them and cleaned their bottoms. And she wasn't paid. Their daughter even brought her childrens down there, and Aunt Becky babysat them. She couldn't say no.

Mr. Joe stuttered real bad; he kept saying to Uncle Tanks, "Ba, ba, ba, by God, you, you and Rebecca won't, won't ever have to worry about anything. We're leaving, leaving the little house to you. You, you, you won't ever be put out." So Uncle Tanks and Aunt Rebecca took them at their word.

So Old Man Joe and Miss Nelly died, and Aunt Rebecca and Uncle Tanks stayed in the house, and nobody bothered them for seven years. Then Uncle Tanks died, and Mr. Joe's and Miss Nelly's daughter came up there and told Aunt Rebecca she'd have to move.

See, I believe either Old Man Joe just lied to Uncle Tanks and Aunt Rebecca about giving them the house or his daughter tricked them out of it. There was a lot of crooked stuff that happened. A lot of white people that owned farms left the old black people that had lived on their place a little house and room for a garden. But they had old low-down-assed childrens, and they found crooked, no-good lawyers. 'Cause old black people didn't know nothing about a will being probated. So the white childrens cheated the African American people out of anything for their retirement.

The daughter's name is Louisa Ann. Maybe I should call her up and disguise my voice so it sounds like her father from beyond the grave. My voice is low enough. I could call her and say, [lowers voice] "By, by, by, by God, Louisa Ann, I never thought, thought you'd be so low, low-down and dirty." I could scare her to death. [laughs] But Mama would say I don't have to. She'd say, "God will require a payment. In some way, some place, Louisa Ann gonna beg Aunt Rebecca for forgiveness."

Now, when I go up to the country, I drive past the rubble that used to be Aunt Rebecca's house, and all it is is a big heap of old lumber in a pile in the middle of a field with a fence around it. It just sits there. I look at it and think of all the memories that's buried there in that big heap, the voices that have been silenced that nobody will ever hear again. Like Uncle Tanks. Like Roosevelt, Rebecca's second oldest son, who died of cancer. Like Willy, their baby child, who died in a violent car accident.

Then I go down and sit and look at Aunt Rebecca, with her thin hands and her gentle eyes, and I think of all the years that she toiled around what was then a house but is now a heap. I think of all she gave, and for a minute I think that she got so little in return. Then I think of the years that God has kept her here with a good mind and with her children that love her, and I know she got blessings beyond what we can ever imagine.

I also think of our little tenant farmer house, really a cabin, on Mr. Paul's farm. All the farm buildings are gone now, except for Mr. Paul's actual house and the shed. Our house that we all loved was tore down to make way for an expensive white man's house. He even graded the land. All us blacks lost our place on the land our families had worked for generations, but I still remember.

Of all the outbuildings, the smokehouse stands out in my mind the strongest. It was made from logs, the first log building that I ever saw. The logs was round and hewed out, so they fit perfectly together, leaving a little hole in the roof for smoke.

Mama or Daddy'd take the fresh meat inside the smokehouse, hang the meat on a hook, build a fire, then close the door to hold in the smoke. When the fire really started smoking good, we could smell smoke coming out. Then after a while, when the smoke really started curing the meat, the smoke and the meat smells mingled to make the most wonderful imaginable smell. I remember standing there, watching the little whisks of smoke coming out at the top of the smokehouse. They rose up, bent to the side, then dissipated into the air. But even when the whisks of smoke was gone, I could still smell that remarkable smell.

We always had an outside toilet that Mama kept real clean. The toilet was framed up with wood, and its outside was tin. When we was old enough to be in school, Shane got this book of children's poems and took a pencil down to the toilet. She sat there and read this book and copied the poems on the inside walls. I learned to memorize by heart from reading what she had wrote on the wall of the toilet. The poems stayed there, even when we moved. Shane gave them to us. Shane was one of a kind.

My first memories be jumbled up, so the time is confused, but I can still see everything in our house. Our house had just two rooms and a kitchen, even though it was two adults and six kids that lived there. It had a double fireplace for heat, one opening into Mama's room and one into ours.

As far back as I can remember, I can't ever remember Mama and

Daddy sleeping together. They slept in the same room, but not in the same bed. When a new baby was born, the knee-baby, which was Jack when I remember, slept in a little iron cot with a mattress made of straw in the room with Mama and Daddy, and the new baby slept with Mama.

Mama kept an old trunk in that room that I can still see. One of the hinges was broke, and parts was worn. That's where Mama and Daddy kept all their important papers—birth certificates, the NAACP material, and the old Bible with names written in it. Mama also kept her few little precious things in the trunk, including a gold bracelet and a pair of gold earrings. She also kept an old quilt top from her grandmama, Ludie Mae, in the trunk. It was real beautiful, with little pieces, Mama's only inheritance. We had a woodstove and a table in our kitchen, and that was all there was to our house.

Mama tried to keep our house pretty. The walls was just plain boards with no paint, but as I got a little older, they got linoleum for the floor. It'd be slick when we first got it, so we'd take off our shoes and run and slide across in our socks. And Mama always managed, one way or another, to keep curtains at the windows. Later on, Daddy ordered us a white porcelain stove with a reservoir, which gave us hot water. Boy, was we proud, tickled pink. The day the stove came, we just looked at the stove, we be so happy. Before, on Saturday nights, we had to heat water out in the yard before we could take a bath. Now we could keep hot water in that stove all the time.

Our house was built on stilts, like other black people's houses, and I'm not sure why they did that. It was cold in the winter 'cause the ceilings was so high, and it wasn't sealed. We'd try to keep warm, but our legs'd be freezing cold. I never had a warm coat until after I married. A coat was always out of the budget. I remember Mama having a red coat, a Sunday coat. My sister-in-law and brother might have sent it to her.

One summer, Daddy took a piece of old screen and cut it up and nailed it to the outside of the window, but we didn't have no screen door for many, many years. Of course, we didn't worry about no flies or mosquitoes 'cause Daddy was poisoning cotton with DDT. Daddy'd come home at night, and that poison would be caked all over his face, all over his eyes, and when Daddy stretched out his arms, you could see the creases in his clothes where his arms had bent. The only place that didn't have that cotton poison was right there in that crease. It was white cotton poison: DDT.

Sometimes his eyes would be real big and sick looking from the heat, and he'd be as white as a sheet. Then he'd be real weak for three or four days. I remember one time he passed out in the field. A guy traveling up the road, he saw the mule just standing up there under the tree. The man went over, and my dad had passed out in the rows. Daddy stayed sick a long time after that.

We'd go to other people's houses, and they had all these bugs. We'd say, "Whoooweee, did you see all those flies in that house? We don't have any." At night we'd lay there in the bed, and we'd have the windows open, and you could smell the cotton poison all night long, and the first thing when you woke in the morning, you smelled that cotton poison. Mr. Paul was the only one that had a tractor that spread cotton poison, so he had Daddy go around and poison for everybody.

Somehow, despite all of these problems, Mama and Daddy raised all us kids, although Mama didn't really have a life of her own. She birthed thirteen kids, but only eight lived. She had her first two kids before she and Daddy got together, and she wouldn't talk about it to us until we got real big. As a girl, Mama'd been bounced from one family member to another, doing housecleaning, washing, working in the fields, and nobody really loved her. Then, the way I understand it now, she was so-called taken advantage of by someone related to the family, and when she was fifteen, just a girl, she got pregnant. She wouldn't tell us who was the father, but I think I know. Finally, she said to somebody, "Something be wrong. I don't bleed every month."

They told her, "Y'all gonna have a baby." She said when she heard that, she was the happiest person in the world. She be so happy, she would've had that baby if she had to go out in the woods to have it. She just wanted *somebody*.

But, when my oldest sister, Luda Mae, was born, Grandpa Lucius and Grandma Sally, but especially Aunt Camilla, took my sister away from Mama and started raising the baby. I guess 'cause they was the closest somebodies my mama had, they thought they had the right to do it. Then Grandpa Lucius and Grandma Sally told Mama that if she got pregnant again, she'd be sent away.

So, a little later, it happened again, and when Grandpa Lucius and Grandma Sally found out Mama was pregnant the second time, they told her she had to leave and sent her to Bessemer. I know Mama was scared they'd take this baby too, bless her heart. So maybe she was glad to go. When Mama got to Bessemer, she stayed with one family, but when the woman got sick, she had to leave. Mama couldn't go back to Grandpa Lucius and Grandma Sally 'cause they already run her off, so Mr. Sid and Mama Bertha, who lived on Mr. Paul's place, took her in. Mama Bertha was pregnant with Lonza Mae and having a hard time, so Mr. Sid told Mama she could stay there and help take care of Mama Bertha. Mama Bertha was much older than Mama, even though they both was pregnant.

That's how Daddy come into the picture. At that time Mr. Sid and Mama Bertha was living in the house where we growed up, and Daddy was living in the little house on Mr. Paul's place that Granddaddy and Mama Lula lived in later. So Daddy met Mama, and they started going together. Daddy married Mama shortly after Tom was born, and Daddy gave Tom his last name, and Daddy was listed on Tom's birth certificate. Even though Aunt Camilla raised my oldest sister those first years, as soon as Luda Mae got old enough to understand, she left her and went where my mother was, and Daddy finished raising her up.

Daddy always let Tom know that he wasn't his natural father, but Daddy loved Tom as much or more than his natural kids. A few days ago, Charlie Mae, Tom's ex-wife, told me that after her and Tom got married, they was in Wetumpka by the five-and-ten-cent store when they looked down by the Fein Theater and saw this man standing there. The man followed them around, then spoke to Tom. "Hey, how you doin'? Do you know who I am?"

Tom says, "No, I don't know who you is."

"I'm your father."

Then Charlie Mae told me that Tom said he considered Daddy as his real father, and when they got back to our house, Tom went in and told Mama, "Mama, I saw a man down there in town that says he is my father, that he was my daddy."

Mama got real, real mad, and Charlie Mae said Mama told Tom, "You don't know but one daddy and that's J. D."

After Mama said that, Tom went outside somewhere, and Charlie found him crying. He told her he was not crying 'cause he was angry at Mama but 'cause he had mentioned this guy, and he wished he hadn't 'cause he thought it hurted Mama.

Even after Mama and Daddy got married, Mama stayed real close to Mama Bertha and called Mama Bertha's three daughters "sister." Mama Bertha taught Mama housekeeping skills, and Mama used to talk to her more than to anybody else. Also, because Mama didn't have no mother of her own to help while she was birthing all these kids, Mama Bertha delivered most of Mama's babies and cared for her afterward.

To me, Mama Bertha goes back as far as I can remember. We all stayed on Mr. Paul Henderson's place at the same time. It was like a big bunch of people that was family. Miss Bertha and Mr. Sid had two boys and three girls. I'm still real close to their daughter Lonza Mae, and if she comes home from New York, she'll come stay with me. We call her Sister.

I remember Mama used to quilt with Mama Bertha and her daughters before they moved. Mama always had this square-like quilting frame that could be lowered from the ceiling so she could work on her quilt. Of course, at first we didn't have no electric lights, so Mama and them quilted during the daytime, usually late afternoon or maybe on the weekends. After we got electric lights, we had just one sixty-watt bulb that hung down out of the ceiling, so at night, when they rolled the quilt up a little ways down from the ceiling, you didn't have much light to see by.

They wasn't no fancy quilts they made, but they was beautiful, and people shared quilt pieces. Back then, anytime when Mama or Mama Bertha and them was ready to quilt, they could find somebody who had quilt pieces to give them, maybe a box of quilt pieces that another woman had collected. They was gifts to each other. So the quilts they made had a little bit of all of us in them. Although Mama couldn't read or write nothing but her name, she sewed the prettiest stitch.

Mama Bertha was darker than I am, a lot darker than Mama. She didn't have long hair, so she always kept it parted down through the center with two little plaits across her head. Her eyes was kind. While Mama Bertha was tall and stocky, Mr. Sid was a little old slender, skinny-lookin' man. He raised sugarcane, and we kids'd be real happy when we'd go over there around October. Then Mr. Sid'd give us canes of sugar. Mr. Sid was like a father to Mama and Daddy, and they was crazy about him.

After a while, Mama Bertha and them moved to what we called "cross the river," across the bridge in Wetumpka. Then Mama Bertha got real sick, and I remember us leaving Mama there to take care of her. I must have been about eight or nine years old when Mama Bertha died. It just broke Mama's heart 'cause she wasn't there when it actually happened. Mama cried and cried. She was as close to being a mama for my mama as she ever had in this world.

Mama had other big sadnesses. A lot of her babies was born dead. There was never even a birth certificate on them. Luda Mae says she remembers Mama having two babies in one year. Mama probably needed medical care, but she just kept working, and the next thing you knowed, she'd be pregnant again, but her body wouldn't be healed from the one before.

There's ten years' difference between Mama's first two babies and Ann Lois, the first from Daddy that lived. One time she had a set of twins. Both died, and another three died really, really early. After Luda Mae and Tom, the ones that lived was Ann Lois, Magnolia, Shane, me, Jack, and J. W., the baby. Mama was forty-five and going through the change of life when J. W. was born.

I think all of us was kind of puny. I doubt that Mama ate enough when she was pregnant. All my life I watched her make sure that we ate before she ate what was left over. She probably did it when she was pregnant too.

Pregnant women back then ate white dirt, what we called clay. Mama and them would go to a dirt pit and dig it out. It was thick, cool feeling, slick, like starch. After Mama dug it out, she'd sit it out on a rock to dry. I always figured white dirt had some minerals people craved. It was a remedy from way back. My mama used to mail it to my sister, so she could eat it when she was up north.

One day Tom, his friend Pullet, and them decides they'd play a trick on us, and they go around to the dirt pile and pee on it. And, of course, urine is salty. Not much later, Luda Mae, Mama, Magnolia, and Ann Lois was sitting there, eating the dirt, smacking, and Luda Mae says, "Mmmm mmm! Ain't this old dirt here good? Got a kind of salty taste to it," [laughs] and Tom and Pullet just killing theyself laughing. But they let it slip out that they'd peed on the dirt, and, Lord, did Sarah whop they butts. But they laughed about it for years when they got together.

Only me and J. W. was born in the hospital. I don't know why we was. Maybe Mama stayed in labor too long or had other complications. Mama never saw a doctor otherwise, no prenatal care, nothing. Just get pregnant, have the baby, get back up, and go on, 'cause she had no mama or no sisters. They had that old custom saying a woman had to stay in bed for a number of weeks, but that didn't work for orphans like Mama. Mama Bertha tried to help Mama with her jobs, especially when she lived right up the hill there, but Mama Bertha had lots of her own work too. After Mama Bertha and Mr. Sid moved away, Mama just had a bunch of little old kids to take care of by herself.

She spent most of her adult life pregnant. She had a baby, then got pregnant again. Black people had lots of beliefs about birthing a baby. They believed that if a woman was bleeding or pregnant, she shouldn't work in no garden because the blood made the plants not bear and made nothing grow on the vine. And she didn't dare fool around with no fruit tree because it wouldn't bear no fruit. Old people even believe those things today. So Mama tried to follow the rules, and after a baby she didn't work in our garden. She could plan her work there, but she still had to work in them cotton fields. Bleeding women wasn't excused from that.

People was tied to the earth back then and believed the earth gave you signs. Like people'd say, "A lot of women's pregnant because the saps rising in the trees." And whether the moon was full or wasting away told if a woman was pregnant. Then after a baby was born, the earth had to tell you it was okay to get up or take a bath. But Mama never had nobody to care about her enough so she could follow all these beliefs. She had to do for us childrens, even against the signs.

She could take just about anything and make a meal out of it. She washed all our clothes by hand and made all our linens for the bed. She was just what you would call an expert housekeeper. Plus, she worked in the fields, and her health was never that good, and she gave birth to and raised all us kids. And through it all, she loved her childrens. My mama went through a lot, but she really knew how to take her goodness from the earth and her childrens. Altogether, I'd say that Mama was my ideal person.

⚡ three ⚡

Whenever the colored man prospered too fast in this country
under the old rulins, they worked every figure to cut you
down, cut your britches off you.

—Nate Shaw [Ned Cobb], 1974

When I was little, I thought all whites was rich, but that wasn't true, and I know now that there were divisions among the whites around us. Some was working-class people, like those who worked in textile plants, and others did things like teaching school. Even so, there wasn't no plantation ladies here. You had to go down south of here, maybe to the Crommelin place or even into Lowndes County, for that. Mr. Crommelin had this humongous amount of land in between Wetumpka and Montgomery, and lots of blacks lived on his land. Places like that was where the plantation ladies was. Daddy thought Mr. Crommelin was powerful and low-down, a force in politics. It's possible the white in the Stewarts come from that place.

Some of these farmers right around us had a lot of cotton, a lot of corn, but they didn't have no antebellum homes and women who sit up pretending they have these big old fat dresses on. There was a place where maybe five or six houses of poor white people lived close together on the road behind Pierce Chapel Methodist Church. And a white woman with all sorts of very temporary men friends parked at night behind Virga Mae. The woman'd meet her friends out in a car.

Us African Americans always acted like we respected white folkses,

even if they was eating shit with a lighter splinter. You referred to them as
Mr. and Miss So-and-So, even the ones without money. But we knowed
what they really was, just exploiters. We knowed that while they sat on
their porches or rode down the road, they was making their money off
black folkses doing their work.

Black people also knowed what they was caught in and what they was
supposed to do. Whites had them any way they went. It didn't mean
nothing to whites if somebody like Daddy, Uncle Tanks, and them didn't
break even, didn't make nothing for a full year's work. "Where's he going?" they said. "He'll have to stay here."

Once in a while you heard of a black man somewhere trying to rent
some land, then work it hisself or rent it out to other tenant farmers, but
in no time at all, he was gone. Whites had him every which way. He had
to get fertilizer, seeds from whites, and he had to get it on credit. He
could not sell one bale of cotton until he paid what he owed to the owner
of his property, so he was nothing but a middleman with no real pull or
authority. He might have been in worse shape than others 'cause he provided for the people that was staying on the place and working the land.
The white system caught him.

Anyway, as a kid, I thought all white people was filthy rich 'cause they
didn't work in the field and we did. They certainly controlled us and
could say, "Go work in the fields. I'll just sit here on my porch and rest
my feet." Today I realize they owned a whole bunch of land but not a lot
of money. Mr. Paul had about three or four hundred acres, but even the
white folkses didn't have no inside bathrooms, including Mr. Paul and
Miss Bernice. Miss Bernice always felt like it was an insult to not have an
inside bathroom, and first thing after Mr. Paul died, Miss Bernice put
one in. I smile to myself when I remember Old Low-Down Wilbert
Atkin's little old outhouse in the back. So we all worked Mr. Paul's land,
and after we brought in the crops, we supposedly got to keep half of the
profits. Supposedly. And for that, Mr. Paul and Miss Bernice had eight
year-round workers.

We also got to live in our little, two-room and a kitchen, wood board
house and got to plant us a big garden to give us the food to keep us
alive. That meant we did the necessary work to feed ourself. He didn't
have to pay us enough to buy food. So having us as workers didn't cost
him much, except for some land. That's why the white farmers had to
keep control. There was no way free workers would live like we did.

We planted patches of peas, butter beans, tomatoes, okra, watermelon, and cantaloupes. We'd raise corn, shuck it, shell it, and take it

over to this grinder, then bring it home and make it into cornbread. That's what we'd eat the most. We also raised chickens and some pigs. Yet even then, sometimes we was hungry. I can remember going to bed lots of nights with a glass or a bowl of milk, bread, and a baked sweet potato. Still, Daddy was a good daddy, can't none of us ever say he didn't work to provide.

Mr. Paul had a smart worker in Daddy. Daddy walked out there and looked at a field, and he told Mr. Paul exactly, to a tee, how to plow the field in order to keep it from eroding. He knowed where to put a corner, how to do the rows, and where to make it straight or curved.

Mr. Paul said, "I'm gonna plant such and such acres of cotton over there."

And Daddy answered, "We can't plant it over there."

"Why not?"

"'Cause we planted there last year. We got to rotate the crops." So one year Daddy planted corn in a field, and the next year he planted cotton there.

Daddy also fixed cars and machinery. I used to go out with him in the yard, when he was up under a car. I guess that's the reason why there was closeness between me and him. Even though Jack and J. W. was boys, they always followed Mama.

When the transmission was tore up in a car, Daddy climbed under it, dropped it out, took the little old steel balls out, and handed them to me. Then Daddy told me, "Give me such and such a wrench, girl," and I handed it to him. I got really good.

I think I hung around with him 'cause he taught me things. People brought things to him to fix—watches, electric fans.

One year Mr. Paul bought a spankin' brand-new tractor. Daddy was happy as a tooth fairy then. He read all the books that came with the tractor and followed the diagrams. Then he ran that tractor so it made rows, fertilized the fields, and dusted cotton for insects.

When I was little, I always wondered why the black man was the really smart one, yet he and his family always ended up with nothing. I watched *real* close as a kid, trying to figure it out. Mr. Paul couldn't do nothin'. Nothing! He was just as lost as a bitsy bug. Mr. Paul and his brothers right around him was just fortunate enough to have inherited this land that we lived on.

But Mr. Paul hurt Daddy real bad with that tractor. At the end of that year, after Daddy and Mr. Paul settled up, Daddy came back to tell Mama what happened. I never seen him mad at Mr. Paul before. "Mr. Paul wants me to pay for half of that tractor. I asked him, 'Why?' and Mr. Paul told me, ''Cause you gonna be using it to do the crops with and you gonna get half the crops.'"

"Oh, Lord, how we gonna do it?" Mama said. "We already is behind."

I believe Daddy paid for half that tractor, 'cause it was after this that Daddy'd go out there to poison cotton for other people. See, those other people'd come and pay Mr. Paul for Daddy's doing it, but Daddy'd didn't get none of the money.

The white landowners had lots of ways to keep the African American workers under they control. The farmer gave the black family on his place a small amount of credit at a store, like I believe Mr. Paul gave Daddy ten dollars or twenty dollars a month to spend, and then Daddy had credit at Mr. Clarence's store. Daddy used it to buy sugar, what else we needed. After he used up the ten dollars, he went in debt. At the end of the year, after we got the cotton in, Daddy tried to pay the whole thing off, but the bill almost always carried over, so we was always in debt. We could move to a different farm around our area, but we'd still owe the store. And if we tried to just go north, we'd better leave at night, and even then the Ku Klux might get us. Lots of the time, after the crops was in, black tenants moved from farm to farm, hoping life'd be better, but it wasn't.

When blacks got arrested, you was gonna stay in jail 'til a white man came and vouched for you. There wasn't no bond, so everybody had to have connections with a white person of some caliber. After arrest, they'd send word to the white man on whose place the black man stayed. So the white man'd tell the jailers, "Turn him out" or "Keep him in," depending on whether the black man pleased him or not.

The sheriff, Lester Holley, knowed every black man between Wetumpka and Rockford and any place west or east—and he knowed whose place blacks stayed on. After Mr. Paul got a telephone, when Holley picked up Daddy for drinking, he'd called Mr. Paul and say, "Mr. Henderson, I got one of your niggers down here."

Course, Mr. Paul knew right off the bat who he was talking about. "What you got him for?"

"Drunkenness."

So Mr. Paul went down and let Daddy out. Blacks didn't dare not have some white man who'd claim them. Terrible things happened in jail.

Sheriff Holley was this tall, sleek, red-haired white man who always wore this big brown khaki hat and drove this big old car with an antenna that swayed back and forth, back and forth. Everybody was scared of him.

Even the sight of his car coming down the road put fear in everyone, including childrens. We knowed all about what people said he did. And they claimed that if he didn't beat you up physically, he beat you up emotionally. The only way he referred to blacks was as niggers.

Anybody else ever beat up Uncle Tanks, they'd have hell to pay with Daddy. But one time we heard that Lester Holley hit Uncle Tanks real hard up the side of his head. Wasn't nothing nobody could do except wait for Uncle Tanks to get better.

So we believe the white farmers and the sheriff and the lawyers all worked together in a system. Sometimes farmers betrayed their black workers when they was old, like with Mr. Chapman and his wife, Miss Chatty. They raised their grandkids because the kids' parents went north to work. There wasn't nobody to do child care up there. Then, when the kids got old enough to go into the factories themselves, the parents came and got them. So the Chapmans was left alone.

Next thing, the white man where they'd worked all these years put them off the farm 'cause there wasn't no working childrens no more. Then he kicked them out of their little, old, run-down shack. He could've let them live there. So the Chapmans had to go off and be dependent on kin. This happened to other old people also.

Sometimes, if the old black couple that was left had been loyal to the white farmers for years and years, the white peoples would let them live on in their little house and give them room in front of the house for a garden. If old folkses was lucky, some other white man might need a caretaker. That's how Granddaddy and Miss Lula ended up in this little house.

Altogether, I reckon that Mr. Paul was fair, at least he was compared to the other white men around. He took Daddy to work for him when Daddy was nine years old, and Daddy stayed with him. I can't ever remember Mr. Paul being nasty or cruel to Daddy, but he was never a man of many words. He'd tell Daddy what he wanted Daddy to do. Some of the white farmers'd openly say the word *nigger*. But I never heard Mr. Paul say *nigger* or *boy*. If he did, he had enough respect that he didn't do it in the presence of Daddy or us.

Mr. Paul generally had a good heart and a good soul. On Christmas morning, we'd hear somebody come up the steps and onto the back porch. It'd be Mr. Paul. He'd be standing there, tall and skinny, real frail looking, with a live hen for Mama up under his arm. Then he'd tell Daddy to come up to the barn and get a calf and maybe he'd have some nuts for us kids. One time Mr. Paul gave Daddy a bull, and for a while Daddy had a pretty good little old herd of cows. Mr. Paul also wanted the black kids to have an education, so he gave an acre of land for a school for black kids. They named it after him, Henderson's Academy.

All and all, when I think about Mr. Paul, separate from Miss Bernice, I think that he and many of the whites did the things they did 'cause they thought that was the normal way of acting, and they didn't want to buck the system. They didn't want someone to say, "You letting that nigger over there get too uppity. You letting him have too much freedom."

But Mr. Paul used us. And I couldn't see no fair in all of it. What I saw was Daddy furnishing the labor of all of us and having to furnish half of the fertilizer and half of the seeds. Plus, we worked our butts off. It wasn't just Daddy's labor that he had out there. Mr. Paul had the labor of Mama and all us childrens too. Also, I know that if something had happened to all of us kids, Mr. Paul wouldn't have hesitated to tell Daddy, "Y'all have to get off my place. You don't have enough labor without your childrens."

We used to sell milk for Mr. Paul and Miss Bernice. God, that was a lot of work, 'cause we had to keep this milk a certain temperature in these special containers until the milk truck came around. To do so, we put water in this big old barrel and put the container down in the barrel with rocks on it to keep it from floating and spilling. Then we poured the old water off whenever it warmed up and pumped fresh cold water to keep the milk cool. We milked all the cows and did the work and sold the milk, but we didn't get no money.

And Mama had to do extra work for Miss Bernice. When Miss Bernice wanted some peas or corn, she'd holler, "Sarah! Go over there and get me about two dozen roastin' ears of corn! Y'all better at pickin' them out than I am." When Miss Bernice had an operation, and she couldn't do nothing, Mama went up there and washed, cooked, and cleaned.

Miss Bernice was a pathetic person from a poor, low-down white family, although she thought she'd risen above them. She had all these sisters and one brother, who was Mr. Atkins, a real racist. Me and Shane used to go up and shell peas and do other work for his wife, and we thought Mr. Atkins couldn't keep his eyes off black girls, no matter how young they was.

When Miss Bernice married Mr. Paul, and with him having all this property and these niggers—that's the way she'd put it—she thought, "Now I'm the lady. *I am the lady.*" She didn't have but this tiny bit of lips, but she'd tickle me so bad. Every time you seen her, she was rubbing this bright-red lipstick across them so she had this little line across her face, and she was puffing her face with powder. Then she'd go out and get her hair did, so she thought she was a fancy southern lady. After she got real skinny following her hysterectomy, she sewed herself a false behind so she'd have hips.

I never seen Mr. Paul touch her, and they always slept in separate rooms. I think it was a marriage in name only, with no sex. She probably was closer to them dogs than she was to him. She always went her way, and he went his. She'd get all dressed up on a Sunday morning and go to church, but he stayed home. He just ignored her. But she always tried to make herself think she was important. She'd go, "I'm going over to so-and-so's house," but peoples just tolerated her because of Mr. Paul. Nobody ever visited her except maybe her sisters every now and then.

Her only reading matter was the Sears catalog and a magazine called *The Progressive Farmer* that came to Mr. Paul. She'd order dress patterns out of it, but that was her life, except for trying to act the lady. She'd stand up there on her back porch and yell down to Mama, "Sarah, I need you to come up here and help me do such and such. Hurry." She not only bossed Mama but all of us. "Shane, Mae Jim, come help me peel these apples." Or "Help me snap these beans."

Most of the time, she had to boss us in a nice manner. Mr. Paul wouldn't tolerate her being too mean. One day she ordered Daddy to get something for her, and Mr. Paul told her, "J. D. ain't doing nothing. J. D. works for me."

Even with Mr. Paul moderating her, I don't know how she slept at night. We was human beings, and she didn't seem to realize it. She never took the time to know who we was. She and others like her didn't know there was a heart in us. They didn't know we had a soul. To them we was just a shell, like robots. It was, "Go do this. Go do that," not knowing that inside there was a heart. Miss Bernice treated her dogs better than us. She hand made a bed for each of them, just like a child's bed with their own sheets and pillow.

Shane and me had a time with Miss Bernice's dogs. [laughs] We had to always get water from their yard to drink. The roots of chinaberry trees in our yard had grown through our well so that the water tasted like chinaberries. We only used it to wash the dishes or the clothes. When Mama ran out of water to cook with or to drink, she'd yell, "Jim! Shane! Y'all come in and go up to Miss Bernice's and get me some water." We had to go up this little hill. Then, when we got to their house, there was this big old gate. These two old dogs—So-so, the little one, and Bruno, a big shaggy shepherd—lived inside the fence.

We was always afraid to go 'cause we knew that if them old dogs was out, they was gonna get us. So me and Shane'd go on up there real quiet, whispering to each other 'cause we didn't want to arouse them dogs. We'd open the gate, go in the yard, and pump the water. It took a long time to prime. Then just as we'd get the bucket between us and start for home, the dogs'd run out from under the house. Big old Bruno would bark real deep, "ruuf, ruuf, ruuf," and then little old So-so would be "yap, yap, yap." We'd be hollering and running, the bucket between us splashing out water. When we got home, we wouldn't have nothing but a little bit of the water left in there.

So Mama'd say, "Y'all gonna go right back up there to the house and get some more water. Y'all know them dogs ain't gonna bother you." By then Miss Bernice'd come out on the porch because she done heard all the ruckus. She'd seen us flying down the hill, the water splashing out the bucket. She'd shout at Mama, "Sarah! Sarah!" in her uppity way. "Tell Jim and Shane they can come on back up here and get the water now. I didn't know So-so and Bruno was outside."

Boy, then we'd be mad; we had to go back and do the same thing over again, except at least this time the dogs wasn't outside. Those dogs must have known we was scared of them and just loved to see us run. Daddy'd go up there any old time, and they never bothered him.

Daddy said things changed with Mr. Paul after he married Miss Bernice. She was the one who kept the books, even though Mr. Paul could write good. At the end of each cotton season, during what was called the "settling up" in December, Mr. Paul'd take what was owed the store and half of all the costs, like for the fertilizer and the cotton poison. So maybe we done made ten bales of cotton before we got a dime out of anything. But with Mr. Paul and Miss Bernice keeping the books, we didn't know if their figures was right. Blacks didn't dare dispute no figures, even with someone like Mr. Paul.

One December, Mr. Paul sent for Daddy and told him to come up there and settle up, and Daddy went up there, and when he come back, he told Mama, "They figured it wrong." Daddy didn't believe what they wrote down. See, Daddy was accurate. In the evening, when we'd weigh the cotton, he'd sit there and weigh it to a tee and write it down.

But after Daddy died, I found where he had wrote down some numbers in this old ledger, how much he paid for fertilizer, how much for cotton seed, and others. So sometimes he did keep track, but he still couldn't dispute Mr. Paul or Miss Bernice.

I remember one year when Daddy came to the house after we got the cotton in. I heard him in there telling Mama, "We didn't break even. We still owe Old Man Paul," and I remember Mama crying. That was the year that we didn't get one thing, nothing. Not even shoes. Some other years Daddy'd get the profits of only one bale of cotton when maybe we did twenty bales. That wasn't more than about two hundred dollars for a whole year's work by all of us. When you think of having to buy clothes and shoes for the six of us childrens left at home, it just wasn't gonna make it. And that year we got nothing.

⚜ four ⚜

She'd be out there with her dress rolled up nearly to her knees, just so she could have a clear stroke walkin. Pushed up and rolled up around her waist and a string tied around it and her dress would bunch up around her hips. She'd be in the field workin like a man.

—Nate Shaw [Ned Cobb], 1974

They had little houses in the cotton fields where they put the cotton, and I remember many times when I was real little, before I could do field work, Mama used to put me in the cotton house and let me sleep on cotton. When I was bigger and we had J. W., Mama'd put him there and would tell one of us to go and see if he done woke up. God took care of us all 'cause snakes and spiders never got us out there. Sometimes Mama carried us along while she worked the cotton, or we rode on the back of hers or Daddy's sack.

When I was little bitty, I couldn't wait to be able to pick cotton. I'd be saying, "Mama, Daddy, I can pick cotton. I can." Mama got twenty-five-pound bags of flour in cloth sacks, and when we got about three years old, she'd make us a little sack out of those bags, string it across our shoulder, and put a rock in to hold it down so we could pretend to pick cotton. She'd say, "Come on, Baby, you can help pick Mama's row." We thought that we was big. Daddy'd say, "Oh, my baby done picked a lot of cotton!" when we had only two or three bolls in the sack. That was our initiation.

One thing, if Daddy was sitting here today, he'd say that he didn't have no trifling children when it comes to getting out there farming. When we went out there, we worked, we worked. Except for Shane. We had this radio at home, and the volume would gradually go down, and you'd have to hit up the battery, and it would come up loud again. Shane tried to memorize every song that came on the radio, then she'd start singing in the field and before long she'd get dreamy and off onto the wrong row. So Daddy'd go back to show her how to hoe, then he'd go back to his work, and she'd start in singing again.

Daddy'd whop Shane all season, and it didn't do not a bit of good. Even now, she'll come home and start telling you stories and die laughing, 'cause she knew she was wrong to not work but she just didn't care. Shane just *hated* working in cotton.

Every day, except for Sunday, we'd work in the fields. I used to be so black working out in the sun. We'd wear the straw hats, long pants, and long-sleeved shirts, and it didn't help any. Also, people's shoulders would be so broke down. We'd stay bent over so long. We tried wearing shoulder pads, 'cause our shoulders got so raw from the cotton sack strap, but it didn't work. We also wore knee pads as we crawled on the ground, picking cotton, but the knee pads came off and our knees was scratched and raw. There was days when it'd be so hot we could see heat devils coming to get us. And half the time when we picked cotton, we didn't have no shoes, and we'd step on the sharp bolls. Our hands and feet got bloody. [laughs] I can remember old crazy Shane singing in the fields, "I ain't got no shoes / you ain't got no shoes / all God's childrens got no shoes."

Me and Shane talked about all sorts of ways to get out of the fields. You might say Shane specialized in that. We was always begging for rain, anything to get us out of working in the fields. Sometimes we'd be looking around while we was chopping cotton, and we'd see this big old cloud coming up. We'd say, "Oh, boy, it's fixin' to rain now." The clouds'd be rollin' 'cross the fields toward us, and we'd be so excited. Uncle Tanks and them would be running out of the fields. They didn't have to chop or pick no more that evening, and the air smelled like rain.

One time the rain crossed the road coming toward us and worked its way up through the fields. Water was running down the ditches. The rain came closer and closer 'til it reached the fence where we was at—and then it just stopped. Stopped. The ditches be full of running water, and I mean it rained! But not on us. We had to keep working.

Sometimes even Daddy'd be happy that it rained. Even though he'd tell us, "Y'all know the longer it rains, the longer you gonna be out there

in the field later," it felt so good for a break. It usually wouldn't last too
long, however. If it came a raining in the morning, then the sun came
out, by evening you had to go back out. Sometimes the cotton balls be
still wet and so heavy in the sack.

We had all these tales about what you could do to make it rain. One
of them was that if you killed a snake and left him hanging in a tree
somewhere, it'd rain. One day we started fixin' for home for dinner
about 11:30 in the morning, and me and Shane was way ahead of everybody else. At that time of year, there's a lot of wild plums out, and they're
real tasty and ripe and yellow. We'd go home early and get us a whole lot
of plums to eat at dinnertime.

The sky was just clear, a good spring day. But while me and Shane was
getting the plums, we run on this snake. We decided to kill the snake to
make it rain. There was this sweet gum tree down by our barn, and we
hanged the snake in the tree and went on to the house.

Everybody came home and ate, and we was finishing up when, all of
a sudden, we heard a rumble. Daddy said, "What was that? Was that thunder?" He just stopped with his fork in midair.

Mama said, "No, the sky's clear as it could be."

In ten minutes it was just a terrible storm, a tornado almost. The wind
was blowing so hard it was like the wind was trying to raise our house up
off the earth.

Me and Shane, we just stopped eating, and we dove into our little
bedroom, and I started crying. I said, "I told you not to hang that snake
up in that tree! Now we fixin' to get blowed away!"

So we went in to Daddy and cried, "Daddy, we killed a snake and hung
him up in the tree, and that's why it's storming so."

But he just laughed and said, "No snake caused it to rain," and
laughed some more. Finally, the rain stopped, but after that, even when
we had to work every day and killed more snakes, we never hung another
one up in a tree.

Old folkses always told us that if you looked at the moon really, really
hard, you'd see a face in it. So we decided it was God's face, and each
month we was out there talking to God at night, telling God all kinds of
things. I'd say what I wanted for Christmas, a doll like Joy's dolls, with
real hair. But all Shane could ever say if she saw the moon was, "Let it
rain. God, let it rain."

Daddy had to plow up cotton a couple of times as part of a government
program. He'd planted over the allotted acreage that they'd given Mr.

Paul. By that time, we'd already done cultivated it, shucked it, and it would be in the process of producing cotton. Daddy didn't get any of the benefits from plowing it up, and he was really upset. We'd put in all our hard labor out there, he'd whopped Shane to get her to work, and we got nothing. They paid the owners not to plant, and it didn't come down to us.

I think the moisture of the earth came from the tears shed by childrens back then. Even though you didn't want to cry in front of other people, you'd get by yourself and cry and cry and cry. Your parents didn't have a whole lot of encouraging things to say because their lives was so beat down. It wasn't like they could tell you, "Go back out there and fight like hell." I'm sure they'd tried fighting like hell, and they was knocked flat. That was normal for poor black people at that time.

Mama had three roles when we was little, but Daddy only had two. He provided for us and was our father, but Mama had to be the mom, the housewife, and a person who worked in the fields. Mama was the boss of the house, no ifs, ands, or buts—at least until we got up to dating age, then she consulted Daddy. But if it had anything to do with farming, except for her chickens and garden, Daddy made the decisions and she didn't interfere.

Mama organized her life around our field work and her woman's chores. She'd get up early and cook breakfast, usually biscuits and syrup or maybe gravy or cornbread. Meat, if they'd slaughtered a hog. Then, while the rest of us ate breakfast, she put on a pot for dinner at noon, our big meal for the day. It'd be cabbage or collard greens, peas, whatever vegetable we had—and meat, if we had it.

Then we'd go to the field, and around 9:30 Mama joined us, leaving the cornbread or biscuits and the vegetable to cook. She chopped or picked cotton for maybe an hour, then went back to the house to finish cooking. The rest of us quit working at 11:30, usually got home about 11:45, and ate and rested until about 1:00. Then Mama went back to the fields with us, and we worked until sundown. That night, we ate just cornbread and buttermilk or maybe sweet potatoes or biscuits and gravy.

Daddy always sat at the head of the table, and Mama walked around, putting food on the table and making sure that we was full before she ate the scraps. Lots of the time, that was it. That's why I think God needed her in heaven, because why else would he take her? Somebody so good and unselfish.

After we ate at night, we'd wash up and go to bed. We didn't have no bathtub, so we couldn't take a bath. Saturday was the scrubbing time when Mama gave us the worse bath in the world. They'd put us in the washtub they'd used to wash clothes, water with devil lye in it, then scrub the daylights out of us. We'd be clean little black childrens on Saturday night.

I remember that I'd wake up in the morning and see Mama standing out in the yard washing clothes by hand. For a long time she didn't even have a rub board to wash them on. She scrubbed until her hands be blistered, but her clothes was so white. Mama was a fanatic about cleaning. In fact, on some Sundays she was just too tired after Saturday washing to go to church.

Mama used to sell eggs for some money of her own, especially around Christmas. All you needed to start raising chickens was a rooster and a sittin' hen. Mama'd use the egg money for little things like thread or baking powder. Then on Sundays she fried chicken and cooked collard greens that smelled so good your heart almost stopped waiting for it to be done.

At times during the day, we'd hear the rooster squawk, the chickens clamor, and Mama'd yell at us as she ran outside. "Mae Jim, Shane, Magnolia, Jack! There's a hawk outside! Y'all get out yonder and run that hawk away! He be trying to get my chickens."

Sure enough, a big, big hawk'd be gliding graceful in the sky. So we'd run out and yell, "Shoo, hawk! Shoo, hawk!" And while we'd be yelling, a little hen'd be running across the yard with her wings flapping, trying to fly. Then the hawk'd swoop down, pick her up with his claws, and start pulling up, its wings heavy in the air. We'd still be yelling, "Shoo, hawk, shoo," but the hawk ain't listening.

Mama didn't give up, and she kept screaming at us, "Chuck some rocks at him!" So we ran around, throwing these little rocks, corn husks, but who could hit a hawk like that? So Mama'd stand there and watch the hawk fly off with her chicken. She'd shake her head. "Y'all be no help. No help at all." But we'd be wondering, do big hawks like that get little black childrens?

She had her garden, and in the summer nobody suffered when it came to food. Sometimes it seemed like fields of food. Peas, butter beans, sugarcane, and sweet potatoes. From Aunt Bertha, Mama learned to make quilts out of old overalls and sheets out of fertilizer sacks, and she also took fertilizer sacks and bleached them out for mattresses, then stuffed them with straw. They itched at first, but after her boiling and boiling and boiling and four or five washings in the devil lye, they be as soft as feathers. Mama made us shirts and skirts from cloth flour bags.

She didn't have no patterns; she just sewed something up and put some holes in it. Daddy usually had only one wearable pair of overalls at a time, so she fixed them with patches from his previous pair.

And she made do with almost no equipment. Way up later in the years Mama finally got a used sewing machine, the pedal kind, but until then she made our clothes by hand. And in the morning she put milk in the bucket and weighed it down in the well so it'd be cool enough for us to drink at dinnertime; then at dinnertime, she put another jugful down there.

Many years later Mama and Daddy got a little ten-dollar refrigerator. It had a little freezer box in the back but no handle to open or shut the door. So Daddy got him a piece of inner tube and a buckle off an overall and somehow nailed it to the wall so you pulled the inner tube to open the door.

Mama had a loving face, with lips that turned up like she was gonna smile. She couldn't sing a lick, but she'd be in the kitchen singing old spirituals as she worked, or she'd be out fooling around in the yard, humming away. She sang "Precious Lord, Take My Hand" over and over:

Precious Lord, take my hand
Lead me on, let me stand
I am tired, I am . . .

Daddy used to have this old guitar, and my oldest brother Tom'd play it, so as soon as Tom got home, Mama asked him to sing the song "If I Could Hear My Mother Pray Again, So Happy I Would Be." That always bothered me 'cause she never saw her mama, but she'd always sing along.

I think there wasn't too many pleasant moments in Mama's life. It seemed that Daddy had the easier part of it, 'cause he could just walk away. He worked five days a week, then come Saturday, he took his bath, Mama ironed his clothes, and he went out—while she stayed home taking care of us childrens. But at the same time Mama also took pride in how Daddy looked when he went out those Saturday nights. Mama said that a man reflected his wife when he went out. Daddy wore khaki, the hardest clothes in the world to iron, and we couldn't afford starch. So Mama made starch out of flour and water, dipped his clothes in it, and ironed them with hot smoothing irons from the fire until she made them perfect, until the creases was almost sharp. Can you imagine, a fire going in a fireplace so the heat will warm up irons in the summer in Alabama?

When we got bigger, we realized that Daddy had other womens, one especially. Mama was totally the opposite of the woman that Daddy fooled with the most. This particular woman lived in town and never had to do the hard work that Mama had to do, and Mama didn't drink much, and this woman partied with Daddy and his drinking buddies.

Mama used cooking to create much of her fun. When she made hominy, folkses came over to eat it with us, then after they ate, the grown-ups sat up and told stories, what I'd call tales today, about what they used to do. I guess I learned to tell stories by sittin' around listening to them. Well, not exactly *sitting* and listening, 'cause they always ran the kids out of the room. We'd hear them talking and talking, then came a big old cackling laugh, down to the bottom part of their stomach. I just knowed somebody'd be telling stories I'd want to hear.

Hog killing was a big day 'cause all these people came over again, and the womens cleaned the chitlins, made sausage, and talked. And it was a big day of eavesdropping for me. Black womens back then said words like *shit* or *ass*, but not the big words that women use now. If a woman'd even thought about saying *son of a bitch* or *motherfucker*, she'd be labeled the worst woman in the world. We heard the term *that old bastard* or *I'm gonna kick his ass*, but not none of those big nasty words that deal with ma-mas.

The womens worked, then sat around and dipped their snuff and fussed in their own ways about something that was going on. "I heard so-and-so and so-and-so was doin' such and such." Typical gossip, that's what it was.

If we kids came where they could see us, they said, "Get your ass on out of here. Ain't nobody talkin' to you. And you ain't even thinkin' about telling what I'm saying. Now go away." But I always moved toward the door real slow, trying to eavesdrop, and with luck I might hear one last word. If they looked up and saw you sort of hangin' around, they'd say, "What you doing? Tryin' to be grown, ain't you? Tryin' to listen to the grown people talk?" During all those times, fixin' chitlins, Mama'd look happy.

Sometimes when we stood out in the yard, helping Mama with the wash, we looked up and saw dust and Virga Mae walking down the road toward us. Everybody knew Virga Mae, but she was special to me and Shane, and Mama knew it. She was a girl about the age of our older sister, but she had this childish mind, like it never caught up with her age. She was just content to play with little bitty kids like me and Shane.

Virga Mae had some sort of nervous condition, and whenever she went outside, she broke off a little switch from a bush, then she kept that switch in her left hand and swished it back and forth, back and forth, as she walked. We'd see her walking down the road, swishing that switch, coming to see us. Virga was very affectionate with everyone she saw and was always trying to touch us. She'd try to pat our face and arms, but we'd squirm away. "Virga, don't be pullin' on me."

Virga Mae looked a little strange 'cause she tugged on her hair and pulled it out, so it was very short all around her face and on the top of her head. And 'cause her mama didn't take care of it, the rest of it was all nappy. Virga lived with her mama and her stepdad, but she loved us.

I remember Mama crying one day when I was pretty little. I couldn't understand what she was crying about. Later on, she told us about it. Five white men lynched this black guy, hung him up and burned him alive. I remember two different stories about why they said they did it. Mama told us that this black man left his wife and a bunch of kids. He was gonna go north and come back and get them. So he went up there and got hisself a job, but when he come back to get his family, the KKK caught him, took him to this tree, and hung him, then burned him alive.

The other story about it I heard was that the whites claimed this black man had said something to a white woman, and they came out and took him to the tree and strung him up alive, then poured kerosene around him and set him afire and watched him burn. Whichever story is right, I know that the lynching and the burning really happened. Daddy told us about it first, then the good white lady, Miss Abby, told me about it. She should know. She told me it was her father-in-law, James Boyd, who said he struck the match.

Sometimes when I was little, I tried to eavesdrop on Daddy and them while they talked. I heard them talk about vigilantes, which was the Ku Klux. They said that if a white man had a problem with a black on a farm, that night the black man could expect to be whopped by the vigilantes. They were this group of white people with sheets over their heads. I was one scared little black girl when I heard this, believe me.

We heard the lynching took place in the little town of Eclectic, and all the older people knowed about it when it happened. The last time that I talked to somebody from that time, that person said that the tree on which they hung the man had lost every piece of bark and every little bitty limb, and it stands there, stark naked. No grass, nothing grows around it.

Also, when it happened, some old black person foresaw the future. "'Cause of its guilt," he said, "Eclectic'll never grow." And he was right. No kind of business, nothing, comes in there. The town's just like it was when it happened. One time they had two traffic lights, but they turned one off. No need. Cotton gins in Eclectic caught fire and burned up all the time with no explanation. The cotton backed up in the cotton houses 'cause of the fires. It was like Eclectic was being punished.

African Americans had great faith back then, and when someone committed a crime that evil, blacks said, "Just give God time, he'll fix it. He'll fix it. We don't know how, but it'll balance out."

Mama was so sure in her belief that God was watching all that happened. She told us, "Be careful what you do. While you out there digging a ditch for somebody you be mad at, you might as well dig one for yourself. 'Cause it'll come back to you." And those five white mens that lynched that guy, they paid for what they did.

But, still, I was real confused about it when I was little. We knowed the man who lit the match, at least that's what I was told. When you think of somebody who done took part in burning a person alive, in your child's mind, you expect to see a monster.

But Old Low-Down James Boyd was ordinary, just like his son, Mr. Bob Boyd, at least on the outside. If Mr. Bob passed by the house ten times a day, he was gonna wave ten times. He was friendly and respectful like that, had a gentle, smooth face, and was the spittin' image of his daddy. So Old Man James Boyd didn't look or act like a brutal person, just an ordinary white man, with this little itsy-bitsy, ordinary wife. The strangest thing was that I'd be over at Miss Abby's—his daughter-in-law's—when James Boyd come over, and I wasn't afraid of him. Maybe it's because Miss Abby made me feel so safe, or maybe 'cause God be watching over me.

But demons was plaguing James Boyd. If what I've heard holds true, he probably saw that poor man burn many nights, many nights. Old Boyd couldn't shake the demon, and the demon wouldn't shake him, but we didn't find out the details 'til later.

Like I said, my first understanding about the race difference had happened when I realized that Mama and them always had to call whites Mr. and Miss So-and-So—but even a white girl as young as Joy called my parents by their first names.

We was also learning about all the different shades of color, but we was still innocent. Magnolia was light skinned like Mama, and when we was mad with her, we called her, "You old half-white thing, you." Then

Magnolia told Mama what we called her, and Mama whopped the mess outta us.

Other black kids did it also. They'd see somebody light and say, "She thinks she somethin' 'cause she half white." But the poor kid wouldn't be knowing what caused her whiteness. Then, 'cause we was dark, they'd say, "You black as a berry. You be a black rascal." But it wasn't did in the context of being mean at all. We wasn't being vindictive, it was just childish rhetoric.

But Magnolia always cried and told Mama. Then Mama'd say, "Bring your behinds here! I'll teach you who's white!" She'd cut us a couple of times with that switch, and we'd think about it before we said it again.

One time Mama be real mad. She said, "I reckon that mean I'm white, don't it? That mean I'm white, huh? If she white, I'm white; is that what y'all gonna tell me?"

"No, Mama, you ain't white! You ain't white!" [Laughs]

It was funny sometimes, and sometimes it was really bad. I was probably around eight or nine years old the first time that Joy called me "nigger."

I realize she didn't know what she was doing, but I got real upset and told her, "I ain't playing with you no more." I knew it was a bad word, something that I heard Mama and them called down through the years. Me and Joy'd played together since we was babies, and it hurt me real bad. I didn't want to be no nigger. But me and Joy and Shane had so much fun together. It was a joy to my ears when I heard her call "Jim, Shane, y'all come up and play with me." Joy brought white dolls with real hair for us to play with. They was perfect, white, like Joy. Me and Shane thought they was so beautiful. We made our dolls out of old iron weeds growing in the dirt.

Me and Shane still got so much joy from playing with our little white friend Joy. Since our house sat close to the dirt road, some mornings we'd wake up and find boxes of clothes that white people done dropped off for us, and our relative who worked for a rich white woman in New York would bring us clothes when she came home once a year. Then me and Shane and Joy dressed up in high-heeled shoes, pretending we was grown-up ladies.

Joy was my idol. She had brown eyes, the color of her brunette hair, which she wore shoulder length with bangs. I wanted her hair, I wanted her color. I wanted all of it. It just looked like the world was better if you be white. When Joy ran, her hair bounced. I used to try to make mine bounce, but all my plait did was hit me in the eye on the side of my head.

It all came to a head one time. One Christmas, Shane and me each got a doll, the only one we'd ever have. But when we looked at our dolls, Shane got a white doll and I got a black doll, and neither had no hair. I was little, probably six or seven, and I began to holler. I didn't want no black doll. I wanted a white one like Joy's or at least one like Shane's.

So Mama told me that there was only two left, 'cause Santa Claus didn't have but two. He had a black one and a white one, so he gave me the black one.

I felt so bad, I beat that doll to death. It was a hard rubber doll, little bitty, with no hair, just lines on it. And I took that doll out there behind the smokehouse. We had a big stick, and I beat it and beat it and beat it 'til I beat off all the legs, the arms off, the head off. And all the time I was beating it, I cried, "I don't want you, you old black doll, you!" I just cried and cried.

The doll was hard, and it took quite a bit of beating to break it apart. Then I went and got me a hoe and I chopped it into pieces, and I buried every one of those pieces in a different hole.

For a long time didn't nobody know what happened. Shane made her doll all kinds of clothes, and I thought her doll was much prettier than mine had been. Finally, one day she was playing with it, and Mama asked me, "Mary Jimmie?"

"Ma'am?"

"Where your doll at?"

I told her and she said, "Well, I bet you one thing, young lady. I bet you ain't never gonna get you another one!" And I never did.

Shane kept her doll up until a few years ago, then she sent it to my daughter Tracy. I beat that doll of mine 'cause I just could not stand the idea that my sister had a white doll and I had a colored one.

❧ five ❧

To me, July Fourth was about the most joyful day of the year. We had this old crank-type ice cream freezer, and we milked the cow on July third, and Mama started making ice cream. All of Uncle Tanks's kids came up to our place, and we ate ice cream the third, the fourth, and usually the fifth of July. We also had milk from Uncle Tanks's cow, so all we really ate was ice cream, ice cream, for three days. During the week we chopped cotton during the day, and in the evening we ate ice cream. And the summer nights were fun back then. When we walked outside at night, it was like we ran into a wheel of sparkles, fireflies. We chased them and chased them and put 'em in jars. During the day we caught butterflies and made cages with our fingers, then we let them fly up and away.

We also loved Christmas. We used to do plays in school about the three wise men, dressing up with sheets so we could be angels and putting a baby in the manger. We tried to decorate at home. Our teacher gave us Christmas wrapping paper, and me and Shane wrapped blocks of wood and put them under our tree to make people think we had presents.

On Christmas Eve, Mama and Daddy told us, "Y'all better go to bed so Santie Claus will come," but instead we went outside into the dark. We had heard the story that said that on Christmas Eve, at midnight, all the cows, mules, pigs, and other animals kneeled down and prayed. So we thought we'd search for the Star in the East, and when it got real dark, we'd go down to the barn to watch the animals pray. But we didn't know which way was east, so we just stood out there, looking all around in the sky everywhere at all the stars.

Mama always tried to make us happy at Christmastime. She made us cakes and potato pies and a chicken with dressing, and we'd have fun just being together with our cousins and do our little gang-type things. Also, we made us some toys. Jack took a stick and made a hook out of the wire, and rolled a wheel around on the ground, and he took a lid and pretended it was the wheel of a car. He'd hold it up and turn it around; he'd reach up and change gears. "Wrrrrr . . . wrrrrr." I can see him now doing it, bless his heart. One Christmas was special. Jack and J. W. got a tricycle to share. Boy, they was some happy little boys.

I can't ever remember Daddy giving Mama nothing for Christmas or her birthday, but later my brother and sister-in-law who lived in New York sent her gifts for her birthday. They sent her red shoes and a red coat, the first coat she ever had.

I started following Shane to school before I was old enough to go, then I hung around outside so much that the teacher finally let me come in. So I began school young; I learned to read fast 'cause I wanted to know everything.

It was a little bitty school with first through the sixth grade, with just one teacher and maybe thirty students. The first grade sat in the first little row and then on up toward the back. Miss Dolby, our teacher, was the whitest person I ever seen who passed for African American. Her hair was always really, really straight, and she walked the way we thought white women walked, like kind of on tiptoes. Miss Dolby was a real good teacher, concerned about us. She came over to the student's house and ate with the family, and if the child messed up in school, the parents knowed it.

Our school was built out of cement blocks, with two outhouses, for the boys and the girls. We went down to Mr. Chapman's house for drinking water. Mama sent us to school with a sugar biscuit to eat, but if we got really, really hungry, we went home. The school didn't have no outdoor equipment, but we played on the hill, sliding down it when it was muddy.

I remember a little girl, Dorothy Nell Chapman—me and her got to be such good friends at school. She had big eyes and always smiled, and if I got to school and she not be there, my day just didn't go right. Whoever got to school first waited for the other, and as soon as I saw her in the morning, I'd be happy. But there were like migrations all the time with poor African Americans. People be constantly moving, moving, trying to find something better. See, we was like a permanent family, but other families'd go to a place and stay there and make one crop, then they be gone. It displaced a lot of friendships between kids and a lot of friendships between adults.

One day I just went to school, and Dorothy Nell wasn't there. I went the next day, and she's gone again. Finally, some other kids told me they moved. Where they moved wasn't a long, long ways, but it was far enough that we couldn't maintain a childhood friendship. I saw Dorothy Nell one last time. We used to celebrate May Day by having a few of the black schools get together. And she be there. We'd decorate a May flag with colored ribbons, and we'd dance around the May pole and weave the ribbons as we danced. We played all sorts of childhood games like hop the scotch, and everybody's parents fixed picnic baskets with fried chicken and biscuits. Me and Dorothy Nell had such a good time. Then, at the end of the day, I had to say good-bye to her, but I didn't know I'd never see her again. Families like Dorothy Nell's had a hard time 'cause they wasn't permanent at all. They had to just go from place to place, and there was fewer places to go.

Mr. Paul had donated the acre of land for our school 'cause he was concerned that things was changing and black kids wasn't getting an education, and Old Man Joe, the man who owned the place where Uncle Tanks and them lived, had this cement block mill, so he gave the cement blocks for the school. Of course, Uncle Tanks worked for him basically for free. Somebody else donated the work for the school, and the county paid the teacher's salary. That's what they'd do for the blacks. If you came up with a school, they furnished you with a teacher.

'Cause Mr. Paul gave the land, they named the school Henderson's Academy. But since the school was started up by the peoples in the community—it was a community school—the county only paid for half a ton of coal to heat it, and the community paid the rest.

Daddy was the chairman of the trustee board and president of the PTA and did just about everything. So he and the other parents had fish fries to raise money to keep the school going. Every Saturday night families'd meet at the school, and Mama and two or three other women fried fish and sold the fish for people to eat. Cousin Tony brought this old gramophone, a record player that you cranked up, and older people, especially Cousin Tony, danced. Cousin Tony rolled and stomped and moved around, the original dirty dancing. Everybody be dancing and flirting. When I see dirty dancing today, I say, "That ain't nothing. Cousin Tony was doing that forty years ago." [laughs] Then Shane was outside, rolling her eyes and sticking out her hip, mimicking Cousin Tony's dancing, and while Shane be doing it, the rest of us just bouncing, laughing, and flirting.

Each week, somebody brought some records of Muddy Waters or Paul Lee Hooker—those was the famous blues singers back then—and they sang in the background of our fish fries. Blues was a way blacks had of expressin' sorrow and love at the same time. It always be something to do with love. "My woman's driving me crazy," or "I want my baby to come back home." Blues was a way of relieving their hostilities and sorrows. Sometimes, when we sat on our doorstep at home at night, we heard someone in the far distance, singing the blues. Or maybe Tom be singing it. The sounds be rollin' over to us through the darkness.

The fish fries at the school be funny 'cause at this time, the old schoolhouse didn't have no lights. They'd always be frying the fish over on the heater, so as it got dark, they had to hold a lamp up to see if the fish was brown enough to turn over. Later, I can remember when they first put electric lights in that school. They hung this light out above the back door, and it drawed so many bugs that at night we'd have to dash through a curtain of bugs to get inside. We all used the back door all of the time. It be like us blacks was so used to going in the back we couldn't change it even for ourselves.

Mama loved to go fishing, and I did too. It's some of my best memories. Sometimes when we'd walk up the creek, the plants be so growed up on the bank that we had to walk directly in the water or we'd jump from rock to rock. We'd come upon the prettiest little old waterfalls.

Me and Mama got lost so many times in the woods 'cause we always fished on these little creeks that run off some river. Mama'd find a creek, and we'd walk up it. We'd be trying to get to a place with a big-sized hole. Anytime she couldn't see the bottom of the creek, Mama'd swear up and down, "There a fish in there under the bank. Let me see if I can hook him." So this particular day we went up this creek and then the creek split, and we went up the split. Then we heard a big clap of thunder. I said, "Oh-oh, Mama. I believe it's coming up a cloud."

"Yeah, it sound like it."

We was still walking, walking, we went in much further, and, shoot, we didn't want to admit that we was scared, that we'd been lost, for a long time. Then it thundered, lightning flashed, and rain fell. Finally, Mama said, "Jim, I believe we're lost."

I went to crying. "Girl, ain't no used in crying. We'll find our way out from here." It be raining hard, and we was like hidden in the woods. But they say, "God'll take care of old folkses and fools." And that was us. We sat under this tree and tried to shield ourself from all the rain, and lightning popped every which way. Finally, the cloud went on over, and the rain stopped, and we started walking again. And every now and then Mama'd say, "Mmmm, that's a dark little hole over there, Jim. Maybe a fish be in there," and she'd throw her line out, even though the sun's going down.

Someway or another, we maneuvered around, and we ended up in this beautiful place with boulders and waterfalls called the Mill Stream. "We ain't lost no more, Jim," Mama said. "I know where we is. We can fish a little bit longer now."

We was wet, wet, wet, but it was in the summertime so we wasn't too cold. So I said, "OK, Mama, but we need to go before it be totally dark." So Mama throwed the line out, and I caught a fish. Naturally, that kept her going for a while.

I liked to fish, but most of the time, I was trying to find something in the woods that I hadn't never seen before. Mama told me about plants while we fished. She showed me wild lilies and the difference between the safe and the poisonous sassafras, and she showed me one plant that would make your hair grow.

Mama was like a bag lady when she went fishing. She wore a pair of Daddy's overalls with all kinds of stuff in her pockets, like rags and a bar of oxygen soap, and a little tarp apron with the tackles in it. Most of the time I be barefooted, but Mama'd usually wear some type of old shoes. Her feet was slightly bigger than Daddy's, so she took Daddy's old shoes and chopped 'em off across the toe so her toes stuck out, and if a hole be in them, she'd put a piece of cardboard in the bottom.

Mama made her fishing poles. She'd find a crooked old stick and would tie some strings on it, but she always tried to find her a real long one that'd reach way out in the water. Later on, she finally ended up with two or three good poles, but she never used a fishing reel. She felt it would've taken the fun out of her fishing.

Also, Mama couldn't afford to buy no cork to fish with, so when she found one from a wine bottle, she made a whole bunch of fish bobbers out of it. She dug worms for bait, and sometimes she used grasshoppers and crickets to fish with. She carried her worms in an old tin can labeled "Eat Well Salmon." Mama couldn't stand not to fish, but fish hooks cost money. One time Mama didn't have no fish hooks left but still wanted to go fishing. I went outside, and she was sitting with the pliers. She had found a big old safety pin and was trying to put a little thread through the top and twist it like a hook.

I said, "Mama, even if you do it like that the fish gonna be able to get back off of it 'cause it ain't got that little sharp thing on the side."

"Well, while he's nibbling, I'm gonna snatch it up."

She finally got it to work and went down to what we called the suck hole behind the house. It be a place where the creek came through with a swirling motion around the roots of a tree. When Mama throwed a hook in there with all the swirling, it sometimes got tangled up with all the roots, and if she didn't act fast enough, she'd lose her hook. That's where she'd lost them all.

A little later Mama showed up back home with the biggest fish she ever caught, and she caught it with the safety pin. She be so happy. Mama had lost her teeth on both sides, and when she really laughed, you could see both places, and you could now. She was tickled pink 'cause the fish she caught was a big mud cat.

For a long time she told everybody about the safety pin and her hook. Joy's daddy came by one day 'cause he liked to go fishing too, and she told him that she caught the catfish with the safety pin, and he asked her, "Why was you fishing with a safety pin?"

"'Cause I didn't have no hooks." So he went into his tackle box, and he gave her a pack of hooks to fish with. But she continued to fish with that safety pin.

We always took a hoe with us so we had a way to kill a snake, and we walked through the woods with the hoe and the little fishing poles on our shoulders. The woods was thick, and as we walked along, all of a sudden, the trees jerked us back. The line be hung up on a branch, and we had to unravel it. It would just be chaos sometimes just to get to the little creek, and we was tired by the time we arrived at our fishin' place 'cause of all we carried.

I think the best times for Mama was when she was out there; even if she didn't catch nothing, she could sit there. I guess I got my patience from Mama, 'cause she walked and fished and walked and fished. She might not catch nothing—or something that was absolutely nothing but a line and two eyes—but she was satisfied. Fishing was Mama's peace. It was like she had this connection out there on a bank somewhere.

It took Mama forever to clean and fry the little fish we got, and she didn't eat fish, at least not the ones she caught. Mama had strange ways of showing people that she loved 'em, and she knew Daddy loved to eat fish but not go fishing, so she caught all these little fishes and cooked 'em up for him. She had to fry them really, really hard 'til the bones was soft, 'cause there's no way you could take them little bones out. Later, after Daddy came home and had supper, she'd say, real proud, "Daddy ate them." I think it was her way of letting him know she loved him.

I loved to go fishing with Mama and run through the woods. I loved the color of the leaves in the fall and collected them for science projects, and I dug up or broke off certain plants for their really magnificent smell.

It was when we was fishing that I asked, "Mama, how did such and such happen when you was little? What happened to so-and-so?" Some things Mama wouldn't talk about at all, and I know a lot of things was really hard for her, but the really big thing that stood out in her mind was that they wouldn't let her go to school. Even though Grandpa Lucius and Grandma Sally sent Aunt Camilla, Mama's half aunt, to a private boarding school, when Mama got to the third grade, they stopped her from going further. They thought she was big enough to work.

Nobody can ever make me believe that God didn't protect us back then. For one thing I saw all different types of beautiful berries as we be playing in the woods and walking home from the cotton fields, but I never thought of tasting them. We just didn't, but we ate blackberries and huckleberries and knowed what hall apples was, and sometimes we ran up on a big walnut tree, a hickory nut tree, or a chestnut tree, and we'd collect the nuts. But with other berries and nuts, something said, "Don't touch me, I'm harmful."

It was like God provided us with the substance needed to survive. It was there to help us, and none of it is there anymore. When I walk through the woods and look for huckleberries, persimmons, or apple trees, they be gone. We had some really good times back then. We took our fun out of the earth. That's where we got our joy. Mama loved the outdoors, her flowers, and to fish. She'd fish in a bucket. Mama felt that there wasn't much joy in life, but what there was, you really needed to take—and mostly that was to fish. And just a little bit of joy made her so happy. Sitting on the fish bank made her as happy as somebody with a

Cadillac and four hundred dollars. And, I think, it gave her the strength to cope.

Mama had this lady friend, Miss Mildred Grey, a big-boned, kind woman, and she and Mama went fishing a lot. And every time they went fishing together, one of them fell in the creek. If it wasn't Mama, it was Miss Mildred. But when they came back, they was so tickled. I asked them, "What happened?"

And Mama said, "Miss Mildred," 'cause she called her Miss Mildred, "Miss Mildred fell in," and she'd laugh. Sometimes the fish done got up under a bush, and they waded out into the creek and got him with their hands. They just had great times, but they always come back wet, and they'd laugh like they was kids.

I think now of the sparkling Mill Stream, the creeks, our land that was so beautiful. You can always tell where there was a old house by some flowers, a few old stones or boards, a chimney connected to nothing. When I pass those places, I think, "What stories do the property around there hold?" It be so full of life for us to look at, but we had so much work to do. In the fall of the year, we had to pick cotton. Spring meant we had to plant cotton. Summer meant we had to chop cotton. Every one of the seasons recommended work for us. But me and Mama tried to enjoy the beauty. I'd walk in the woods behind Mr. Paul's, especially when the leaves turned colors, and Mama'd go fishing. Mama always wanted to go fishing.

✦ six ✦

Teach us to listen to sounds larger than our own heart beat:
That endure longer than our own weeping in the dark.
—Lillian Smith, *The Winner Names the Age*

We kids heard about Daddy and his other women in different ways. I know Mama knew about at least some of Daddy's other womens, and I think Mama felt beholden to him 'cause he married her when she had two kids, and he gave Tom his name and raised both of them like his childrens. So Mama and Daddy had certain understandings.

The only time I remember Daddy staying away from home all night was when he had got put in jail for drinking. Those times somebody came to our house the first thing in the morning to tell Mama that Daddy was in jail. Then Mama went up to Mr. Paul and told him. Mr. Paul didn't have no phone at that time, so he got in his car, went down there to Wetumpka, and when he came back, he had Daddy with him.

I know that what Mr. Paul did was wrong, exploiting us, but he was not a bad person. He was the only white man I knowed who died and left property to one of his workers to make sure that the tenant's family would always have some place to stay.

At first I was confused about how Mama could accept Daddy as he was, but over time I just came to believe that Mama was a really wonderful, beautiful, warm, loving person, and somehow I felt like she really didn't care about Daddy's running around. Maybe after giving birth to thirteen children, she really wasn't concerned about him going out there in the streets. Or maybe she just didn't let it hurt no longer. Certainly, Mama never told us nothing about no sex, and I couldn't imagine Mama and Daddy making love.

I really and truly don't believe that sex was that high on a lot of black women's priority lists when just survival was so hard. Maybe a lot of them got to the point where they could do without sex. They had their home, they had their childrens there, and then, also, where was it for them to go? What options did they have?

Daddy felt real strong about not letting men hit their wives. If a man come to him and said he wanted to marry one of Daddy's daughters, Daddy'd give him a talking to right then. "You see my daughter," he said to the man who wanted to marry me when I was older. "I'm gonna tell you something. You'll see that when you take her away from here, she don't have no marks on her. She ain't been mistreated. Now if y'all get to the point where the two of you can't stay together, I want you to bring her back here to me the same way you took her. No bruises from no beatings. Y'all mistreat my daughter, y'all have hell to pay." Daddy didn't believe in no knocking a woman around. I'm pretty sure other fathers did the same thing, but Daddy really meant every word of it. So Daddy tried to protect us.

But no question, Daddy really was a bad little man. I remember one time when Magnolia, my older sister, started to see this boy. Now, when somebody come to our house, Mama always asked them who their peoples was and where they lived. Magnolia had met this boy at church, and he came that Saturday night, not on a date, just to sit there and talk. His name was Paul.

So Mama asked him, "Who your mama and daddy, Paul?" and it turned out she knowed his mama. His mama's name was Bertha Robinson. Mama said, "Oh, that's Mr. Gene Robinson's daughter," and Paul and Mama talked about his peoples. Daddy was out somewhere.

The next morning, Sunday, we sat at the table like we always did, eating chicken, our favorite meal. There would always be gravy, and sometimes, if we could afford it, we had rice, but usually it would be chicken, gravy, and biscuits. Daddy sat at the head of this long wooden table, us kids sat on each side, and Mama walked around, putting food on the table. She started making some more gravy—we'd eaten all we had—and she stood there, stirring at the stove.

"J. D., you know Bertha Robinson, don't you?" Mama asked.

Daddy said yes.

"One of her boys come over here last night to see Magnolia." We heard this noise, a clump, and we glanced at Daddy. He had dropped his bone in his plate; that's what had made the sound.

Daddy turned around and he said, "Who, whose son was that?"

"Bertha Robinson, Mr. Gene Robinson's daughter. Well, her boy come over here last night to see Magnolia."

"What's his name?"

"Paul."

I can't remember exactly what happened then, but what I think happened was that we finished our meal and went on outside to play. Anyway, we was all outside there, and, all of a sudden, we heard this big clang from inside the house. Mama never said bad words, but we heard her yell, "You bald-headed bastard!"

We looked at each other. Daddy came out rubbing his head and called Magnolia into the house, but we all flew in with her 'cause we didn't want to miss whatever was gonna happen. Daddy looked at us. "I didn't call all y'all in. I just called Magnolia." But he didn't make us go out, and he told Magnolia, "That boy can't come over to see you no more."

Magnolia is this really quiet child, really, really quiet. She stood staring at Daddy. Then Daddy said, "They say that boy is supposed to be my son."

I have to give Daddy some credit. If he got caught doing something, he'd go and tell the truth about it. Later on, Paul came back down to visit us, and Daddy sat him down and told him. He said, "I don't know if it's true or not, but if your mother said that you's my son, then I have to believe her. And I was told years back that you was my child." Paul took it really good. I'd be angry, but he wasn't.

And you know Mama, bless her heart. After Daddy told her what they suspected, we thought we'd never see Paul no more. But Paul continued to come to the house, and I guess he felt a need to build some type of relationship with us. He really is a truly wonderful person. When my brothers died, he was there for us. I really feel blessed to have him, and Mama learned to love Paul. She really and truly did. When Mama died, we put Paul's name in the obituary. Sure did.

One time Daddy went to Santuck, just a little old place without a post office, just a bitty place with nothing but dogs trotting along the road, and there was a general merchandise store there run by Old Tomas Bass. We had two stores around us; Daddy usually went to the other. The road ran right down one side of the store, and an old ditch went along another. A black man, Mr. Jessie Bozeman, and his wife, Gussie, had about five boys and just one daughter. The youngest boy, Olson, was about ten or eleven years old, and we knowed him real good. Mr. Jessie went to Jude Tomas's store and got some goods on credit, and the family owed Jude Bass some money. Jude Bass went over to Mr. Jessie's house a couple of times and demanded money, but Mr. Jessie says, "I don't have none."

An old black man named Fred Jones had a little old bitty one-room shack that was right behind the store. Mr. Fred would sit on a bench in front of that store seven days a week. The whites didn't pay no attention to Mr. Fred, but he always listened, and that's how us blacks knowed what was happening, him and Evander, the black barber in Wetumpka.

One day, Jude Bass come right out to Mr. Fred and said, "We're gonna go out and gonna teach Bozemans a lesson." They were the people that owed the money. Mr. Fred didn't have no way to warn nobody.

Jude Bass and his goons went over to Mr. Jessie's, rounded the family up, and took them into the barn. Then, as they held guns on the others, they pounded each one over and over, including little Olson, our friend. They beat Mr. Jessie until blood come out his eyes and they swelled shut. They battered all of them nearly to death. Mr. Jessie never really recovered. And Mr. Jessie and them knowed the people that beat them up. Matter of fact, one of them was the farmer they worked for.

The next morning Daddy went out to Santuck for something, and it wasn't long before he come back to the house and walked into the kitchen. He whispered to Mama about the beating 'cause he didn't want us to know that a thing like that could happen. But we heard Mama crying, "Lord have mercy. Lord have mercy." Later, kids came to the house and told us what happened. "Y'all know where Olson live? Somebody went over there and just beat him up real bad." We kept wondering for a long time why somebody would go in and beat up Olson.

After they beat up the Bozemans, the store owner and them went along like nothing happened, like they'd done nothing wrong. Night riders was like the Ku Klux. Those low-down whites was organized in different ways. I can't remember which it was, but Daddy talked about one of those white lodges in Wetumpka. Whenever he mentioned a white man he didn't like, he said that man belonged to that lodge and if you saw such a lodge in a town, you knew the Ku Klux was there also.

When I got older, I heard Daddy talking about what he called the low-down White Citizens Council. Everybody knowed it was nothing but the Ku Klux Klan, and they do the dirty work for the rich. They met at the courthouse, just as obvious as could be. Even advertised in the newspaper. Sure did. When people say it's just poor whites that belong to the Ku Klux, they're just wrong.

Daddy mostly did business at the other store where Mr. Paul gave him credit. It was run by a funny little guy who wore his pants pulled up to his armpits and who tickled me. He was from around here, but he went off to St. Louis and came back with a wife, and both was real nice. Him and his wife walked real fast, and all the time they walked, he whistled. And all the time he worked in the store, he hummed a tune no one had ever heard before.

There was some low-down people back then. I swear, if I go to heaven and see them there, I know I won't want to stay around. I can't understand some white womens. One woman around here had a black half sister; they had the same white father. The white one knew that she had this sister, and sometimes they visited with each other. But the white woman exploited African Americans terrible, and her husband was one of the ones going around and being a night rider. I don't understand how a woman can lay down beside her man and knowed he had just went out there and hurt somebody.

But her husband has had to answer for what he did, like the mens that beat the Bozemans. Like Mama always said, "God don't like ugly. Just give God time." That woman's night rider husband suffered quite a bit before he died, and she suffered a lot too. When I heard about it, I wondered, "Did she ever think that maybe God was making her suffer for some of the things that the old man did that she knowed about?"

Another thing strange back then. The white mens never wanted to marry womens that was strong. They always go for these womens that was real meek. Every one of them, except for Old Lady Bernice, was very meek and very timid looking, especially the ones that didn't work. Like Old Lady Francie, Lady Cissy, Lady Nelly—they never hit a lick out of a snake. That's what they said back then when somebody ain't never worked nowhere. You never hit a lick out of a snake.

Miss Francie was married to James Boyd, the one who lit the match when they lynched the black guy; [he was] Miss Abby's father-in-law. Miss Francie was just a poor soul. Not poor in terms of material things. She had a beautiful house, but like in timid, lost. She always wore this little old wig. [laughs] And her husband, the lyncher, had a big old Hudson, which he never drove over five miles an hour. For somebody who was so low-down, he was the slowest driver. He'd burn somebody up, but he wasn't gonna run over nobody or get a speeding ticket.

After Mr. Paul died, I started coming up to the white cemetery, 'cause it was near our house. I thought about how long the people'd been dead, what happened to the souls of the bad ones. Me and Shane tried to peep into a couple of graves. We especially went to visit the grave of a baby that they didn't give no name.

There isn't an African American body in the white cemetery. I reckon every body in there would raise up even in the daylight, then walk away, if somebody black be buried there.

All those white people we lived around, they didn't know how close I was paying attention. It was like I wasn't a real person, maybe like a shadow, but I watched and learned. A new family moved in around here, and the woman was black, but she looked like she was white. She and her husband got run out of Lowndes County by the Ku Klux Klan because of how light she looked and that she was married to a black man. One day I was up at the store and so was this black woman who looked white and so was Miss Bernice.

Miss Bernice went up to the other woman and said, "Hmmm, I don't believe I know you, do I?" The black woman who looked white didn't have a black accent. She said, "I don't think so," and she told Miss Bernice her name and where she lived. So Miss Bernice said, "Well, my name is Bernice Henderson, and when you're down my way, come see me." So the black woman thanked Miss Bernice and left and walked down the little dirt road toward where she lived.

Then Tomas Bass, the owner of the store, said, "I heard you telling that woman that you'd like for her to come and see you. When did y'all get to where you're entertaining niggers?"

I stood there listening. Miss Bernice just went all to pieces. "Why, she ain't no nigger!" she sputtered.

"Yes, she is. They just moved in from Lowndes County."

Well, she got all upset, but I got tickled. Oh, it was funny. I thought to myself, "That'll teach her."

The white folkses in the area had different divisions. There wasn't no rich whites living around there, but there was still categories. Miss Bessie Hendersen was a schoolteacher, and she associated with other schoolteachers. She never married, and she lived near us. People called her an old maid, but she belonged to a garden club and some little old societies. They might have been the women's Ku Klux for all I know. Eventually, all Miss Bessie's relatives around here died, and I was all she had. So in her old age she came to think of me as kin.

The whites that worked in textile mills was poor by white Wetumpka standards, but they was well-off by black. In fact, Miss Bernice's brother and sister-in-law worked at the textile mill I worked at later. We kids used to go up to their house on Saturdays and work for them and hear them talking. They was making a fairly decent living, enough that you could tell they was accomplishing something.

The subject came up one time while we was there that there was not any blacks working in their cotton mill, just a few working outside as janitors. I listened real careful, and it really started to dawn on me how much injustice there was. Because we was out there, we was the ones that was making the cotton for them to send through these plants. We had the hardest part, and we wasn't getting anything for it. I didn't become totally aware at that moment, 'cause I was young, but it started me thinking even more.

And those white womens wasn't so meek all the time. One time they got together and did some of their own low-down dirty work. This black woman worked for these white people, and I guess one day after the white woman left for work, she came back home and caught her husband having sex with the black woman. Apparently, the guy brought his ass back home to do it every day. Some people said the black woman was prostituting, but I don't think so. I think she was caught in a situation where she didn't have no say-so.

So the white woman got together with her white women friends, and they told the black woman, "When the sundown comes, you better be out of town." The black woman had a husband and a bunch of childrens, but she had to leave. They ran her out. Later, her mama died, and they told her she couldn't come home for that. So she lost her kids. Her husband raised them. The one who should have been run out of town was the damn [white woman's] husband.

Someway or another there was always these myths about black women, that black women was supposed to be more sexual than the white woman was. Even to this day they have these ideas. So African American women was in danger back then. White men sat around and talked about what it was to sleep with a black woman, and they thought black women couldn't turn them down. When I got to be older, I understood that on several of the farms around, white mens fooled around with the black girls. Sometimes the girl went ahead and was submissive so her family had a place to stay. We was just lucky that Mr. Paul was a good person, but even that didn't protect Shane.

I learned to love this one white woman, though, Miss Abby. From my earliest memories Miss Abby was a wonderful woman. It was against the code for blacks to go into white people's front door, and my family always had to go to the back door of Miss Bernice's house. Sometimes, me, Joy, and Shane played on Miss Bernice's front porch, but if we went into the house, we had to go around to the back. But with Miss Abby it didn't make no difference. If she was in the front yard when we came over, she said, "Come on in," and took us through the front door.

She was so pretty. She had black, curly hair and always kept it cut real short so it fell into waves, and she had a big, soft, gentle face with large jaws so she talked all the time like she had a mouth full of something. Her words would slide. "Jiiim, I want you and Shaaane to cooome in heeere and dooo such and such a thing." It was like she pushed half of the words out and swallowed the other half. Her voice always sounded so loud and authoritarian, but really she was so gentle. She never had no kids, and she treated us like we was precious.

So, me and Shane went up to watch her TV a lot. The news came on at 6:00 and went off at 6:30, then *Highway Patrol* came on, and, believe me, there was these two little ole excited girls sitting there watching it. Miss Abby baked the best pound cake, and she gave us a slice and sometimes even a Coca-Cola. Then when the show was over, she said, "Okay, you girls get up and gooo to the house, but I'm gonna staaand here and listen until I think y'all done got home." So she stood at the back door, and we went down this trail which would run back into the road, just a little piece from our house. Of course, it was dark.

Later on, when we finally got a TV of our own, we'd watch 'til the TV signed off at night, when they played "The Star Spangled Banner." Mama was happy too. She loved the soaps.

Altogether, Miss Abby was an extremely warm, wonderful person. But she married a scoundrel. I knew it even as a kid. He didn't mistreat any of the kids that stayed on his place, at least not until later, but he didn't treat Miss Abby with no respect. He constantly belittled her. Miss Abby was a working-class person; she didn't have no education, but her husband, Bob, and Bob's daddy had plenty of property. They made their money off cotton and corn. But what he had, Bob didn't share with Miss Abby. He'd talk to her, but he didn't never consult with her like an equal. That's how she got taken so bad. She'd no idea what he had because he wouldn't let her know.

But Miss Abby was genuine and respectful. That's what made me see her beauty. I heard a lot of white people use the word *nigger*, but I never heard it from her. Some whites did it thinking you didn't hear them, but sometimes I came up when Miss Abby was talking to somebody else, and she didn't realize I was listening. Something about some African American'd come up, and Miss Abby would always say that "colored man" or that "colored woman." She'd not call them "boy" or "girl" like other whites called a black person, even when the black person was three times older than them.

Miss Abby's mama and most of her sisters was good to blacks also. Miss Abby got her gentleness and her goodness from her mom. Before Miss Mack, Miss Abby's mama, got sickly, she'd come and go, staying with her daughters in Montgomery, then with Miss Abby up in our neighborhood. But when Miss Mack got pretty old, she lived with Miss Abby and Mr. Bob.

The night Mr. Bob come and got me, because of what happened with Old James Boyd, the lyncher, I went up to Miss Abby's and stayed there with Miss Mack. Miss Mack and Miss Abby was innocent—it was Mr. Bob's daddy that done the burning.

I'll always remember Miss Mack's bedroom. I stayed with her a lot at night, and as she combed out her white hair and as I made up the bed, we talked. She'd ask me questions like, "What y'all be learning in school, Jim?" and I'd tell her. The first night I tried to sleep on the sun porch, but it didn't work. After that we'd climb in bed together, but before we went to sleep, we'd talk.

Miss Mack believed a woman should be submissive to her husband. "A wife's meant to follow her man, Jim," she'd say, "and my daughters learned what I taught them, thanks to Jesus." Miss Abby lived like Miss Mack taught her. I can't ever remember Miss Abby showing me anything that Mr. Bob gave her as a gift, but she worshiped the ground he walked on.

Miss Abby be so funny. Bob had a big chair that sat in front of the TV, and he used to wear these nice khaki pants. One day, Miss Abby showed me what she did. She took the cushion out from his chair and laid his pants carefully between the cushions. "Let him irooon his ooown pants," she said.

Bob always tried to control her. They lived in Wetumpka for years and years, and he wouldn't let her work. At first I thought it was really cool, that a woman just got to be at home, but then I realized it was a domineering thing. He didn't want her to be independent, but after they moved up to the country, she went to work and worked in a lunchroom.

I heard a rumor that Bob had an outside child by his brother's wife, who lived nearby, and he held it against Miss Abby that she couldn't have childrens. I think Miss Abby knowed about the child. I also learned real recently that when Bob got drunk, he'd beat Miss Abby, and she hid out in the cornfield many nights. At least she knowed Bob was unfaithful, and it must've hurt her, as devoted as she was. There be some low-down mens, and Bob be one of them.

Then, when Bob died, he hurt her one more time. He left all his property to a nephew. His will said Miss Abby could use it while she lived, but when she died, it was to go to his nephew. When Miss Abby found out what Mr. Bob had did, she said, "Low-down rascal," took her little tan dog, and just walked out. She left the house, the furniture, everything.

Altogether, I call Miss Abby a "unsung hero." There was a lot of white people that did things to help black folkses back then. But they knew they had to live in the white world and that they could even end up losing their lives if somebody actually knowed what they was doing. So some of the white people helped blacks behind the scene, where it really didn't show.

A couple of years ago I walked back through the woods 'til I got to the rubble of Miss Abby's house. I climbed up to what had been the hardwood floors and had to ease my way across, 'cause it was caving in. Vines be growing over the walls that still was standing.

I looked at the hardwood floors and old linoleum from the kitchen and remembered. I believe when we are children, God gives us a young mind so everything is fresh and new, and it stays with us when we get older, more than what happens day to day. So I remembered how I'd take the dust mop and run it over the floors. I liked to clean her house and pretend it was mine. For the time I was make believing I had a wonderful house. Besides, Miss Abby's house always made me feel warm and safe. I always felt welcome there. On Sundays, Miss Abby always cooked a dishpan of biscuits and fried sausage, then she invited all her sisters, their husbands, and their childrens for sausage, biscuits, and syrup. She wanted us to come too. So I'd go up to eat. She'd tell us, "Come over here and get yourselves something to eat."

Of course, there'd be times when I'd be over there and Miss Abby's mother-in-law, Poor Soul Miss Francie, and father-in-law, Low-Down James Boyd, the lyncher, come over. The strangest thing about it was that I wasn't scared of him. I believe God just has his way of protecting people, and he made me not afraid.

But I was real confused because Daddy and them told us how James Boyd and four or five other men took this black man, stringed him up from a tree, poured kerosene on him, and set him afire. Later, Mr. Bob himself confirmed it to us, but when I was at Miss Abby's and he was there, it just didn't fit. In my child's mind I expected to see a monster, but James Boyd looked and acted like his son, and Mr. Bob treated us decent, at least to our faces. If Bob drove past our house ten times a day, he was gonna wave ten times, and James Boyd, his father, was just like that. I'd be looking at Bob's daddy and thinking, "How could this man here do that? He don't look like no monster." You'd think it took a very brutal person to burn somebody alive. But, still, in that great getting-up morning, if James Boyd heads upward and I'm there, I'm gonna say, "Now, how in the world did he get up here?"

Later, Miss Abby married again, the sweetest guy, named Mr. Joe. He was what I'd call her soul mate. I think the years with Mr. Joe sort of made up for what happened before. Miss Abby and Mr. Joe was both working-class people, and they loved animals and lived in an old house surrounded by them. They raised goats, dogs, cats, birds, and black hens, and they covered each square inch of the walls with a picture or knick-knacks of a cat or dog.

Finally, Mr. Joe died and Miss Abby went to a nursing home, but I'd visit her, and sometimes she'd remember me. She'd talk to me about how she wanted to be cremated like Mr. Joe. After she died, I wanted to go to the ceremony they had to remember her, and when I asked where it would be held, her remaining sister told me that I wasn't welcome. I guess 'cause I'm African American. So I'm trying to find out where they scattered her ashes and go there by myself.

Even with some people like Miss Abby around, there was a lot of evil. Sheriff Lester Holley thought he was judge and jury down there in Wetumpka. If he put you in jail, we believed you stayed there until he got ready to let you out. You didn't go before no judge, and he owned this huge bunch of rocky land where he used to make prisoners clear up all the rocks.

African Americans always felt whites cared more for their dogs and cats than about them. That's just how Holley felt. A black person was less than an animal to him. He had no problem degrading a black man, calling him a nigger. We thought he'd even beat a black man to death. And the blacks felt they didn't dare raise a hand to a sheriff 'cause he'd just shoot them down.

When I got old enough to understand, I learned of the rumors that a sheriff would keep a family of black womens for himself, usually someone who was really, really light colored with long, straight-looking hair.

There wasn't no way that womens could say no to a sheriff, 'cause if you did, you was gonna end up in jail.

And even when night riders beat the Bozemans up, people didn't talk too much about things for fear that it might get back to the wrong person. I know that Mama did not let her anger show to the point that we would see it. We might let it slip. She knew the danger we faced all the time. Back then, when I was young, there wasn't nothing blacks could do about the violence, nothing to do but wait and watch. It was like in this old black hymn: "You can't hurry God, you just have to wait. You can't hurry God." So the old people watched and waited, and if they heard tell of one of the low-downs getting sick, they said, "Yeah, God's coming. I told you, just give God time, and he'll fix it."

Old Sheriff Holley went to the Elmore County Hospital, and one thing that black people did back then, if they knowed some white man had been really, really bad to the people that worked on his place or if he had acted low-down in some other way, black people would watch real close and spread the news about what they saw. The blacks around there was curious to see how bad Lester Holley suffered, so those that worked in the hospital kept a constant watch over him, then they reported out to other black folks, who told others.

Sometimes Holley begged, begged people to find some of those he'd wronged so he could plead for their forgiveness, and sometimes he yelled, "Get 'em back, get 'em back. Don't let 'em get me." It was like all the peoples that he had hurt or killed came back to torment him. Holley laid there and begged to die. He asked God, "Why? Why aren't you taking me? I'm ready to go." By and by, people came to the conclusion that God was making him suffer while he was still alive for all the things that he had did on this earth to hurt people. Then, finally, he died.

Maybe it was just fate or maybe it was God's will, but those low-downs died horrible, horrible deaths. I think death should be the ultimate, peaceful sacrifice, and they died bad, real bad.

seven

*They make butterfly cages of interlinked fingers. Swallow
tailed memories hover inside, disturbing a breath of a place
with remembrance, then the women open their hands, and the
soft creatures flutter up and drift away.*

— Fran L. Buss, 1988

Daddy was Baptist and belonged to Sweet Water Church, and Mama belonged to New Style, the Methodists, but we always liked to go to Daddy's church. The Methodist people was more laid back, but the Baptists, boy, they'd be kicking, shouting, filled with the spirit, really getting into the service. The Methodist church was not as loud. With the Baptist, when you was like a half block away, you heard the services going on. They opened the windows, and the sound flowed out real good, and they preached and prayed. They've gotten so sophisticated in all the churches now, they got the big old drums and pianos. Back then, there was no piano, and the people sang this good harmony. And the preacher, he didn't have no microphone, but you could hear him a half a mile away.

We loved going out there to Sweet Water 'cause funny ladies worshiped in that church, especially Miss Lena Westbrook. Miss Lena used to shout and tap out her spirit with her feet. Miss Lena always wore these shoes without a heel, and her foot was so big that you couldn't see the shoe, her foot stuck out all the way around, and it be going up and down, up and down. The preacher'd be preaching, the people be singing, and right before Miss Lena start to shout, she'd reach up there and just rip

93

the hat off her head. Then she'd go into this spell with her arms stiff and straight out. She'd walk up and down the aisles and shout and shout. For a long time the ushers tried to hold her, to keep her safe while she be so happy and filled with the spirit.

Mr. Lige Hardy, one of the deacons, was about the same height as Daddy, and Daddy wasn't no more than about five feet, three inches. One time Mr. Lige decided that this time he was gonna hold Miss Lena down, but when he grabbed Miss Lena, she knocked him wide across the room. And we never did see him hold Miss Lena no more. They got to a point when Miss Lena stood up and ripped off her hat, the sisters told the ushers, "Just take her glasses off, fan her, and let her go. Let her go." Miss Lena be knocking and falling while they struggled to get her glasses off, but once they did, she couldn't hurt herself, and they let her express her feelings. She'd shout and shout and shout, [laughs] then finally she'd say, "Hummmmm," and begin to wind down.

Oh, I tell you the truth, we kids done sit back there snickering and laughing and going on, and when she got to the point where she was at the end of her "Hummmmm," I looked at Shane and Shane looked at me, and we fell out laughing. We got in trouble a couple of times 'cause Daddy saw us breaking up.

Us kids never got happy. We was too crazy to get happy. Nobody did but the adults, and that'd just be the womens, not the mens. They shouted for all sorts of reasons. Some of them be shoutin' 'cause they done found their man going with one of the sisters in the church. [laughs] Also, of course, at that time we kids had no idea about some of the things happening with some of them womens and some of the mens. There be some of the most devilish preachers, especially with the revivals. If a preacher be good looking, the womens felt like whatever he wanted to do, they was justified in keeping the preacher happy. Them little sapsucker preachers.

The womens wasn't allowed to do anything in these churches except get happy. The deacons sat on one Amen side of the church and the deaconesses, the deacons' wives or widows, on the other. The choir stood in front of the church. The preacher sat in front with four seats for visitin' preachers, and the people and childrens sat on benches, with aisles.

I never in my life heard a woman lead the service. The deacons'd be the ones that started the church service with prayer, and if the deacon was down praying and the spirit hit one of the women, she'd say, "Continuing prayer," then go up there and pray. But as far as her sitting up there, she didn't.

Daddy wasn't a religious person, although he'd go to revivals. One time he was going good until they made him a deacon, and then he just stopped going. But the church that he was born and raised in is still there. Also, it was the normal thing back then that whenever a woman married, she'd change her religion to her husband's, but Mama didn't. She stayed a Methodist.

We kids really looked forward to the all-day sings each summer. Each church had a different annual note-singing day, and people who had moved came back for the Sunday scheduled in their home church, the church where they'd been raised in. We got to look forward to two all-day sings, the reunion at Daddy's church at Sweet Water and the reunion at Mama's church, New Style.

Note singing used no instruments, just four or five people. One person started the singing, then another person began, then another sang, and then the first person joined again. A long time ago many people could note sing, but a lot of the old people who did it died. They've been trying to get more young people in it, but you can't just pick it up. It took a lot of practice.

When I was a real young child, Mama and them let us play and wander around the outside while the grown-ups were in church. People went in and out as they listened to the note singing, and they nodded their heads at each other and smiled. It was summer, and the windows was always open, so as we ran around the churchyard, we heard the beautiful sound of them singing. After the singers once joined together, they'd be in perfect harmony.

I remember Old Perfect Jackson. Perfect Jackson would sing, then go outside and get him a drink of whiskey, and go back in there and rock the church with his music. Another little old man who was half white, with hair as straight as an arrow, shined with singing.

Later, as we got older, we used the sings to flirt. We never went inside; we was too busy looking at the boys. The same with revivals. If we was already inside, we looked out the window, and if we spotted any boys, we announced, "Got to go to the toilet." The outdoor toilet was way down in the woods without any light, so as it was getting dark, you be taking a big chance when you pulled your drawers down out there, but we'd did it in order to get outside with the boys.

There was lots of romance going on, older kids in the cars that wasn't supposed to be there. Daddy threatened to kill us, but Shane didn't care. Shane'd take a chance on anything, and if anybody accused her, she'd just say, "No, it wasn't me. I didn't do it," looking 'em straight in the eye.

Those was some revivals back then, and when we came back, we'd stop at the watermelon patch, and Daddy got us a good one. Sometimes Uncle Tanks, Aunt Becky, and their kids stopped by after the revival, 'cause the watermelon patch was up on the road. I just loved revivals.

But do you know what stopped me from laughing at people at church? I heard my mama shout one time, I did. I saw her shout, and after that I never laughed at people no more. I don't know why it happened, but I remember it was at New Style. When we got ready to go to church that morning, Mama looked different. I don't know whether Mama was worried or what it was. Mama often cried silently in church, but that day, when the man started preaching, she got up and shouted. We started to cry 'cause we was scared. We childrens always made fun when someone else was shouting, but we thought something bad was happening this time.

When we got home, we asked, "Mama, why was you shouting?"

She just shook her head and said, "Shoo. Get on out of here." So she had cried and shouted, and we cried with her. Just boo-hoo, sitting there on the bench, sobbing. After that, I never laughed at nobody else shouting.

We have good memories. Each year, when we got a new dress, I'd put it on soon as I could, and Mama'd say, "What you doing with that dress on? You ain't going to church." One year, when I was about nine or ten, we went to Wetumpka after the cotton was in, and Mama bought me two dresses. I can still see them dresses and smell their newness. I came home and put one on, and I felt so pretty, I walked up to the cemetery and back, then I put on the other one and did it again. After that I be satisfied.

Sometimes, when all our cousins got together, we'd be a yard full of kids. We'd run in the cotton fields, up and down the rows, just flying. Our plaits be bouncing as we run. We'd catch june bugs, tie a string on its legs so that it'd buzz and fly around in circles like a little airplane. Sometimes we had two or three strings of june bugs, and they all got tangled up. Then at night, we'd catch lightning bugs and put them in a jar. They was beautiful. Oh, you'd walk outside and it was like you done run into a wheel of sparkles, all the lightning bugs.

Me and Shane also climbed all sorts of trees and Muskie vines, which have fruit like grapes and tastes real good. People put up a big old rack so the vine'd grow up it, then they pick the fruit from underneath. The vines also grow wild out in the woods, where they run up a tree. We went hunting for the vines, shimmied up them until we got in the tree, then we shaked, shaked, shaked the vine, and somebody on the ground picked the fruit up.

Virga Mae, the girl with the childlike mind, came to see us, swishing her switch down the road. She loved to play our games with us; her body was big, but she was just a little girl. We had this smokehouse made of logs, almost like the toy kids put together, and we set sticks behind it and made us a playhouse.

Sometimes Mama gave us permission to go to Virga Mae's house. She lived not too far from the white dirt spot, so Mama'd say, "Take this sack and go on up there to the dirt ditch and get some dirt." So Virga Mae'd go to the dirt ditch with us. We always had a really neat time together while we was walking. Virga could talk, and she was very, very loving, especially to animals. Sometimes she showed us a bird with a broken wing or some other little animal she cared for.

Mama used to have them headaches, and I shudder every time I think about them. She lay there and thumped her head against the bed, pounding it in pain. I remember real good her telling us kids to take our hands and put pressure on her head, as much pressure as we could. So we'd be standing there around the bed, trying to hold all our little hands around her. She'd be crying, and we'd be crying. Boy, she had a hard time.

When Mama wasn't sick, she really liked to hear the stories, the serials she'd listen to on the radio, the soap operas. She especially loved *Young Dr. Malone.* And sometimes, when she'd get those headaches, she groan and beg us, "Please call Dr. Malone," not knowing he was just made up, that it was radio fiction. When Mama started getting those headaches so bad, everybody told her it was her long hair, that was the reason the headaches was so terrible, so she really cut her hair one time, but it didn't make no difference.

Then one morning Mama got up and big old water blisters come up onto her legs and her hands and in her mouth, just out of nowhere. They virtually covered her whole, entire body, and she got this big old blister on the roof of her mouth, and it busted. We sat there and cried, Mama was so miserable. Daddy even took her to the doctor, and nobody could figure out what was wrong. The doctor thought it might be the change of life. The blisters went away and came back. When I was an adult, I started thinking of them in terms of the pesticides Daddy was spraying, wondering if they was connected.

There was all kinds of suffering that people lived through. Lots caused by other people. Mama was kind, and she always acted loving toward people, but other blacks played their part in the suffering. One morning, we was in the kitchen real early, and we heard this shot ring out. We knew right off the bat it was a shotgun 'cause we recognized it, and nobody used rifles back then. We heard people hunting all the time, and we really didn't pay it any attention, but this was different. Mama said, "Hmmm, I wonder what fool is shooting this early in the morning?" It was like 6:30 or so. We went on with our work, but it was a really disturbing sound. A little later, Mama was still thinking about it. "That gunshot sounded strange," she said.

Then somebody came by the house, I don't remember who, and that person said, "Virga Mae . . ." Our friend. The person said, "Crazy Old Mason—her stepdaddy—killed Virga Mae this morning."

Boy, we wailed and Mama cried! Our hearts just broke that morning. We learned Virga Mae's mama was there when Virga Mae's stepdaddy killed Virga Mae, but the mama never told quite what happened, the reason why her husband killed that girl. Of course, at that time me and Shane didn't know nothing about no incest. We knowed of people dying. People died all the time, but we never heard of anybody we knowed being killed. Virga Mae was our good friend.

It's hard to believe that her mama didn't know what her stepdaddy was doing to that child, sexually molesting her. I don't think Virga Mae's mind was probably mature enough even to know that what was being done to her body shouldn't have been done.

Nobody knowed nothing about this man, her stepdad, but he must have had a little money because he owned their own place and was able to build a house out of cement blocks. It was unusual for a black person to be able to do that, so I figured maybe Virga Mae's mama let what happened with Virga Mae go on because of the house it let her live in. The house had two bedrooms and a little living room.

The funeral was just so, so terribly sad. It was at Sweet Water Church, and she looked so very, very small. I looked at her left hand, where she held her switch, and it looked empty. Her hair was still short around her face where she'd pull it out, and the rest was nappy as always. I stared at her and wondered why would this happen. She was just a child that wanted people to like her. It was so cruel.

Me and Shane went back up there to the house, and, oh God, that house was so sad. Old Man Mason shot her behind the door. We always heard that if blood got on the ground when somebody was killed, every time it rained the blood rose back up again. We wondered if that would happen for Virga Mae. Later, we searched for stains but weren't sure we found them. When we went into her house, it was like we could see her spirit there, and then we went outside and saw her out in the yard, down by the hog pen.

We was all grief stricken, everybody was. A lot of the older people thought, "Maybe if I had did something, I could've stopped it. What was it I seen that I ignored that would leave this child dead?"

Everybody in the community knowed her. She'd go see people at different times. We'd be sitting there at the house and see Virga coming with that little switch, swishing it back and forth. When she actually reached a person, she'd switch them gentle-like across the legs. That was her compassionate way of letting them know she knew who they was. And she always wanted somebody to touch her, to show affection. I believe Virga Mae's stepdaddy died in prison.

Now there's hardly any black people staying on the land where we share-cropped, but when I was growing up, it was a living community. Folkses had been going north or to Montgomery for work for a long time, but our place was still alive. We blacks called it New Style or Sweet Water, after our churches, but I guess it had no name to whites. They just saw it as a few farms up in the country.

But it was alive to us, and we all tried to take care of each other, providing food or help when something went wrong. As we got older, one of my sisters would watch the younger kids at nights, so when a neighbor got sick, Mama could leave us and walk to wherever that person stayed and be with them 'til the sun come up. Then she'd walk home, cook our breakfast, and do her work around the house and in the fields. She was just like that.

When a woman had a baby, the rest of her kids wasn't gonna be lacking nothing. Neighbors'd make sure they had the same meals, their clothes was going to be washed and ironed, and their houses was going to be cleaned. Daddy used to take Jack and J. W. and cut loads of wood for people that was sick. Even if old people lost control of their bowels and had to be cleaned like a baby, they were took care of. If a father who was farming got sick or died, some neighbors'd show up to help with the work. At least the family didn't have to worry about the crop not being brought in. Other families'd rally around.

My friend Zeny Catron was raised by her stepmama. Zeny's mother died, leaving seven kids, and their daddy remarried to a woman who had some kids herself. But about two weeks after they got married, the daddy was killed in a logging truck accident, and that stepmama kept all those kids and raised them and put them through school. Zeny always talks about her stepmama with so much compassion.

There was a place for peoples in our community. There was important people like Evander Anthony, the only black barber in Wetumpka. His shop was right there among the businesses of town, so even though he just cut black peoples' hair, he was the person that knowed what whites was up to. And if somebody needed someone to sign their bonds to get out of jail, he'd be there.

There was even a place for strange people, like Ezra Who Sleeps in the Woods. Me and Shane was scared of him 'cause he was like a hobo, and he didn't have no home. They'd find him in an abandoned house somewhere. We'd just be going about our normal business, and all of a sudden we'd see this raggedy, straggly person with long hair and a beard coming down the road. He'd stay for a few minutes, maybe get some food, then he'd just disappear. We thought he was spooky so we'd get to fussin', but Mama'd say, "Aw, y'all quit actin' crazy 'cause he ain't gonna bother y'all. He ain't dangerous."

There was this whole migration of families back then, all the time coming and going. Peoples'd raise a crop two or three years on somebody's place, then they'd move on, hoping for somethin' better. Then here come another family. It was an ongoing thing. There was only a few stable sharecropping families, Daddy and Uncle Tanks and Cousin Will's and Cousin Ansley, which was Mattie, Daddy's distant cousin. By the time I got very big, Old Man Paul didn't have but one house that tenant farmers stayed in, and that was ours, so he didn't have people moving around. But others did.

As it happened, we realized there was fewer and fewer families being replaced when a family left. We kids knowed because when the adults left, the childrens left with them, and they was kids that we growed up and went to school with. When they started leaving, it was hard, like with my little friend Dorothy Nell.

A lot of the childrens wasn't living with their biological parents but with grandparents, aunts, or older brothers and sisters. The parents had done left and went north to make a better living. Then, as years went on, if the parents didn't come back and get the kids, when the childrens got old enough, they left and went north their ownself. So there was fewer and fewer peoples in total.

Also, when the old white farmers died out, whoever came in may not even want to have sharecroppers, so even if there was people who wanted to work, there wasn't a place. There was a lot of white farmers that was getting out of the cotton-growing business, so blacks was disappearing, disappearing.

Other changes be happening. When I was just little, they was changing from mules to tractors, and with tractors fewer peoples could do more work, which probably encouraged more white farmers to put more croppers off their land. I know Daddy loved his tractor, and he'd go around and do work for other farmers. Today, when I see the machines, cotton pickers and cotton choppers, it just makes my blood boil. 'Cause I know that if they could invent one now, they could've invented one then, and we wouldn't had to be out there breaking our backs.

Also, over the years some of the few African Americans that owned land was cheated out of it. That happened to one man. He had a lot of land, for a black man, but he sold a little piece of the land to a white man. Then the white man came back and told him that he had lost his deed and needed another copy and they could go down to the court-house and get the deed made up if the black man would sign it again. But the black man couldn't read or write, so the white man had the deeds made up giving him almost all the black man's property, and the black man signed it. After he found out what happened, he went running around to different people, trying to get his property back, but because he done signed it, it was gone.

But we was a community back then when Daddy and Mama was alive, and we was growing up. The grandparents that was raisin' kids didn't have to worry about the child because everybody in that neighborhood was going to be in the corner with that grandparent, teaching those kids what was right and what was wrong. People shared responsibility for the children.

I be laughing and telling somebody what always amazed me when we was growing was that we could be over at somebody's house playing, and we'd do something wrong and got our behinds spanked, and by the time we got to the house, Mama already knowed it, and we didn't have no telephone. We couldn't figure that out. I guess we must have come in looking guilty. Mama'd say, "Yeah, I know you did something wrong. You're in trouble with me too." Either she could tell by looking at us, or they used the can with the string on it. [laughs]

It hurts that my grandkids are being raised up in a mostly white world. I feel like they are losing their cultural identity, and by the time they have grandkids, there's not gonna be none. I will probably never be this proper English-speaking person, and I wouldn't want to be, 'cause that would mean that I'm trying to be something that I'm not. But when I see [my grandkids] being taught to speak perfect, I think, who are they speaking it for? You don't have to do it for me. There's nothing wrong with speaking perfect English, but there's a loss. I just sit up sometimes and think about all the things that we lost—a whole community taking care of its kids, loving them, disciplining them, that's a big cost for change. Me and Shane and other kids growed up together, and we carved our initials in our chinaberry tree. Then the other kids vanished, we got bigger, and the whirlwind come and it all disappeared.

One day in May 1956, Old Man Paul went out to the barn and just fell over. We was over yonder in the field, chopping cotton, when we heard Old Lady Bernice hollering, hollering: "J. D.! J. D.! Come quick, come quick!" Daddy ran all the way over there from that cotton field, and when he got over there, he found Mr. Paul out there in the barnyard collapsed. Daddy took him to the house, but Mr. Paul wasn't breathing.

When we got there, Daddy looked at us. "Mr. Paul's dead." We went to crying, having a fit. Mr. Paul was good to us, and he was a gentle man. Also, Miss Bernice couldn't be trusted. I boo-hooed as the hearse came and got him. Of course, we went to Mr. Paul's funeral, but we had to sit in the back. We did go out to the grave with everybody and stood around, watching them put him in the ground, and we came back later to look at the flowers. Miss Bernice lived eleven years longer than he did, and she messed up a lot in those years.

She was scared of staying alone after he died, so she told me to come up to the house and stay with her. She had a room with a cot that they never used, so I used to sleep on the cot. I did it, but I didn't really want to. There was nothing to do up there at night, plus she didn't want me to come until almost time to go to bed, and by then it was good and dark, and I wasn't too happy about walking outside. The house smelled stale, like a old person's house, but it wasn't dirty. Miss Bernice wasn't no nasty old person.

When we worked over in the fields, we had to come by Mr. Paul's house on the way home, and it be so funny. People used to joke that Bernice only mourned Paul until she inherited his money. Several times Daddy'd come into the house at night and say, "Old Lady Bernice making me sick."

"What she doing now?" Mama asks.

And Daddy'd go mocking her, mimicking Bernice. "She up there slinging snot, saying, 'Oh, I sure do miss Paul. I sure do miss Paul.' " So Daddy'd be mocking how she be crying, and the next thing we know, she'd be spending money, spending money. As long as Mr. Paul had lived, they had a very primitive life, but Miss Bernice wanted to be the lady. Mr. Paul wasn't dead in his grave a good six months before she had that house remodeled, and she went out and had furniture reupholstered and bought beautiful mahogany twin beds and a mahogany dining room set with a big, beautiful china cabinet. She'd had just a regular old tin sink with no cabinets in the kitchen, a old table that probably was Paul's grandmama's, old chairs. Nothing more. Mr. Paul had a pump in the well that pumped water into the house, but there was no bathroom.

So she changed all that, fixed everything up, and bought a brand-new car. By that time Miss Bernice thought she really was *something*. She'd answer the telephone: "This is *Mrs.* Paul Henderson speaking." She was the lady.

And she got more and more superior acting with Daddy. Mr. Paul had stopped her from using her power as his wife to make us feel like servants. When she'd boss Daddy, he'd say, "Uh- uh, J. D. works for me." But now it was like Miss Bernice just went kind of batty. She'd be making all kinds of demands on Daddy. "Bring me this. Bring me that. Put this here. Put this there." Stupid things, like she wanted the garden one place one year and another the next.

Sometimes Daddy said, "Mr. Paul never told me to do that."

Then she answered, "Well, Mr. Paul is not living no more. Miss Bernice is the boss."

And at the same time she fixed her house all up, and there was only one person living there, she didn't do nothing for our house. For all those years we had done stayed in it, and there wasn't enough room in our house for all of us.

Miss Bernice just went crazy, thinking she was so high class. She virtually turned everybody against her, including Old Man Wilbert Atkins, her brother, and her nephew, just by thinking she had done hit the millionaire status.

Finally, Mr. Bob, Miss Abby's husband, who had known Daddy and every one of us from babies, saw what she was doing. So he came and told Daddy, "J. D. You don't have to take that. You can move over to my place. You can farm, you can raise cotton and corn and anything else you want to over there."

Miss Bernice kept on pushing and pushing and pushing, until Daddy finally said, "We moving." He told Miss Bernice, "If you can't do no better than this for us, we'll just move." So, when I was about fourteen, we did.

Then after we moved to Mr. Bob's, we passed by our old house once. Miss Bernice took the house that we had been staying in all our lives and was putting a porch across the front and making the back porch into a bedroom. Miss Bernice hurt us bad, but she also paid a heavy price for the way she treated us. God don't like ugly.

Even though his father, James Boyd, was the lyncher, Bob treated Daddy and other black men with some respect. And, of course, Miss Abby was kind to us all. I enjoyed where we moved. It had two hickory nut trees in the yard and was surrounded by a woods that I used to sit in, especially in the fall. We had a good-sized barn and a gutter that ran down from the well to the animals, so we didn't have to tote the water to them, and the house had three bedrooms.

Later, we moved back to Miss Bernice's, and late one night, after all of us was in bed, Mr. Bob came to the house and knocked on the door. "Can Jim come over to my house for the night and stay with Miss Abby's mama?" he asked Daddy.

"Yes, I guess. She's sleeping. I'll get her up."

As soon as I got my clothes on, I went on over to Mr. Bob's and Miss Abby's house, back in the woods. I could tell Mr. Bob was upset, and when I got there, Miss Abby was up and crying. Miss Abby's mama, Miss Mack, was staying with them and was in the bed sick.

This was the first time Miss Abby asked me to spend the night with her mama. "Jim, go back yonder onto the porch and sleep. I just wanted somebody here with Mama," she said.

I asked her, "What happened? What's the matter?"

"Papa," that's what she sometimes called Mr. Bob's dad, James Boyd. "Papa just blowed his brains out."

"What?"

"I can't tell you about it now. I'll tell you about it later."

"Okay."

I was scared after she left. I thought, "God, why would he do that?" And the little porch back there where she told me to sleep had all these windows around it. They were screened in so that in the summer they could let the windows open, and in the winter it was like a sunroom back there. I was so scared. I finally went in there where Miss Mack, Miss Abby's mama, was sleeping, and I got in a chair and stayed there in the room with her. Partway through the night Miss Mack woke up and saw me sitting there and told me, "Come on. Get in bed with me." It was after that night that I stayed with Miss Mack a lot, sleeping in her bed and talking before we went to sleep.

At that time Miss Abby still couldn't drive, so the next morning Mr. Bob brought Miss Abby back home, then he went back to his parents' house. Miss Abby gave me a bunch of phone numbers and told me to call them about what happened. One was to Bob's brother in Seattle. I was to tell him to come home immediately, that his dad was real sick, but really his dad was dead.

Then Miss Abby told me what happened. By that time Mr. Bob's daddy, low-down James Boyd, had been sick for a couple of years, and he'd tried to commit suicide several times, but they had always caught him and stopped him. Lately, he had gotten so weak that they just never dreamed that he could get up and get himself something to kill himself with.

But he had another shotgun that they didn't know about, and it was hid in that room. He was also taking some kind of medication, and Miss Abby says that they think he stockpiled the medicine up and took just enough to give him enough strength so that he could get the gun. Then he put the barrel of the gun underneath his chin and raised his foot far enough to pull the trigger with his toe, and he blowed his head clean off. His wife was sleeping in the next room.

"Jim, this was the god-awfullest mess I ever seen in my life. It was just horrible," Miss Abby told me. "He blowed his head all over the top of his house. I never thought Papa'd do that to himself. He has hurt Bob and Miss Boyd so bad."

Later on, Mr. Bob told us why his dad was in such bad shape. His dad helped lynch that black man years before. Mr. Bob told us, "Not only was Papa there, Papa was the one that struck the match. Papa prayed to die 'cause of it." He was terrorized by what he had did. Nobody knows what demons plagued him. If it holds true what I've always heard, he probably saw that man burning many nights, many nights.

Mr. Bob told us the whole story. They caught the black guy, and five white mens hung him up in a tree. Then they poured kerosene on him and stood up there and discussed who was going to strike the match. They were gonna burn him alive. So Old James Boyd said, "Sure, I'll strike the match to the nigger." He was the one who did the deed.

It's strange to think of him and Miss Abby in the same family, although I don't know how close they was. I always got a sense that it was something that wasn't quite right in their relationship because she hardly ever called them "Mama" or "Papa" as if they was hers. She always referred to her mother-in-law as "Miss Boyd." I think they looked down on her, at least James Boyd did.

Old black people talked a lot about James Boyd's death. They said, "See, give God time. Give God time. God'll fix things and then it'll be done." And it happened. Each of the low-down men that lynched the black guy got sick and dragged on years and years, waiting to die, to be released from his suffering. Some went five or six years waiting, some went for ten, and death wouldn't come. Like James Boyd they begged to die. Living was so terrible for them.

Yeah, after James Boyd killed hisself in 1959, the old ones said, "That's the last of those low-down sapsuckers that burned the guy."

It's hard, 'cause when something happens like the lynching, you want justice quick and swift. The crime was done swift, so you don't want to wait around. Lately, I thought that's God's way of testing us to see if we will believe. I got involved with the civil rights movement and the union movement 'cause I want justice to prevail. But I believe in my heart that although God wants us to fight for it, justice is coming, no matter what we do.

·

❧ eight ❧

For black people . . . had learned a long time ago that to stay
willingly in a beloved but brutal place is to risk losing the love
and being forced to acknowledge only the brutality.
—Alice Walker, *In Search of Our Mothers' Gardens*

I started developing breasts when I was like ten years old, and by eleven I was really big chested, but we couldn't afford no bra. I had this humongous chest, so I took a flour sack and pulled it down over my head to flatten my breasts out. I'd pull it into a band across my chest, and I didn't have no bra until I was grown.

One day, when I was fourteen, I went to the bathroom, and when I looked down there, I saw blood. "Oh Lord," I thought to myself, "I'm gonna die!" My period come on, but I thought I was bleeding to death, so I ran into the house, yellin' and hollerin' to the top of my voice.

"Gal, what in the world wrong with you?" Mama said. I be crying so hard I couldn't tell her. All I could do then is just let down my panties. Mama said, "Aw, shit, I thought you was talkin' about something. Ain't nothing wrong."

I could always talk to Shane, so I told her, "I went to the bathroom, and I done cut myself or something 'cause there's something in my drawers."

Shane started laughing. "You ain't cut yourself. It's your menstruation." She showed me what I had to do. Back then black people was really superstitious about menstrual cycles 'cause they thought people could use it for witchcraft, so it was very important how you cared for the rags. You didn't put 'em down nowhere. If you took one off and couldn't wash it out right then, 'cause water and soap was scarce, you washed them out every night, then you let 'em soak in water, and the next morning you had to boil 'em.

Every now and then, you heard this rumor: "So-and-so done got hoo-dooed."

Then somebody else'd say, "Yeah, they got ahold of some of her menstrual rags, and then they done messed her up, so she's acting crazy and having fits." Then, when I got older, I heard: "Miss Estelle is a witch doctor, live down in Redland. She's the hoo-doo woman." Over the years she became really wealthy from tellin' her fortunes and doin' her hoo-doo. If a man left a woman, the first thing they'd say was, "Child, oh so-and-so done took so-and-so's husband away, and you know how she got him? Honey, she hoo-dooed him. But so-and-so's going down to Miss Estelle's trying to get him back." Every time some husband or wife left, you heard that they got "hoo-dooed."

One time Tom came home and drove us to an annual picnic, then, when he was driving us home, he pointed to a house. "That be where Miss Estelle lives." I stared. It looked just like a regular house, with nothing scary. But people come over to it from all across the country.

So my period started, my breasts grew, and I kept growing, but I thought I was really ugly, 'cause I couldn't do nothing with my hair. But then, when I was starting junior high in the seventh grade, Mama put the straightening comb in me and Shane's hair. You needed a Fresh Apple Tobacco can for the straightening comb. Daddy chewed tobacco, but not the right kind, so we got a can from other people. Mama taught us to put the can in the coals of the fireplace or in the stove, then stick the comb down in it and get it hot. The can kept the ashes out of it. You could lose a lot of hair if the straightening comb be too hot when you stuck it on your head. A big patch of hair'd come out, but after Mama straightened our hair, we thought we was pretty, we thought we was fine.

When I was twelve, I started being bused into Elmore County Training School, the African American junior and senior high school in Wetumpka. It was a shock. First of all, if you had to ride the school bus, half the time the bus broke down on the way to school, and maybe it was noon before you even got there. They didn't have no other bus to pick you up.

Where I'd grown up, everybody in the community around me had been in the same boat financially, so we didn't worry about showing off.

But the city kids didn't want to have anything to do with us country kids. They called us names and told us we didn't know how to dress.

But it wasn't just the other kids. Blacks labeled blacks. If you came out of the country, you was labeled by the teachers too: "This child ain't gonna ever amount to nothing 'cause she just came off of the farm." And because we was needed in the fields, we couldn't start to school when the Wetumpka kids did. One literature teacher said I was really good 'cause I could interpret what I read real well. She always encouraged me, but the other teachers put me down.

Also, the childrens had to buy their schoolbooks, so lots of the times we didn't get no books. I used to try to borrow books from other kids, but they'd tell me, "I'll help you if I can, but I gotta have my books to study at home."

Mama and Daddy knew it was hard on us 'cause we'd tell them how we was treated, but there wasn't nothing they could do. Mama said, "Well." Nothing else, just "Well." Daddy'd been a trustee in our country school, but at Elmore County everybody on the trustee board was from Wetumpka. I read everything I could ever find. Sometimes when we was living at Old Man Paul's and Old Lady Bernice's place, we woke up in the morning and a box of newspapers, magazines, or even a bunch of books had been left out along the road. I be always so happy! I loved to look at pictures, but one time I found a romance book about slavery and a black man laying down with a white woman! They had sex together, then she protested that he was coming there to her house.

I thought, "Wow! I wonder if there's more books like this!" I couldn't believe that somebody wrote about slavery, and I read it two or three times and found it absolutely fascinating. Then later on, as I got older and older, I found other books that dealt with slavery. I tell you, I wondered if those white folkses who left Mandigo at our house knowed what they was doing!

One morning we was in the kitchen, and Mama was standing at the stove with the frying pan in her hand. *Clang,* she dropped it. It startled us all, and we looked at her. She looked down, and when we did, we saw she stood in a puddle of blood. She stared at it a few seconds, then started to pass out, and we grabbed her. It turned out Mama had cancer, but they gave her a hysterectomy, and then they sent her to Montgomery and gave her radiation, so we thought it made her better.

I think in Mama's mind, she believed that she'd been cured. I don't think she even fully understood what cancer was. And I believe that was one of the things that maybe prolonged her life. She didn't understand that every day this thing was constantly spreading further through her body. So she didn't have to fight the fear. She didn't have no more symptoms for maybe a year.

In the meantime things was changing in lots of ways for us. As we began to go to junior high, I lost my white friend Joy. 'Cause there wasn't no other young white kids around where we lived as a child, it had never dawned on me that black and white kids went to different schools. I had just thought Joy and I went to different schools because she lived in town and I lived in the country, but as I began junior high and rode the school bus into town, it finally dawned on me.

Joy was growing distant from us in other ways. I guess she didn't see a reason why we'd stay best friends. I guess she just thought our childhood was over, and we wasn't meant to be friends after we got older. Of course, there always be hints of problems. One time Miss Bernice made us tomato sandwiches, and we was sitting there eating them and drinking some tea. I said, "My tea ain't sweet enough."

So Joy said, "Let me taste it."

But before she could take my glass, Miss Bernice swooped over and said real fast, "Don't ever drink after one of them."

"Why?" Joy asked. "But why?"

"Just because. Don't do it."

Then, another time, Joy was going to spend the night up there at Miss Bernice's, and Miss Bernice wouldn't let me stay with her. Joy questioned the rules. She did. But maybe Miss Bernice's teachings finally got through. There must have been some reason they didn't let her come see us no longer. It was not like we had a fight.

I guess her parents told her, "You can play with her when y'all little, but you can't be her friend as you get big." Maybe it was 'cause Jack and J. W. was getting bigger, and Joy's family was afraid to have her around them. I tried to find answers for why Joy no longer wanted to play with me. I wanted to know why. Why? People'd say, "'Cause she's white and you black." I didn't hear from her again for twenty-something years, although we lived not far away.

But Miss Abby stuck with me and helped me make it through high school. She always encouraged me, and sometimes I think that if we had stayed on her place, I might have got an education, 'cause she was always worrying about it. She'd say, "Nooow, don't be over at that school just meeesing around," sliding out her words. "You be over there to get an education. You don't want to stay out there in them coootton fields the rest of your life." She fixed me up used clothes to help me go to school.

Miss Abby also gave me a different kind of gift. I must have been twelve. Me and Miss Abby was in the kitchen, and she was baking a pound cake. The TV set in the living room by the fireplace was on so we could see it, and somebody said something about Rosa Parks being arrested for refusing to give up her seat on the bus in Montgomery.

Miss Abby was stirring the cake; she stopped and said real strong, "That colored woman in Montgomery, the one they be talkin' about, the one they arrested for not giving up her seat on the bus, she shouldn't have to give it up. She paid her money just like anybody else did. She should've been able to sit where she wanted to sit." Miss Abby stirred some more and said, "Plus, they be hypocrites. She look like the same color they is." She meant that Rosa Parks was a light-skinned black woman.

I didn't understand exactly what was happening at that particular time, but there was a lot of talking, almost a commotion. "Did y'all hear Dr. King's house be bombed?"

"Did you hear about all those black folkses that be at Holt Street Baptist?"

"That old low-down White Citizens Council rallied. They say ten thousand. Ain't nothin' but the Ku Klux."

Miss Abby also took me to her mama's, Miss Mack's, funeral, way, way down in the country where they was from. Miss Mack had died in the hospital, from old age, I believe. I can still remember how the church looked. It was just a pretty, little old white church, white and clean and plain.

At that time, other than going to Mr. Paul's funeral, that was the first time I'd ever been in a white church. We sat in the back at Mr. Paul's funeral, but Miss Abby walked me right on up in the front with her. And the peoples there treated me real nice.

Some pretty bad things happened for Shane. One of the families that was real important to us had me, Shane, and Magnolia work for them a lot. They had a big garden. One time, when Shane wasn't old at all, she went to work for them without me or Magnolia. When she came home, she be crying. I asked her, "Shane, what's wrong with you?"

"Old Sapsucker, he be pawing me. Grabbing me with his low-down hands. Rotten old dog." She kept crying.

Somehow it happened again, so Shane was all afraid to go up there by herself 'cause he was always making some sort of sexual innuendo toward her. Dirty old man, he just couldn't keep his eyes off black girls, no matter how young they was. So, finally, Shane told Mama, but Mama just said, "Stay away from him. That's all you can do."

Then Miss Abby's husband, Bob Boyd, also messed with Shane. Overall, he treated people decent, but when he started drinking, he'd become a problem. I guess it was the way he was brought up by his old father, his dad being the lyncher and a part of the Ku Klux Klan. Maybe drinking brought out the racist or molester in him. Turns out, when he'd be drinking, he'd be violent to Miss Abby, but we didn't know it then. She'd be out there hiding in the cornfield, just like Grandmama did.

But one time he'd been drinking and came down to our house, and he grabbed Shane's breasts. Shane got real upset. "Can't trust none of them rascals. I'm gonna leave, and I ain't never coming back!" See, we'd trusted Mr. Bob. Shane told Mama, and Mama told Daddy that she never wanted Mr. Bob at the house again, but Shane had got to a point of age where these low-down white scoundrels tried to take advantage of her.

Shane graduated from high school in '59, when she was seventeen. She was the first one of our family to graduate, and she was very proud. Back then, people believed if a child finished high school and went north, the riches of the world be just waiting for them. We all went to her graduation, and she was very happy about that, but she kept saying, "I'm gonna leave from here. I'm gonna leave from here. I'm going with Tom when they come."

I thought she be fooling. I said, "You ain't doing nothing. Daddy and them ain't gonna let you go nowhere."

"No, I'm leaving. If they don't let me," she said, "I'm still gonna leave."

When Tom and them got home, we was all sitting and eating just a day or two before Tom and Charlie Mae was going back north, and Tom said, "Shane wants to go back to Albany with us." It was a big shock to me.

We all looked at Shane. "Well, there ain't nothing here for me," she said.

Charlie Mae said, "There's a woman's doctor up in Albany, and we'll take her to see why she gets so sick when she has her cycle each month."

Daddy started shaking his head no, so Shane started begging Mama, and Mama said, "You better talk to your daddy."

"No, Shane don't need to go up there," Daddy said.

Then Mama spoke up. "What she staying here for? To stay in them

cotton fields for the rest of her life? To be bothered by all these mens?"
We looked at Mama.

So finally Daddy said, "Alright. Alright." And, really, he couldn't stop
her anyway; she was grown.

Shane had just gotten to the end with everything. She was fed up. She
hated chopping cotton, she hated picking cotton, she hated picking
peas. All Shane wanted to do was sing. I don't care what she had to do,
she was gonna find some kind of song to sing. But she was just tired of
down here.

I thought Shane'd always be around to bother me. I couldn't imagine
life without Shane, but she packed her little things and put them into the
car. Right before she left, she come over to me and said, "Jim, I'm gonna
get me a job. I'm gonna send you some clothes or money for them. I'm
gonna send you a dress to wear to the prom." Sometimes, I think Shane
left primarily to try to make it better for me.

Then she got into the backseat of Tom's, and they drove off, waving
at us as they went up the road. I just stood and watched them go. I didn't
have nobody else. She kept me in trouble all the time, but she was so important to me. Shane was like this free spirit who gave me life. I missed
Shane so bad.

That fall I was going into tenth grade. It was just a real big empty feeling. God, I ached I so missed Shane. I just never would've thought she'd
leave. When Shane got north, she went to work in a store, but she had a
wild streak, and she and Tom had bad conflicts if she stayed out late.
Charlie Mae did take Shane to a gynecologist, and he said her womb was
real twisted and fixed it.

I kept missing Shane real bad, but I didn't know what else to do so I
stayed in school. In fact, I was so ahead of my age so that I was gonna
graduate from high school at sixteen. One day the mailman came to the
house with a huge box that had my name on it. It was the first piece of
mail I ever got. I opened the box. It was this really pretty pink dress and
pink shoes to wear to the prom, and it came from Shane. They cost forty-
five dollars, Shane's salary from a whole week. I just stood there, staring
at them, they was so beautiful. I kept that dress for a very long time.

1. Luda and Lucius Damous, Mary's great-grandparents, Elmore County, Alabama, ca. 1900

2. Mary's father, J. D. Freeman *(right)*, and an unidentified farmer, Elmore County, Alabama, ca. 1958

3. Sarah Easter Freeman,
Mary's mother, ca. 1956

4. Shane Freeman,
Mary's older sister,
ca. 1966

5. Mary and her sisters Magnolia Lovejoy and Annie Lois Lyles, Montgomery, Alabama, 1998. *Photo by Fran Buss.*

6. Aunt Rebecca Freeman, a constant presence during Mary's childhood, Elmore County, Alabama, 2002. *Photo by Fran Buss.*

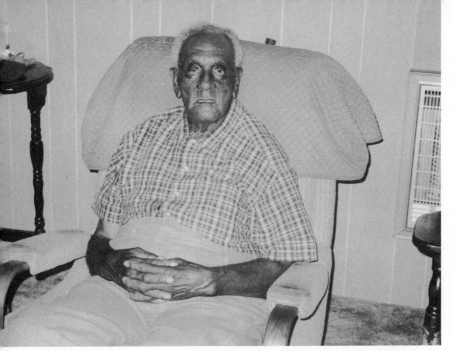

7. Grady Canada, nephew of Ralph Gray of the Share Croppers Union, Camp Hill, Alabama, 1998. *Photo by Fran Buss.*

8. Addie Mae Robinson, a relative by marriage who told Mary the story of her mother's birth, Eclectic, Alabama, 1998. *Photo by Fran Buss.*

9. Mary with textile worker and union activist Myrtle Cauley, 1998. Cauley went to work at the mill at age fifteen and lived in company housing her entire life. *Photo by Fran Buss.*

10. The Amalgamated Clothing and Textile Workers Union presents Mary Robinson with a charter confirming her union's official membership in the AFL-CIO, Montgomery, Alabama, ca. 1977. Harold (Hal) McIver of the AFL-CIO is on the far right.

11. Harold McIver *(right)* of the AFL-CIO, coordinator of the union organizing drive at union steward graduation at the West Boylston plant in 1977, with ACTWU associate education director Bruce Raynor *(center)* and union international representative Henry Mann *(left)*. *Photo courtesy of the Kheel Archives at Cornell University.*

12. Willie Townsend, employee at the West Boylston plant of J. P. Stevens, receiving a union steward certificate from Bruce Raynor, ACTWU, 1977. *Photo courtesy of the Kheel Archives at Cornell University.*

13. J. P. Stevens boycott rally, Birmingham, Alabama, 1978. West Boylston plant workers would travel to places like Birmingham where there were J. P. Stevens outlets. Their marches, which often joined civil rights and church leaders, were an important part of the boycott because they got public attention. *Photo courtesy of the Kheel Archives at Cornell University.*

14. Mary Robinson at the J. P. Stevens stockholders meeting in Greenville, South Carolina, March 4, 1980. Union members armed with voting proxies attended the meeting and testified about bad working conditions and discrimination in the plant. *Photo courtesy of the Kheel Archives at Cornell University.*

15. Mary's family, Eclectic, Alabama, 2000

16. Mary Robinson,
Montgomery,
Alabama, 2007.
*Photo by Amy
Guttensohn.*

✧ nine ✧

Dat's de very prong all us black women gits hung on. Dis
love! Dat's just what's got us uh pullin' and uh haulin' and
sweatin' and doin' from can't see in de mornin' till can't see
at night.

—Zora Neale Hurston, *Their Eyes Were Watching God*

Magnolia was courting this boy named Cecil Smith, and one Saturday night when I was fourteen, she asked, "Mama, can I go to the fish fry with Cecil?" Cecil was standing there. "Let me go with them," I said. I knowed that if one of Mama's girls was going out and Daddy hadn't given permission, she'd always send one of the younger childrens along.

I can remember it real clear. I had this little old dress on that Mama had made for me out of fertilizer sacks. The dress was starched so the skirt spread out, but it fitted tight in my waist, which was real small, and I looked very, very grown up. So we went on to this fish fry back in a pasture at some people's house. I just walked in the house and saw several people I knowed, then I noticed this tall guy in a uniform, sitting across the room. I looked at him, and he be lookin' at me. Finally, he came over and asked me what my name was, and I told him, "Mary."

He said, "My name's James. Can I come over to your house tomorrow?"

"I don't care."

So I didn't think too much about it, and the next morning, Sunday, we got up and went somewhere, and when we came back to the house, this car passed by the house driving real, real slow. It went on past, turned around, and then came back, still drivin' very slow.

I was inside the house when the car stopped, and I heard Mama go outside. She asked, "Who y'all lookin' for?"

"I'm . . . I'm lookin' for a girl named Mary." By that time, I walked out, and he said, "That's her." So I stood out there and talked to him for a few minutes. Then he left, and I went back inside. Mama said, "Come here. Who told you you could court?"

James was in the army reserves, and after we met, they shipped his behind off to St. Louis. When he came back, I'd gotten out of school, I was sixteen, and we dated. He was my first boyfriend. We'd go out to fish fries on Saturday nights, where we'd eat and dance. And at that time James and his brother and his brother's wife's brothers had a gospel singing group that be really, really good. They had a program at a church somewhere every Sunday, so we'd go to these singings. I especially remember them singing:

Some bright morning when this life is o'er, I'll fly away
To a home on God's celestial shore, I'll fly away.
I'll fly away, O Lordy, I'll fly away
When I die, Hallelujah, by and by, I'll fly away.

One time be really funny. Grady, James's brother, had bought this little Renault, a small car, and it was so sorry. There was a bunch of us, and we was going to a sing and was all dressed up. The car wasn't running real good, and when we started up a hill, it wouldn't pull. So we got out and walked up each hill, then at the top we got back in and rolled down. We laughed a lot and made it on time.

Back then, for some reason or another, peoples thought singers was *it*. And James was so handsome. The other girls be jealous. When Shane finally came back home and met James a long time later, she started playing and laughing and acting the fool. She thought he was the best-looking thing she ever seen, she said. She was just a clown.

James was my light at the end of the tunnel. He was this big, tall, handsome person, and every weekend he wore his army uniform. Back then, it was the dream of the African American girl to marry a guy in the service, no matter who he was or what he looked like. If he be in the service, that uniform could make him look handsome. Being the wife of somebody in the service meant all these wonderful places was waiting out there for you. He was my first boyfriend, and I was a virgin, but I'd been reading all these romance novels and thought I knew all about love. I believed I was living in hog heaven. When I knowed him about a year, he asked me to marry him, and I said, "Yeah." I was head over heels in love. I thought he was the best thing since ice cream.

I didn't have to get married, because I wasn't pregnant or nothing, but I needed Daddy's permission 'cause I was just sixteen. So I went to Daddy, but Daddy said, "I ain't signing for you to get married." After he said that, I defied my Daddy for the first time in my life: "If you don't sign me to get married, I'm gonna run away from home."

I stayed real close to Miss Abby and went over to her house lots. So I went over to tell her that me and James was gonna get married. She was always very blunt; she wouldn't hesitate. "You ain't pregnant, is you?"

"No, ma'am."

"Well, I'm not happy about y'all getting married, you're too young, you need to go on to school." She looked at me real close. "But you know I'll support you. If this is what you be determined to do."

One day during this time Mama, Daddy, me, and the others was driving past Miss Bernice's, and we saw she was fixin' up that house where we'd been staying in all our lives. I think she wanted us back and was trying to entice us. After that, somehow or another, she talked Daddy into moving back there. Maybe he did in memory of Mr. Paul. So we left Mr. Bob's and moved back.

Mama was more satisfied with me getting married than Daddy and helped me plan to get married on our new front porch over at Miss Bernice's. Oh, we all loved that porch. We used to sit out on it, and Mama planted hedges across the front. By the time she moved, the hedges be so pretty and thick. It was just unpainted wood, but we thought it was wonderful.

We got married on August the twelfth of '61. The wedding was real simple, wasn't nobody involved in it but me and him and his daddy. His daddy was a preacher and performed the ceremony. I wore the pink dress and shoes Shane had sent me, and I thought I looked real pretty. Mama and Daddy was there, Aunt Rebecca and them, and quite a few people, although Shane couldn't come down from New York. We stood on the porch, and the crowd stood in the yard. Miss Bernice didn't bother to come down, but Miss Abby cooked my wedding cake, and her and Mr. Bob was there. They even got out of the car and stood with the other people, 'cause I looked out and I seen them.

But I was really, really disappointed that Joy didn't show up. I knowed then that it was something that was very, very, badly wrong—that two little kids could grow up and play with each other and know each other so well, and then, when they started growing up and getting into adulthood, they lives had to go separate ways because of some stupid rules about race. I also knowed there was so many black womens out there that had raised white kids, even nursed them, then the white kids growed and somehow it changed. It was really wrong. So, when Joy didn't come to my wedding, then she got married and nobody told me, I knowed it was over.

After we got married, me and James left my house that night and went straight to his mama and daddy's house. They had one little room his daddy added on. There be six girls and James's parents in the house on our wedding night. Then I must have got pregnant the same night I got married.

It was a hard way to learn about sex those first days. I kept thinking to myself that somebody's listening and trying to figure out if we was doing anything. In fact, I had a hard time dealing with sex for a long time. I just never could get nothing out of it. I thought it was just a waste of time. I reckon that's the reason I had kids so fast, because I didn't know how not to. I knew that sexual intercourse was the cause of being pregnant, but I didn't know nothing about the sperm and reproduction.

It was awful, living in James's parents' house. I didn't have nothing to contribute to the household and felt awkward. If I wanted something to eat, I didn't want to just go into the kitchen and get it, and now I can kind of see why they'd resent me. They didn't lose a son, they gained another person.

I also tried to go over and help Mama and Daddy out with the farm. Daddy'd had a falling out with my brother Jack, and there was nobody to do the crops but Daddy and Magnolia. I'd go down in the daytime and help them pick cotton.

The army reserves called James up because of the Bay of Pigs, and he was sent to Arkansas. Of course, I was already pregnant. I stayed with James's folkses for a while, then I went back home and stayed with Mama and Daddy. Then James came back for me, and on January the third, 1960, we left for Fort Smith, Arkansas, with a friend of James. I was excited 'cause I'd never been out of the state, and I peed all the way to Arkansas.

I was never sick during my first pregnancy, but I couldn't go from here to the mailbox without having to pee all the time. Pee, pee, pee. And back then the bathrooms was segregated. Blacks couldn't stop many places when we was traveling. The rest stops was for whites. So James had to stop on the side of the road for me. I'd squat down behind some bush somewhere and hope I didn't spray my feet and nobody'd come by so everything I ever had be exposed.

Back then there wasn't any interstates, so all we had was plain roads, and we had to go through a really, really rednecked little town, Cullman, Alabama. Black people did not go to Cullman, 'cause they'd kill you there in a heartbeat. But this guy we was traveling with had an auntie that worked for these very rich white people, and they protected her. She was the only black that was in that town. She fixed us something to eat, and we stayed with her the rest of the night. I wasn't even scared.

Now, I was scared in Mississippi. I was scared in Mississippi. No doubt about it, I was scared in Mississippi, and we had to go through there. It had a terrible reputation—that's where they killed Emmett Till, and a few years after we went through, in 1964, they killed those three Freedom Summer workers. I remember James telling me, "Shit, you better pee before we get in Mississippi 'cause I ain't stopping, I ain't stopping." But a few minutes later he be pulling onto the gravel, and I was heading for some black-hating, Mississippi bushes.

When we finally stopped at our house in Fort Smith, I was excited. It was the first time I ever been in a city, my first time in a place where houses with sidewalks sat next to each other. The neighborhood was segregated but nice, with painted houses and mowed yards and flowers. The place where we was living was up on the hill, and we could see maybe eight blocks to the downtown.

We rented a bedroom in Miss Wilson's house. She was very slew footed, that's what we call it. One foot looked like it was going east, and the other foot looked like it was going west. She was short and bull legged and shuffled when she walked, but a very nice little old lady, who let us have privacy. She also gave us access to the rest of the house, the kitchen, the living room, and the bathroom, which was good, given my peeing problem. Miss Wilson used to tell me, "You need to walk." So we'd walk to the stores on the corner and to her son's house.

'Cause I was pregnant, I went to see a doctor, for the first time ever. I remember when they made me get on the table. I was so tensed up, in complete knots, and they said, "Relax. Relax." And I'm laying there saying to myself, "I'm so embarrassed this ain't even funny. How you gonna relax when someone's looking at everything you ever had and ever was gonna have?"

I was away from home and scared when Jamie was born, but a friend with a baby and Miss Wilson helped me a lot. They told me what to do with the navel cord and how to burp him after I fed him. Me and James was very proud of him and named him Jamie Lovell, after James.

Jamie was born in May, and then we came home in August that same year and moved into this old house that was right next to James's daddy's. It had a acre of land, two rooms in front, and this long kitchen that you stepped down into that ran the length of both of the rooms on the back. The house wasn't sealed, with just rafters, so it was real cold. In the winter we all slept in the one little room with the fireplace and tried to keep warm. When I'd go to the kitchen, I'd freeze to death. There wasn't nothing there but the little old woodstove. When the weather got good, I planted a big garden to keep us eating.

After Jamie was born, it was just babies, babies, babies. Fitzgerald was born in December of '63. I named him after President Kennedy, who'd just been assassinated on the twenty-second of November. The next child was Ron Deron, who was born July the thirty-first of '65, then I got pregnant with my last child [Tracy]. I had the first two in the hospital, then the last two with a midwife, and, believe me, they hurt. The babies was enjoyable, but also a burden, 'cause I had to do so much to take care of them. I'd work for money, then I'd come home and try to chop wood to heat the house, then take care of them. James just had no getup about him at all when it came to working. He took after his daddy.

James's daddy had run around all those years, calling hisself a preacher, but he'd always looked for somebody else to take care of him. This trait escalated from him to his kids, especially the boys. Even now, they don't have jobs. James's mama never worked at a job, but she had twelve kids. Only nine be living.

Our marriage might have gone better if we'd stayed away in Arkansas or somewhere else, but we moved right next door to his parents. James's mama and daddy'd set up an argument between me and James, then James'd tell them about it, and for about a week or two they'd treat me like I'm the Big Bad Wolf.

James's mama, daddy, and sisters used to accuse me of not being faithful 'cause of the color of my kids. "We know Fitzgerald ain't none of James's 'cause we ain't got no dark peoples in the family" and "We know Tracy's not none of James's 'cause we ain't got no light-skinned people."

Tracy, my daughter, was born in '66, when I was twenty-three. The day before she born, we sat down at Mama's house eating chitlins, then, when we came back home, I started having pains. So Lazy James Robinson went and got Miss Harriet Pearce, who we called Aunt Had, this old black midwife. I went in labor and was in labor an awfully long time, and of course the midwives didn't have nothing to give you for pain. I was in all this severe pain, and each time I needed help, I looked at Aunt Had, and she was just sitting there at the fireplace, not moving. She made me so mad. Every now and then she'd come back and raise up the sheets and look down there, then she'd go back and sit by the fireplace.

So finally Tracy was born, and the only thing Aunt Had said was, "Mmm hmm, a split tail." That was it.

The next morning James Robinson got up and went down and told Mama that I'd had a girl the night before, and later in the day Mama came up to the house and stayed there with me. Then for a couple of days she'd walk back and forth.

About two weeks later, 'cause we needed the money so bad, I went back to work at the club where I'd been working. It was about early December and terrible cold. One night it was the coldest that I ever remembered in all the history of my life. This guy lived across the street from us. His wife and children said he was mean, that he'd get drunk, beat them, and run them away from home. Their house stood up off the ground, so there was spaces between the floor and the ground. That night he came in drunk, drove them off, and laid down in front of the fireplace and froze to death. They found him the next morning. So that's how cold it was, and I had these three little boys and a new baby girl.

James came to pick me up from work that night, driving our old car. He left the kids with his mama. We didn't have no heat in the car, and it was so cold I prayed, "God, please don't let the car break down." If the car froze up on the road, we'd die.

We made it home and picked up the kids, but then we didn't have no wood for the fireplace. I was scared to put the kids to bed 'cause I thought they'd freeze. They say when you freezing, you just go to sleep. I kept trying to keep them awake, and they kept crying. I remember sitting there holding Tracy, the baby, and being so depressed and scared.

James Robinson had gotten so sorry by then. He was so damn lazy and just as sorry as hell. We didn't have no wood to burn 'cause he be too lazy to earn money or chop wood. So he went out there and found some old tires for a car and put 'em on the fire. Now, tires burn really, really powerful, so the fire was dangerous, and we had to worry about burning to death. That's how sorry James Robinson was.

James was also hard on the kids. He had this way of yelling and screaming at them, and I don't think people should do that to kids. It makes them nervous and makes them feel like they is less than they actually is. So him and I differed a lot on that. I say that if you're going to punish kids, just do it, but don't do all this hollering and putting them down. I'd stand up to James about the childrens, and he'd say, "Don't tell me how to raise my childrens." But I fought for them.

You aren't born strong. I believe you have to acquire it. It's something that you have to make. I didn't have no strength when I was married. If I had any of the strength I got later, I would've had that sucker's ass out on a limb somewhere. He would've been hanging up by his balls. That is the truth. But I had no self-esteem; I had no self-worth; I felt like I was a baby factory, that was all. I couldn't figure out what was happening.

I said, "God, why?"

✦ ten ✦

There was a sense of power, in a place where you didn't feel
you had any power. There was a sense of confronting things
that terrified you, like jail, police, walking in the street. . . . So
you were saying in some basic way, "I will never again stay
inside those boundaries."

—Bernice Johnson Reagon, 1990

D addy talked about the NAACP all the time, how the NAACP was gonna change this and do that, and he went to his Wednesday meetings. He always said, "They gonna make things better." The NAACP did have a chapter there in Wetumpka, and I remember Daddy telling me, "Now, you don't go saying nothing to Joy."

"Nothing about what, Daddy?"

"Nothing about no NAACP." This was before the bus boycott in Montgomery in '55, before people wanted it openly known that they belonged to it. We kids talked about the bus boycott after it began when I was twelve, and somehow we knowed it was essential to our future. So we'd ditch school, get in some older kids' cars, and end up in Montgomery watching things. But even if some of our teachers figured out what we was doing, most of them was from Montgomery and was supporters.

We'd go downtown to see all these people, mostly womens, and they'd be standing around waiting for somebody to pick them up. There was this strip in Montgomery on Perry Street, where all the black businesses was located. The organizers set up a system where volunteers would go out in cars to Perry Street, pick up peoples boycotting the buses, and take them to work. Perry Street was where the people'd wait. Sometimes we'd see a bus go by that was almost empty. A lot be dressed in white, so I thought they was nurses. Being a nurse was a real high-status job, but unfortunately that wasn't it. They was maids in people's houses.

But God's got a way of protecting you. When I think back now, I'm glad that the teenagers back then was not as militant as I became in later years with the union. Because if the young people would have been that militant, a lot of people would have died. Young people today wouldn't have put up with the conditions like that.

As I got married and we went to Arkansas and returned with Jamie, things started really heating up with the movement. Dr. King be put in jail, the Freedom Riders be beaten, whites be rioting in Alabama. Every day the headlines was saying the students were protesting one thing or another. Dr. King was really strong, and there was sit-ins and boycotts. By then activists was even demonstrating in a lot of the little cities around us, like Wetumpka. We was willing to go out and risk our lives. We didn't care.

At that time people talked the most about getting the right to vote. There was always droves of peoples who wanted to vote, masses of people, but the Voting Rights Act didn't get passed until 1965, so civil rights people was trying to get folkses involved. Mama never would register to vote. I don't know why. She was such a good person, but I think she was also fearful for us kids. I guess she'd seen so much that she didn't have hope that it'd ever change.

So the NAACP had been encouraging people to register to vote during the voter rights movement. They'd go out into the community and talk to them. They managed to end the poll tax. I registered to vote the day I turned twenty-one in 1964, that very day.

I walked right up the steps of the white Elmore County Courthouse, the steps where the Ku Klux had rallied, right past where their low-down Confederate flag was blowing, through the door, and right past the so-called whites-only bathroom. White people still worked at the counter in the registrar's office, but a whole bunch of black peoples was waiting to register. When I finally got to the head of the line, the woman gave me the paper that asked me if I was a citizen, what race, my date of birth, if I had ever been convicted of a felony.

Once I got the registration form filled out, I took it back up to the counter, and the woman there told me they'd send me a paper telling me where to vote. I felt wonderful. I felt really, really proud that I had power.

I was so proud of the old people that couldn't read and write that came to register. They was not ashamed to go over to the counter and say, "I can't read so I brought my daughter to help me." That's where the civil rights group came in. Their workers went out to the country in an old van and picked up these people, maybe four or five at a time, then helped them fill out the papers. People was coming out of the court-house jubilant; they was laughing and excited. Young people. Old people. All people. They was running down the courthouse steps, calling to each other, "Yeah, I can't wait until the next election comes up. I'm gonna get some of these suckers out of office!" They was just joyful about it, very, very happy.

It had been denied to us for so long, and people had died so they could vote. It seemed to me that to dèny people the vote and then use government to control them was a form of slavery. If I didn't have noth-ing to do with the political process and others could use it to control me without my say-so, it was like being bound. Then registering was like a bond being broken. We knew that the next time an election came up, we'd have that little bitty piece of power that the vote afforded us. I made sure every one of my sisters and brothers and their families was regis-tered.

The first time I voted, they was trying to tell us that we couldn't take nobody to the booth with us if we didn't know how it was supposed to work. The polling place in Eclectic was in this little fire station, and it was pouring down rain, just streaming. They set it up so they only had one booth in a little old room away from the main part of the fire sta-tion. So you walked in this door, then immediately turned around and went outside, back into the rain. That way nobody had no place to stand out of the downpour as they waited. I saw it as their way to discourage people from voting, to make them say, "I ain't gonna wait here and get drenched."

It was gushing down rain, just pouring, and people was trying to sit in their cars while they waited, but I'll tell you, that was one time when we demonstrated to them white folkses how determined blacks was to vote. I remember some of the old people that was waiting. Uncle Bart, who was real elderly. Uncle Herman. Those was James's uncles—little old mens with a bent-over walk. Uncle Bart was short and walked with his hands folded behind his back. He had to be in his early eighties. I guess they stuck with it 'cause they'd seen such suffering and meanness. I reckon for them this was the ultimate thing in their lives—to see this stone rolled away so that their children wouldn't have to endure what they'd endured, so that their children wouldn't be torn apart 'cause of the color of their skin. They stepped out in the rain or tried to wait in a car. The young ones would jump out of the car and run in there to vote, but the old ones would just slowly shuffle to the firehouse door. So they got real wet. It was my first election, the first time I ever voted.

We saw the violence and the attack on the 1961 Freedom Riders in Montgomery, Birmingham, and Selma on TV, so peoples just assumed that when they saw a black person and a white person together, they was part of this civil rights thing. It polarized relationships. A lot of white people who'd been friends with blacks broke off the friendships. That might've had something to do with what happened between me and Joy. But not with Miss Abby. She stayed as close to me as always and continued to be real friendly to blacks.

Then in the spring of 1963 we watched Old Low-Down Bull Connors in Birmingham as he aimed fire hoses on childrens. His police and them hoses knocked the kids down the street with so much pressure that the water took the bark off trees. Then big dogs attacked little kids. Sometimes I felt like if somebody had gave me a ticket and said, "Get on this boat and go back to Africa," I'd have said okay. 'Cause I didn't see no hope for blacks at all.

Then it was September 1963, after we'd been to Arkansas and back, and I had Jamie and was pregnant with Fitzgerald. We was living up in Eclectic in this little old house, and it was a Sunday morning. Suddenly, they came on the radio and said there had been an explosion at the Sixteenth Street Baptist Church in Birmingham and that there was four deaths and some other injuries. I think they knew then and there it was a bomb, but they didn't want to tell nobody it was a bomb 'cause the tension was already real, real high. But that night on the news on TV, they showed them taking those little girls' bodies out of the church.

Way before this I had already questioned where was God, and that night I felt like I could damn God right then and there. We always had grown up with the understanding that you trust and believe in God. Then here was four little girls that went to church that morning, to worship him, and some son of a bitch goes in there, plants a bomb, and just blows them to smithereens.

I felt like if God was this superpower, why didn't he stop it? They say everything is did for a reason, and I could find no reason in that. No reason why four little girls that got up that Sunday morning, that had trusted and believed in their parents, who'd said, "You get ready, you go to Sunday school, you praise God and thank him for the things you got," should get blown up. Some no-good, low-down bastard plants a bomb in a sanctuary and just blows them away. I started wondering then, thinking, "Maybe God is a white god." That hurt me so bad.

Another time that really, really hurt me was the twenty-third day of November 1963. I was pregnant with Fitzgerald and watching *As the World Turns*, a soap opera, when all of a sudden they come on with an announcement. "We interrupt this broadcast to bring you a special bulletin from Dallas, Texas." I sat there on the floor and was folding some clothes, then they said there had been a report that the president of the United States had been shot.

President Kennedy had really cared about us blacks, and it was just like the whole world stopped. I stared at the TV and thought to myself, "Naw, that's not what they said. I know that can't be what they said." In a few minutes the TV went completely off. It was no more broadcasting and no service. Then they came back and said, "We take you to Dallas, Texas." They went on and did some commentary, and then in a few minutes they came back and said, "We've got an unconfirmed report that the president is dead." I tell you, I sit there, and when I knowed anything, tears be just rolling down my face, and I'd never even felt them. That hurt me so bad. I cussed God. I said, "You don't give a shit about what's going on with no black people."

Then after that come the death of Dr. King and Robert Kennedy in 1968. I was still living in the house with the two bedrooms and had all four kids. I was also watching the TV when Dr. King was shot. It was about 6:00 in the afternoon. They interrupted it just like they did with Kennedy and said that Dr. King had been killed in Memphis. We was just like stunned; people was at their end. Then we watched the riots, the cities burning. It was such a sad, sad time that I think lots of people have almost tried to blank it out of their mind. It was like they—we—lost all hope.

I just didn't understand how these things would happen and God wasn't intervening. Then I saw things like kids starving in Somalia, in Africa, and I wondered to myself, "How can you be a god and a just god and then sit there and watch this go on?" They said in the blink of an eye he can do all these things, and I knowed I had no right to question him, but I did. I thought of the saying that he never promised you that the road would be easy, but I also thought that he also ain't never promised me that somebody would blow it up every time we made a step. In some ways I didn't believe no more.

But it didn't always all seem so hopeless. There was times of triumph. After [President Lyndon] Johnson signed the Civil Rights Act in 1964, the one that was supposed to outlaw segregation, I decided to integrate Cotton's Barbecue Pit. Cotton's was this real famous little old restaurant out in the country up by Eclectic. But the restaurant was for whites. If you be black, you had to go to the back door and get your food from there. No stools, nowhere to sit down. And you may have to stand there 'til everybody in front's served.

But after it was made illegal, I just decided one day it was time for Cotton's to be integrated. I parked in the back so it would've been much easier for me to just go to the window where we always went, but I felt too much pride. I walked straight down the side toward the front door. Cotton's had windows all down the side, and under those windows he growed all these beautiful roses. I walked right past the roses where the white people inside could see me coming. Then, standing tall, I opened the front door, went inside, and hopped up on a stool. People looked at me real, real strange, but I was determined. Finally the person asked me, "What y'all want?" I answered, "A barbecue sandwich." It took them a while to get it for me, but I sat right there until they brought it and ate it there. For years and years and years black peoples had to take the food from the back, but not no more.

Then we was part of the march from Selma to Montgomery in 1965. Me and James's family didn't go to Selma on Bloody Sunday, the day Sheriff Jim Clark and his troopers beat down and gassed those hundreds of marching peoples, men and women, even kids. The first one they clubbed was John Lewis. Today he's a congressman.

After that clubbing, blacks and whites came from all over the country to make the march go on, and partway down the highway the Ku Klux shot dead this white lady, Viola Liuzzo. They wounded one of the black men she was riding with. Viola and this guy was going to pick somebody up for the march.

We was still living in Eclectic, and there was not a lot of coverage in the media about what was happening. Of course, the local news was not touching it, and the national news that told about it was still very conservative, maybe two seconds of footage. But after Viola Liuzzo was killed, the more local news covered it in a very negative manner. It wasn't like she was this hero for being down here trying to help blacks get equal rights. It was like she was a person who shouldn't have been here.

I remember it so good. The news came on at 12:00; then at 12:15 they had this little old talk show with this white woman named Inez Brooks as commentator. It was on TV, and I'd be cooking or cleaning or feeding my kids, maybe washing their faces. That day the people called in and voiced their opinions about Viola, and they belied her so bad. They said she was a "nigger lover" and that she should have been home in Chicago with her childrens. They said, "She got what she deserved." Others said, "She should've been charged with child abuse for leaving her kids." Their viciousness took the focus away from what the civil rights movement was really like. It was like they called for more violence, and Dr. King advocated nonviolence. They said that no mercy should be shown to anybody white found consorting with blacks.

We decided to go to the march, especially after Viola was murdered and people was so cruel; all of us except James's mama. She was like my mama. She warned us, "Y'all gonna mess around and get your heads busted up." But we was energized, a whole bunch of us went. James's daddy thought it was important 'cause he was a preacher, although not a real one, according to me. It looked like everybody in Eclectic went down. Peoples called each other up and went out to folkses that didn't have phones or cars.

The NAACP chapters organized it so that one group of marchers would relieve another, marching in shifts, and whole bunches of folkses was always walking. When we finally caught up to the marchers, it was like wall-to-wall people. They came from everywhere—from New York, California, and Detroit—and they came with energy. After what happened when they'd crossed that bridge in Selma, when the marchers was beat, it brought new marchers out. When it hit the news, people got mad. People came out of little bitty towns like Wetumpka. Then Viola was killed, and people decided it was time to walk. I said so too.

So we marched with them, and the number kept growing. People sang and carried flags. I will never forget what it was like when we got into Montgomery. Something drove people, and once they started coming up Dexter Avenue, I could look at their faces and see all the things that they had endured. Someone who was there that day said it right: they said they saw 150 years of pain, discrimination, torture, and being beat down just slowly roll off the people and roll down the street.

It was amazing to see people's faces. Old and young. Some people had actually walked the whole thing. They rested and slept but walked it. People cried, and even the speakers, when they started to speak, they got so choked up that they'd have to stop. It tore them up to look down at all the shining faces.

We was like right in the center of the people, close to the Safety Building, and as we was coming up the street, we looked over there on the lawn and saw these Ku Klux with hoods on standing there, but Dr. King and the other speakers told everybody to act nonviolent, preaching nonviolence.

The Klan yelled obscenities, but it was like the black people didn't even hear them. Other than to look at them and keep marching, nobody acknowledged the Ku Klux. But I think if nonviolence had not been so constantly drummed into blacks, there'd have been a bloodbath. But even though everybody in the march at that time had a right to hate, a right to be angry because Viola Liuzzo had been killed and people'd been beat down by state troopers, Dr. King had so constantly preached nonviolence that violence didn't break out.

And God is good. God is good. He took all that anger that was inside peoples and turned it into something that was beautiful and joyous. He let us know, "You have won a big part of this battle because you kept going on even in the adversity, even with the killing, and all those people being beat up and made bloody, you have won." And we did. These was people with a lot of mileage out there. They was housewives, they was truck drivers, they was glass plant workers. I saw old people coming in on sticks. These people didn't just make a difference in the lives of the people here in Alabama; they made a difference in the lives of the people across this whole world, all the way to South Africa, where black people said, "What we live with is wrong."

And people sang all kinds of freedom songs. "We Shall Overcome," "Ain't Going to Let Nobody Turn Us Around," "Keep Your Eyes on the Prize," and all the freedom songs.

I saw some video footage on the march from Selma during an anniversary celebration of the Voting Rights Act; this woman I had met was in it. She was in her twenties in the video, and she was singing, "Ain't Going to Let Nobody Turn Us Around," and she bent her arm, throwed her hand up with joy. Her head was back, her face shined, and she was talking to God: "I ain't gonna let nobody turn us around."

There be a long line of unsung heroes. When we was working on this book, we talked to Mrs. [Catherine] McGowen [her story is mentioned in the introduction] about the Montgomery bus boycott and the Lowndes County voter registration drive. She was the hospital cleaning woman with the two little boys who risked so much. And we talked to Mrs. [Annie Mae] Brodie. She be the mother of the first soldier from Elmore County who was killed in the Vietnam War. She told us about her fight to get him buried in the Wetumpka Cemetery and their march through Wetumpka.

We talked to Mrs. [Daisy] Varner, who tried to get Sheriff Holley prosecuted after he supposedly beat her son and left him to die in the Elmore County jail, how she called in outside civil rights groups, trying to do it. And we talked to Debra Bracy, the woman a little younger than me, the one who be part of the first group to integrate the Wetumpka High School. She told us how her house was firebombed and the sacrifice her family made for the struggle, how, despite everything, her brothers and sisters helped found the first NAACP youth group in Wetumpka. Then we went way back to earlier organizers, and we talked to Grady Canada about his sister and father and uncle, who tried all those years ago to get a sharecroppers union.

Yes, there be a long line of unsung heroes.

⊹ eleven ⊱

O Jerusalem, Jerusalem, . . . how often would I have gathered
thy children together, even as a hen gathereth her chickens un-
der her wings.

                                       —Matthew 23:37

Things was real bad for me with James back then. And it was compli-
cated, partly 'cause of my kids. I loved my kids and wanted the best
things in the world for them. I wanted them to grow up and be strong
and healthy, and they was just little bitty fellows that was dependent on
me. I felt inadequate 'cause I didn't have no strength at the time. So with
me not having any, I couldn't give any away.

I did all sorts of work to keep us going. In fact, I learned how to swing
an ax as good as any man, and I could pull a plow. It was hard, but it's
good to know you can survive if you need to. I also tried to work at different jobs to bring in money. The first cleaning job I had was in Alex City
[in Alabama]. All the people I cleaned for was decent to me, and the husbands all worked during the day, so that wasn't a problem. I heard of cases
where womens'd go to people's houses to clean as maids, and the wives'd
put down five or six nickels or something just to try to catch them, but
that was the first thing you learned. You don't touch nothing. If you found
any money, you take it right to the woman. And, of course, Mama and
them always taught us that we don't steal under any conditions. But with
these cleaning jobs, I couldn't get minimum wage. I think I got paid three
dollars a day, but one of the women gave me children's clothes.

Then I started working at this resort area. I cleaned cabins on Saturday and Sunday, and I went back to work in Alex City on Monday, then worked that week at different houses. When I cleaned at the lodge, it was segregated. I used to think, "Yeah, here I am making beds, and I can't even sleep in one of them." Then I started working in the kitchen, preparing food, and if I decided to buy some of the same food that I prepared, I had to take it in the back somewhere and eat it. Not 'cause I worked there, but because I was black.

I worked in a sewing factory for one day before I decided I'd rather starve. I was determined I'd not go so low. It was down in Tallassee. The first thing in the morning, one of the girls put a needle through her finger, and a man had to come and dismantle the machine before she got her finger out. Then people worked so fast. If you did pockets, you got a split second to sew it on, and you was required to do something like twenty dozen. I could tell the womens that had worked there a long time because their backs curved over and their necks was stiff.

At the end of the day the lady in charge said, "You been really good today."

I said, "Well, I'm glad you think so 'cause I won't be back tomorrow. There's some things I just won't do." That was one of them.

James wasn't working even before Daddy died, and Daddy'd tell me, "That boy is sorry. He ain't no good." By then I knowed Daddy was absolutely right. There was lots of times when I told Daddy, "I wish you'd let me run away from home instead of marrying." Daddy's remark always was, "No, you was grown. And you was hardheaded."

James didn't care what happened to us. He'd buy this furniture, and you'd be sitting there, when a couple of months later a truck'd pull up. The people'd say, "We come to repossess such and such." That was the most embarrassing part. I never will forget one time James had bought this TV, and I was sitting there watching one of the stories, the soaps or serials, when the people came to the door and said, "We come to get the TV. Y'all didn't keep up with the payments."

I just stood there and looked at them, then I said, "Can I finish watching my show?"

"Nope." They came and took it in the middle of my soap opera!

When I finally got myself a real job at the country club and bought my own furniture, nobody came and picked it up. We had a house, and they foreclosed on it, but I kept my furniture, and now Jamie has it.

I believe the lowest part of my life was when I was pregnant with my baby boy and I got mumps. It like to have killed me. Then old James beat me so bad I left the house in the rain. I decided I was gonna walk down to my daddy's, but this neighbor woman came out and said, "You out here pregnant and y'all got them mumps? You gonna kill yourself and that baby! You know you ain't got no business out here trying to leave home!" So she finally convinced me to go back, but at that point I really didn't care what happened. I didn't. I couldn't of went any further down if I'd dug a hole my own self.

James got really violent, even when I was pregnant. I think he was jealous, especially then. He wanted me to be big and waddlely, but instead I never did look pregnant. Matter of fact, I looked better when I was pregnant than when I wasn't. Every man that ever saw me looked at me twice. My skin was just as smooth as velvet, my hair got so thick, and I never showed, 'cause I was always broad in my hips. People always said, "That gal be carryin' that baby in her breasts."

When I was pregnant with Jamie, I wanted to look like other pregnant women so I bought the maternity clothes with the hole in front but almost never wore them. Still, James wanted me to look like the rest of the womens—big. He got even more upset 'cause I'd go out and play ball with the kids. It threatened him.

I think that some of the lowest points ever in my life was when I was married. I do. I felt like I was shut in. I felt really, really helpless, and I felt like God was punishing me for some reason or another, and I couldn't figure out why.

Also, James had all these ambitions, but he be too lazy to follow through on them. He did go to trade school for a while, and while he was doing woodwork, he made Tracy this little old bitty chair that was solid oak, a heavy little chair. One time when Tracy was a little baby, James come in ranting and raving about something. "I'm gonna take my children and I'm leaving."

I was learning to stand up: "You can leave any time you get ready, but you better not never take one of my kids. You ain't taking them nowhere." Then he reached down and grabbed Tracy up. I told him, "Y'all set one foot out that door with my baby and I'm gonna kill you."

I guess he said to hisself, "She ain't gonna do it," so he started to walk out the door. I couldn't see nothing but that little chair he'd made Tracy, and I grabbed it up. I think God gave me strength from hell. I raised it back, and when he stepped down, I busted him across the head with the chair. I actually broke the oak chair on his head. As he fell, I grabbed my baby and got away. Blood streamed down his face.

My God, I really killed him, I thought, but he staggered up. James ran his behind over to his mama's, then she come running out. I felt that was the worse thing she ever did. We was always taught to respect our elders, but she had no business interfering. But she comes running to my house. "What's going on between you and James out here!" she yells.

Everybody called her Dear. That was her name. "Dear," I said, "let me tell you something. If I need you, I will call you. That's one of James and me's problems. Everybody's always interfering. Now you get out of my house, you go back to yours, and don't you ever come out here and interfere with me and James again." So she turned and took her little old self on back out the door and went home, and after that she never came out and interfered again.

Every time James done beat the living hell out of me, all I could see was that these are my childrens, and I needed to protect them. It was always strange. I was like this old sittin' hen, the way she gathers all her little babies under her wings. When James did something really, really cruel, I'd just want to hold my kids and make sure that everything's alright with them. They'd be crying and I'd be crying, and I'd just want to hold them.

James was smart. He didn't start doing the worst things 'til after Daddy had died, 'cause, like I said, Daddy'd told James the same thing he told Ann Lois's husband. That if he beat Daddy's daughter, he'd have hell to pay. Daddy'd kill him if he had to. So James Robinson didn't start doing the worst until my daddy was gone. And, when Daddy died, I lost my protection.

But God does something wonderful for a woman who goes through hell with the father of her kids. Even though the kids look so much like their father he could've spit them out, God makes it in your heart so you see them as your children, not his. You look at their face and feel love. In my heart James didn't have nothing to do with them, even though they looked just like him. I conceived them; I did the whole thing.

There's a bonding between a mother and child. I always heard when we was growing up that when a woman gives birth to a child, her life hangs by a string of thread that's very, very thin. And going through that experience forms a bond that's just extremely deep.

Tracy was born in 1966, and the civil rights movement was easing off some when I went to work at this country club on the lake. I worked for this Greek guy called Jimmy Katisshca, a very nice person. Louise Purter was another African American woman who worked for him, and she was big on civil rights too. Louise was in the kitchen, a short-order cook, and

I was the salad person. Me and her worked together later on at [the J. P.] Stevens [textile company].

One night some civil rights activists was having a meeting, but at the country club we didn't get out of work until about 10:00 or 11:00 p.m. Louise always talked real fast. She told Mr. Jimmy, "We-need-to-get-off-early-tonight." I wanted to be straight with him and told him why, and I be really, really astounded.

He said, "Y'all think that you the only ones that have to fight discrimination. When my family first came here to the United States, we was called terrible names." He said, "When I was going to school, I encountered all kinds of racial insults from white kids. So any time that y'all need time off for something like this, just let me know a day in advance and I'll work it for you." He said that.

I watched him at the country club, and I think that was the first time I knowed we wasn't the only ones who had trouble. If some of the whites had a problem, they said, "I want to see the manager." Then, when Mr. Jimmy walked up, they looked at him like they didn't believe he was it. I remember this one guy saying that he wanted some different kind of salad, and he was mad 'cause we didn't have it. He said, "I want to see the manager!" Then, after the problem was over, Mr. Jimmy looked at us and said, "Damn redneck!" [laughs]

Anyway, we went to that meeting. These civil rights workers wanted blacks to apply for jobs they knowed blacks couldn't get in the past, where employers only hired whites. They was trying to break the discrimination thing in the workplace, like in textiles. So I said, "Yeah, I'll try it."

This white lady, Mahilia, lived across from me, and she worked in the plant that Miss Roberta and Mr. Wilbert, Joy's grandparents, had worked in. The only job blacks had there was working outside on the loading dock. So I decided to try to get inside, and I told Mahilia that I was going to go down there and try to go to work at the plant. It was called West Boylston then. At first she wasn't encouraging, but I went down and filled out the application.

They said, "Do y'all have any experience?"

"No, but I'm willing to learn. Give me the opportunity, and I will learn it."

The bosses was geared up for that. They knowed that blacks was gonna try to get in. So they asked me, "Do you think you can wind?"

I'd never done winding before in my life. "I don't know, but I'll try."

In about two to three days they called me down for another interview and did everything they possibly could to keep me from taking the job. They told me I'd have to work the third shift, even though my kids was little, but it worked out fine 'cause I rode to work with Mahilia. Then later on, when Louise and another black lady came to work down there too, we carpooled.

Louise was a good friend. She was married and had four kids, three boys and one girl. She was a very vocal, tall, strikingly attractive black lady, and she was a hard worker, working two or three jobs. I guess she felt a lot of frustration, as lots of other blacks did, 'cause of the fact that you was constantly working but was always stuck working for minimum wages and sometimes even less than that. So Louise got really involved with civil rights and was a politically astute lady.

I left the country club first, then Louise also went to work in the textile plant, even while she was still working at the club. Later, when it came to the union, Louise signed the card right away, and got other people to sign. She was not a scary person; she'd stand up and argue with a sign pole.

Daddy and Mama'd moved back to Miss Bernice's when I got married and went to Arkansas with James. Then Daddy and Miss Bernice had another falling out, and Mama and Daddy moved up to Eclectic, not far from us. Once they got to Eclectic, all the farming was over, so Daddy went to work in Montgomery for the city department, pouring asphalt on roads. Before long J. W. left home, but Magnolia had Pappy, her little boy, and she continued to live with Mama and Daddy. It was just Mama, Daddy, Magnolia, and Pappy.

I never told Mama about my problems with James 'cause I knew that would worry her so bad. I'm glad she never did know the type of person that he was. Mama loved to go fishing with James. He'd come over and say, "Mama Sarah, you wanna go fishing?"

"Yeah." Mama never made connections that James didn't have a real job. She thought work was like farming, that at a certain time in the year you had to do this and at another time you had to do that. And since you had to work so hard, you should take what little joy that is there. And to Mama that joy was fishing. So she was never really suspicious that he could go fishing just any time.

I went into the textile plant to work just about two weeks before Mama died, but my doing that was a big step up for blacks, and when Mama found out, even though she was laying there on the bed and almost at the point of death then, it made her so happy. She knew I be working where Old Lady Gladys and Old Man Clement had worked, and they'd seemed so well off to us.

The cancer'd been in there inside her for all these years, just growing. We took her back to the doctor, and the cancer had spreaded practically all over her body, but still they never told us it was going to kill her.
I couldn't believe that until after I seen her get down into the bed. That's
when I finally come to the realization that something that bad was wrong
with my mama.

It was hard for her to take care of herself. She didn't have no bathroom. The things we take for granted now—an electric stove, a bathroom—it's hard for me to know that she never had them.

Mama fought a good fight. She fought a good fight. Toward the end
she'd lay there and just grunted, that's all. "Mama, why you grunting?"
we asked. "What hurts you?"

"Nothing. It's just 'cause I'm so sick. That's all." She had a couple of
bottles of medicine that she took, and that was it.

'Cause I was working and had little kids, I stayed at home until the last
days, but I lived right down the road from Mama's. Magnolia, who was
with Mama, cared for Mama day and night.

When I seen that Mama wasn't gonna get any better and that all she
could do was go down, I started asking God, "If you gonna take her anyway, go ahead and take her now. Don't keep leaving her here in this kind
of situation." We was all sitting around her on the night she died. It was
on a Sunday, the twenty-sixth day of March. Aunt Rebecca was sitting at
the head of Mama's bed when Miss Mildred's husband came over. Miss
Mildred was the lady who was Mama's fishing partner, the friend she kept
falling into the creek with. Her husband's name was Mr. Johnny Gray.
He'd been drinking, but he wasn't drunk, and he walked up there to
Mama's bed. He always called her Miss Sarah, and she called him Mr.
Johnny.

He asked her, "How you doing, Miss Sarah?" She just nodded her
head a little bit.

So he told her, "I'm gonna pray for you," and she nodded her head
again, never saying nothing. People knowed he'd been drinking, and
somebody said, "Come on away from her. You been drinking,"

But Mama told them, "No, let him stay."

So Mr. Johnny knelt down at the foot of Mama's bed, and he started
to pray. When he was done, we looked at Mama. She'd closed her eyes
and wasn't breathing. Aunt Rebecca said, "I believe she's gone." It was
just that quick.

I figured that God sent Mr. Johnny there to get her. He'd sent him
just long enough to take our minds off her, so she could go. They had an

old saying that something happened just "long enough for death to sneak in and get her."

Still, the most amazing thing to me was that she died such a peaceful death. At that time I never cried. I never cried. I never cried, and it was years later when I cried. But still, when she was actually gone, it felt just like my whole world had fell apart. I had all my kids, Tracy was a baby, James wasn't no good, and I had lost my mother.

The day of the funeral we sat there waiting for it to begin, and I just felt like my whole life had collapsed. I didn't know how I'd keep going, but I couldn't just give up with all these kids. After a while I looked around, and the church was really, really full.

It was just a simple ceremony, but the minister said something that helped me deal with death a little bit better. He said that when we lose somebody good like Mama, we always wonder why things like that have to happen, but then he said, "Have you ever went out into a flower bed and picked a bouquet of flowers, the prettiest ones that was there?" He paused. "Well, that's the way it is with God. God likes pretty things too. And sometimes he comes and picks the very best thing that he can find. See," he said, "God's just like us, he wants pretty things, and he wants good things. And Sarah Freeman was both of these."

After that I got to where I could deal with the loss of somebody real close to me a little better. I always think about God picking flowers, and I've told a lot of people what the minister said. It's the best way I know of putting it when somebody's going through the stage asking why it had to happen.

Miss Mildred spoke about Mama, talking about what a good friend she was, how she'd do anything for anybody, then we sang a song Mama loved:

Precious Lord, take my hand, lead me on, let me stand
I am tired, I am weak, I am worn
Through the storm, through the night, lead me on to the light
Take my hand, precious Lord, lead me home.

It was a song we always sang at funerals, and when we did, everybody fell apart.

Mama is buried at New Style, her old home church, and Daddy's buried next to her, then my brothers and Uncle Tanks and Aunt Rebecca's boys and her grandson. It's on a hillside by a tree, and you hear birds sing. When Mama died, Daddy went in and staked off enough spaces for all the children.

Mama wasn't always hugging us and saying, "I love you." We've never been really affectionate, but she loved us so much and wanted us to love each other. She knew what it was not to have nobody, no brother, no sister, mother or father, that's why she loved so many different people. I can say this with a pure heart. Mama didn't leave this world with no enemies but a lot of love. In her fifty-seven years she loved more than lots of people who live longer than one hundred.

Still, I questioned God. I knowed I was not supposed to doubt God's plan, but I couldn't understand his motive, why he ever put Mama on earth, why he let her suffer. I knew that was a stupid question because I was born out of her, but it seemed like there was so many things that she should have had and didn't. She brought a lot of joy into people's lives, but it seemed like she had so much sorrow, especially not ever having a mama of her own. I just have to believe she went to heaven.

Sometimes things was hard for us with Daddy after Mama died, and he wasn't part of our lives as much as we would have liked. Then James, his aunt, me, and our kids was on vacation, traveling up to see Luda Mae, and James called home from a pay phone for some reason. The rest of us waited in the car. Then James came hurrying back. "We're gonna have to go on home right away."

"What's wrong?"

"They found your daddy this morning. He's dead." I was stunned. Daddy was sixty-nine. It was late, and we'd drove all the way there, but we turned around and drove back.

Nobody ever associated him with heart trouble. Daddy'd always been so outgoing, and he worked even after he stopped farming. He did landscaping for the town, and when he died, he had this little patch of a garden out in the yard with collard greens and tomatoes. And he kept everything up.

After Daddy died, I felt like I was an orphan. Daddy'd been the storyteller. He sat up at night and told ghost stories and made us laugh. He used to love to joke about preachers. We loved the stories, and when we actually went to church, we sat there all tickled, remembering all Daddy's jokes and stories.

In his will Old Man Paul left Daddy and Mama the place where we was born and raised at, along with sixty-three acres of land, but nobody informed us about it. Finally, Mr. Bob, Miss Abby's husband, told us that Mr. Paul had left Daddy land, but he still didn't tell Daddy nothing about how much it was. It was enough for ten acres for each of us kids and then some acres for Mama and Daddy to stay on when they was old. But Mr. Bob, the lawyers, and Miss Bernice sure didn't let us know that. And Daddy sure didn't know that he should go down and look for the will in the courthouse.

After Mr. Bob told Daddy about Mr. Paul leaving us some land, Daddy went over to Miss Bernice and asked her about it. I don't know exactly what happened, but Daddy was mad. That's why we moved over to Mr. Bob's. Miss Bernice also told Daddy that Daddy couldn't do nothing with the land as long as she was alive, but that wasn't true. Daddy couldn't do nothing with the land unlessen Mama agreed for him to do it. That's what it was.

Mr. Bob had always said he'd like us to work for him, so Daddy went to Mr. Bob and told him, "I want to get way from Miss Bernice just as quick as I can."

I didn't find out how much land it was until I went down to the courthouse much later. Then I seen the will. Mr. Paul had wrote down that he left sixty-three acres of land to J. D. Freeman, then he described that land and stated that the remainder went to Mr. Paul's wife, Bernice Sterning. But part of it all was that as long as Mama was living, Daddy couldn't sell it without her signature.

Like I said, after Mr. Paul died, Miss Bernice went wild buying new things, new furniture, a new car, and fixin' up her house, with a bathroom, special cabinets, fancy woodwork, and other changes. She just had her life did up. Now she was really *the lady*, but in the process she turned off everybody until nobody had nothing to do with her. Years went on, then for some reason she decided she wanted to sell the farm and move away. I don't know where she thought she'd go. By then Daddy knew he had the house and some land. After a while, Miss Bernice thought she'd found a buyer for her part of the land, but the people who wanted to buy it actually wanted the place where our house had been. They told her that they'd buy her place only if they could also have what was really our land.

Later, the guy that bought it told me his ownself that he'd told Miss Bernice, "If I can't have all the farm, I don't want none of it." So he just walked away from the deal.

After he said that, Miss Bernice came all the way up to Eclectic to talk to Daddy. After she left, Daddy came to where Mama lay sick. "Old Lady Bernice wants to buy the land."

"Too bad," Mama says. "I ain't signing shit. Mr. Paul left that place to you. How many white men die and leave a nigger anything?" That's what she told Daddy. She wasn't signing nothing.

Not much later Mama died, and I really don't think Daddy understood how it all happened. According to the man who owns the land now, Miss Bernice called him up and said she believed she could get the land. Then Miss Bernice went to Daddy, told Daddy that somebody wanted to buy her house and her part of the land but that person wanted all of it, which included the place where our house had stood.

I think Miss Bernice had concocted a plan in her mind. "If I can get J. D. to sign over this sixty-three acres to me, saying to him, 'I want to sell my place and the only way I can sell it is that I get this land that Paul left you,' then I won't have to actually go through with the sale and then I'll have all of it. I'll get it back from them niggers." That's what I believe Miss Bernice was thinking, but I'll never have no proof.

So Miss Bernice gave Daddy five thousand dollars and got him to sign it over to her. Five thousand dollars for sixty-three acres of land! He signed the sale alright; I went to the courthouse and found his signature, but where he signed it, it didn't say that it was sixty-three acres. I believe Daddy didn't know what he was signing. I also found Mr. Paul's will, but it was too late to challenge it all.

I believe the peoples up in Wetumpka, the lawyers and all, was in cahoots with Miss Bernice. No telling how much property was given to African American people by some whites, then the black people lost it because they didn't understand anything about how a will was supposed to be did. So I went to the guy who bought it, and he showed me the canceled check that was wrote to Daddy for five thousand dollars.

He also told me, "I didn't buy the land from your daddy."

"I know you didn't."

"I never wanted the place where Miss Bernice lived. I never wanted that. I wanted this spot right here." He was standing right out there in the yard where he built his big old house, right exactly where we used to live. What he did was legal, but he still got it wrong because he knowed there was other peoples involved and he knowed that Daddy was an uneducated black man. He could have said to Miss Bernice, "No, I don't want you to do this." He knowed it was worth much more.

It was a terrible thing Miss Bernice did, and Daddy was wrong also, but God really put something on her because of selling us out and selling our land like she did. Miss Bernice's scheme backfired. The saying goes, "Oh, what a tangled web we weave when first we practice to deceive." Miss Bernice practiced to deceive Daddy and Mama out of the land, and she did it knowing all the time that every improvement around the place and all the work there had been done by Daddy and the rest of us.

The way I understand the story, after Miss Bernice got the land from Daddy, she went to this guy who owns it now, and she told him she was ready to sell it. So he wrote her a check and bought the whole thing. Then she sold her cows to Mr. Lester Warren and made arrangements for him to pick them up Monday morning.

Somehow by Friday she finally realized what she had did. She had nowhere to go, nothing, nobody. She called the guy who bought her house and land and said, "I've changed my mind. Come get your check. I didn't cash it."

But he said, "No, I'll take you to court if I have to. It's my place now."

She started crying and begging and going on, saying, "I made a mistake, I made a mistake. I don't want to sell it. Paul came back to me and told me, 'Don't sell it.'" I guess she was seein' Paul's ghost. She must have been tormented.

"No," he said. "I got the land. I'm gonna keep it, and if you give me any trouble, I'm gonna take you to court." Later, the man stood in what's his land now and told me what happened, and Bernice knowed who she was dealing with 'cause she knowed he had plenty of money.

That Monday morning Mr. Lesley Warren planned to come out to Bernice's house to pick up the cows. He called her first, and he didn't get no answer. He thought she might be out in the barn, so he decided just to go on down to catch her. So he drove over and pulled in the driveway that leads to the back porch. He got out and looked at the house. Miss Bernice lay there halfway out the door. She was dead. She'd shot herself in the head.

I never could totally accept Daddy's part in what happened. Mama had died without ever having an electric stove or bathroom, but after he got the five thousand dollars, Daddy basically gave it to his girlfriend. Daddy redid his girlfriend's house, and I believe he paid one of her son's tuition in college—with the land that was our inheritance! Instead of to Mama or us, it went to her and her children. If he had needed money for medical help, I wouldn't have had no problem with him selling the land if he had to, but he did it for the wrong reason.

I had been so close to Daddy when I was little, but when that happened, it's like something changed in my heart. Not a day goes past that I don't think about my Mama in some way, but something has to happen to remind me of my Daddy.

I go back and I look at the land now, the sixty-three acres, all the hills and trees that we climbed. The new owners just swooped our past off the earth; they tore down our house and wiped up our poor little childhood and threw it away.

We don't understand God's creation. We get out there and take a bulldozer and bulldoze down the earth, just like they did to the location of our childhood. But see, in my mind, when I look at the place, I see the little hill that used to come down to our house from Mr. Paul's, and when I look at it I see me and Shane walking up to get water with old high heels on, then the dogs chasing us back down the hill. I see the little creek running back there. And I remember when me and Mama used to go into the woods, and every year when the azaleas bloom in front of my house today, I think about the wild azaleas back among the trees and how we'd go out and break them off and put them in a big old fruit jar on the table.

And I remember the sweet shrubs that smelled like a very ripe apple. The smell was so strong that when the wind was blowing in a certain direction, you could just walk outside and smell this wonderful smell. Sometimes Mama'd say, "Jimmie, let's go over yonder and see if we can find one of those sweet shrubs." We'd find it, look around, and promise to each other, "Next year we'll remember where they is at," but we always forgot and had to wait 'til we could follow their smell again. Yes, God gives us claim to the earth that we love.

⤚ twelve ⤙

It is just possible that the white man is no longer the center of the universe.

—Lillian Smith, "Buying a New World with Old Confederate Bills," 1942–43

It was night when I first went to work in the textile factory in Montgomery. Only streetlights lit the door, but I could hear the clang of metal grinding before I reached the entrance.

A big-boned, real nice, white lady, Joyce Bice, taught me how to wind, to put this little machine on my hand, take the end of the yarn from the spool, and get it to the cone, my finished product. Then I passed the cone to someone else. The problem came if the yarn broke. Then you had to make a knot and lay it back on a roller. I had sixty spindles I was supposed to keep running, and I got really good at it.

After I learned my job in the winding room, I went into the spinning room 'cause I was fascinated at the spinning process and learned it my ownself. On my way to my break I worked with it. Finally the supervisor noticed it, and when somebody was out, he asked me if I wanted to try to run the spinning frame.

So they put me in the spinning room, and I worked there for years. I enjoyed spinning better than the other jobs, but it could have problems. If a thread fell down, it messed up your whole frame. The thread started flying to other threads and pulled them down in this domino effect, so the spinner lost the whole damn frame. Then you closed it down and got the fixer. Sometimes the previous worker had left a big mess, which you had to fix before you could start your own production.

We was paid by the pound, so they could really screw people up by taking us off the machine we was used to. Workers could get really, really good, then they'd put us someplace else.

A bunch of us be riding to and from work—me, Louise, Mahilia, Ida, and this other lady. We all got wired from our job, where we just wore the coffeepot out, drank coffee, coffee, coffee, and took NoDoz. After they put up the fire escapes, and before they didn't let us go out no more, if somebody on a floor beneath us couldn't stay awake, we tied a string around the NoDoz box and dangle it down.

While we rode home together we talked. Sometimes we be mad 'cause our machine done broke down so we couldn't make production. Sometimes we got moved off a machine for some stupid reason, and it cut down on our pay. The day-to-day working in the mills was so hard on us all. I ached from the strain and the bending, and I spinned in my dreams. A lot of people drank or took nerve pills or smoked dope in order to go to sleep.

What really disgusted me was that those machines seemed to have more knowledge than I did. I looked at them and be thinking that I was looking at a human being, somebody that was very, very smart in order to make a big old monster of a machine like that. So every time I ran a spinning job, it was a challenge to me. I knowed I had to work hard, 'cause if I didn't, it was going to beat me. I felt I had to beat the machine.

And we worked under bad conditions. They didn't have no air conditioner until the union and OSHA, the Occupational Safety and Health Administration, come in, so sometimes I felt like Daddy looked when he had heatstroke back on the farm, like the mule was standing in the shade of a tree and I was laid out on the ground. Then Stevens came in and bricked up all the windows so us workers couldn't even look out no more.

I couldn't block the noise, so I just tried not to think, and I got so I did my work without even thinking of it. Of course, cotton dust be floating all through the air and made it hard to breathe. About 11:00 at night I could look at the wall in the spinning room and see it completely covered with dust. We brushed and blew dust off our skin or clothes, but we couldn't blow it out of our insides, and that killed a lot of the longtime workers.

For a while we run rayon and polyester, but that could be just as bad on your lungs as cotton because pieces of the rayon broke up in flecks so they looked like itty-bitty shimmers of glass floating through the air. Once rayon's melted down, it's plastic, and we wasn't even aware of what kind of chemicals was accumulating in our lungs. We breathed whatever was in there eight hours a night. Also, the machines vibrated the wood floors and jarred the workers' insides like a jackhammer.

Most of the people that worked there couldn't afford real good shoes, and they stood on their feet all day, pushing boxes filled with rope. The boxes weighed 150 pounds empty. They had rollers, but you still strained, and some didn't roll good, and you had to push real hard. So people's backs got stressed, and lots of workers' legs ached from varicose veins. There was so much pressure and strain.

But we developed a sense of loyalty among the workers, white and black. If one of the spinners saw another get in a mess and her job was running good, she helped the other spinner. And we not only worked together, we socialized together, white and black again. We drank beer, told jokes, and laughed and talked, like me and Mildred, we run off at the mouth. Sometimes we sat in the parking lot, talking. When I was still living up in the country, my friends drove all the way up to see me on the weekends.

When I first went to work at the textile plant it was owned by United Elastic. Management was people from the South who worked in the plant and was more sympathetic than after the owners sold the plant to J. P. Stevens. Almost immediately after that we lost some of our holidays, and managers came down from the North, like from Tennessee, so they weren't really aware of the problems we had as textile workers. And we got no benefits, no insurance, no sick leave.

J. P. Stevens was a runaway shop. They founded their first mill in New England in 1813, but they left the North 'cause they knowed that they was going to have to have unions there. So they started coming south in 1946, three years after I was born. One by one, they closed dozens of plants up north and brought them south. By the time I worked in one, they had eighty-five plants. Many ended up in North and South Carolina, two of the worse states there was for workers. Not Mississippi. I guess they figured, "Ain't no use going down there 'cause 90 percent of the population be black."

Stevens had their own little company towns surrounding the plants. They owned the store, the little houses that they rented out to workers, even the doctor. Almost like living in slavery, except the workers was white until after the civil rights movement. Before the movement the only blacks that worked there was outside and in the card room, the most dangerous place.

Textiles was the most important industry down south, and the plants put a monopoly on wages. It be easy for Stevens to take advantage of their workers. They was vulnerable. Almost nobody who worked there hadn't had a hard life—like being poor, not having no education, family violence, or illness. When we began organizing, we had about five hundred workers, 60 percent womens and 40 percent mens. Many of the womens was divorced and responsible for themselves and their kids. 'Cause so many hadn't graduated from high school, Stevens thought they could just push them around.

They definitely discriminated against women. The highest-paid workers in there was the fixers. Now Johnny Adams was a fixer who did good—but most of them didn't do nothing. Because my friend Mildred be a woman, they wouldn't consider her as a fixer, even though she had seniority. "File you one of those discrimination suits so the company'll think twice before they give it to a man next time," I told her, but she didn't.

See, they wanted to keep a woman down so she couldn't be independent and didn't have no power. There was no womens in supervision, in management, but there wasn't no reason that a woman couldn't do the work. Besides, the supervisor mostly just drank coffee.

The men thought they had the advantage over womens and made wisecracks or told us dirty jokes when we didn't want to hear them. They used anything they could to come onto the young white womens, and rather than saying anything about it, many womens just kept quiet and took it.

Some of the womens got involved with one or another redneck supervisor, but then it got outta hand. If it started causing difficulty in either one's family life or if the woman wanted it stopped and said, "I'm not gonna do this no longer" or if the supervisor got tired of her, they just found a way to fire her or make her life miserable so she'd quit. That happened to one of my white friends, and it contributed to her drinking.

The whole sexual stuff burned me up. I noticed that black womens, including myself, or older white womens would work real hard, learn our job, and be making production on a machine real good, so we'd finally be making money, then suddenly the boss'd walk up and say, "I'm moving you over here to these other machines."

"Why?"

"'Cause I'm putting so-and-so on it." You'd look around to see who so-and-so was, and nine times out of ten, it was some nice-looking white girl. So we'd be over there on the new machine, and time passed and we got good at our job and started making some money again, then that same white girl looked over and saw us doing okay and she decided, "I want that machine." So she went to the boss, and he moved us again.

Seniority just had no place, so they could just do that. Plus, blacks wouldn't have had no seniority anyway 'cause up until a short time before I went to work in there, there wasn't no blacks inside. The only blacks that worked there before was working in the back on the docks, where it be cold in the wintertime and hot in the summer. Either that or in the dangerous card room, where they'd get their limbs cut off.

The sexual harassment kept going on and on and on, and if a nice white woman come there, the white supervisor'd slide up to her too and tell her, "If you do what I want, it'll work out good for you." It just burned me up when somebody be pawing you, and they got octopus arms. Made you want to just slap the taste out of his mouth. I just didn't feel a man has any business having that kind of power over womens.

Also, when textiles had been finally forced to take African Americans into the plant as workers, Stevens came up with a new way of discriminating. They speeded you up or gave away your machine. And if they said something sexual to a black woman, there wasn't no black supervisor she could go to. I was real happy when Louise Purter, my black friend from the country club, came to work with me. I wasn't so alone.

At first I was just thankful to have me a job that would pay me what I thought I was worth. Then I found out that it didn't pay nothing like I was worth. I started seeing what was wrong, and I thought that if anything could be done, I'd have to be part of it. But I didn't know what to do.

My baby brother, J. W., had gone to Ohio and worked in a union plant there, and he told me they had tremendous benefits. They got paid real good, had sick leave, insurance with dental care, eyeglasses, and a credit union, all 'cause of a labor union. He said it was like he'd stepped out of hell into heaven.

I couldn't really find no information about unions down here, but I had a set of encyclopedias, and I looked up unions and found out what they was. Also, there was a glass plant down here that had good benefits, so I knowed good conditions were possible.

Some of the old workers told me they had a union long, long ago, but the people who wanted it was harassed. The union met in people's houses, and the company sent spies. It happened to my friend Diane. They didn't fire her, but they made work so rough on her she wanted to quit, doubling up her production 'til they just about drove her crazy.

Finally the union was voted down; somebody set a casket in front of the plant and said, "The union's dead, we're going to bury it." After that the company fired all the active workers. It was hard for Diane to join us in another drive, but eventually she did it.

I made so many friends out of that plant and later out of our union drive. I had this one white friend, Margaret Austin. We got to be so close. Me and Margaret worked straight across from each other on this long winder. I was faster, but we'd start working together and go down these hand-knotters at the same time, talking like mad. Then we took our break together. She was the nicest white girl, as good as could be. But if either of us was sick and missing, the other was absolutely miserable. Our supervisor, Ronnie Gilmore, told me, "Y'all gonna kill me, you and Margaret." If Margaret came to work, and I wasn't there, she went home, just like that. She told Ronnie, "I'm sick, I can't stay." [laughs] I usually done rode with somebody else, so I couldn't just go home if Margaret wasn't there, but I was just pathetic, just pitiful without her.

I went through some terrible times while I was working with Margaret. James wouldn't work and really started acting the fool, getting more violent. I'd have to deal with him, try to work and care for the kids, and sometimes I didn't know if I could do it. But Margaret was always there for me.

I never will forget the night, about 9:30, when I started into the plant as usual, and this little old short, bewildered-looking fellah with curly hair stood there in the near dark. And he held all these leaflets in his hand and talked to several peoples. I was nosy, I always been, and I peeked over several shoulders, and they was leaflets—fliers for the union. I still didn't know too much about unions, except they was supposed to help, so it was like, "Oh, okay," then, "Yeah!"

The bosses stood by that night watching who was going to take one of the fliers and who wasn't. During the day they could spy real good, but it was harder in the night shift. Me and Louise Bailey, this overweight white lady that was my friend, we got our flier and walked right straight through the lobby reading it.

The noise inside the plant was absolutely horrendous. It hit you in the face even before you went inside. The only way you could talk to somebody once you got inside the plant was to be right in their face. Still, we could look around to see how the workers responded to the leaflets.

Some of the workers picked leaflets up outside, but when they realized what they were, they balled them up and throwed them onto the floor. So we knowed them was people that didn't want it.

For the next couple of days and nights, on all three shifts, the union guys—Henry Mann and his helper, Foots—was out there. So on all three shifts they was out there. Finally one day I got a chance to talk to Henry, the organizer. He said, "We're gonna have a meeting at 7:00 tonight at [the motel] Howard Johnson's. Could you get the word out to people to come?" A lot of people showed up. I looked around, and there was more blacks than whites, but gradually more whites started coming to the meetings. Henry started telling us what unions was about and what they could do for us, and everybody got excited. Then Henry said, "When y'all go back to work, every one of those boss mens is gonna know who was at this meeting. Because there's somebody here tonight that's a spy, that's not here for the union. They're here to go back and tell the boss who's at the meeting. That always happens."

And, sure enough, the bosses knowed. They knowed who exactly was there. "I know you was at the meeting tonight. I know." Real blatant.

But we acted like, "So, ain't nothing you can do about it." The civil rights movement had fired us up. "We ain't taking no shit no more. Uh-uh. You ain't gonna give me no grief over it."

We learned later that somebody from our plant wrote the Amalga-mated Textiles and Clothing Workers Union (ACTWU) and asked them to send a organizer. Henry said they got a letter from somebody, but no-body ever knowed who it was that wrote that letter. Nobody ever said, "I was the one that contacted them."

Henry Mann came out of the mills hisself, from the Opelika mill in Atlanta, and his peoples was union backers. Henry said his daddy led the weavers out of the mill in 1956 and was blacklisted. Henry went to col-lege, then became a shop manager, then organized the workers, so he was blacklisted too.

So after Henry hit the gate, I hit it with him. I got very, very active in the organizing drive, especially me and Marva. Marva had two little kids, she was a single mother, African American, and was brave. She lived in the housing project with her mother. Her mama had been a maid all her life and hoped for more for Marva, and Marva was determined. If some-body thought of something, Marva'd try it. Plus, she didn't have no hus-band holding her down, so she could be militant, I mean *militant*.

Louise Bailey, this big, blond lady who I was with when I first picked up a flier, was fifty-five when we started. Louise went to work in that plant when she was sixteen, when it was on the edge of Montgomery, and raised three kids on it. Her mother-in-law started [there] when she was only eight. Louise'd put in all those years, then they took someone with six weeks' training and gave that person the same pay as Louise was making. It wasn't fair, but could Louise raise hell. I mean she could *raise* hell.

So then the boss mens started to try this divide-and-conquer strategy. They brought their people down from North Carolina and started having meetings on all three shifts trying to work out some method to stop the unions. They went to the white people and said, "If that union comes in here, you may have a black supervisor."

But Louise Bailey answered them back. She tickled me so bad. She had a heavy voice and spoke real southern. She had this soft, round body, blue eyes, and wore fluffy, feminine dresses, but, oh, could she cuss. Now, we had Woodrow, the white supervisor. He kind of walked slew footed, with a butt like a iron board, flat as it could be.

When Woodrow told Louise that she might have a black supervisor, trying to scare her, Louise said, "Goddammit, Woodrow, if I can work for your so-and-so ass," and she flopped her feet, slew footed, "I can work for any damn body, black or blue." Everybody just rolled laughing. We started meeting on Tuesday nights in the motel where we had our first meeting. We sat on folded chairs, mostly older white women in the front row and the younger blacks behind. Stevens employees was trying to organize all over in different plants, so if Stevens even got a wind some plant was going to try it, they give the workers a five-cent raise or six holidays instead of four, a half-hour lunch break, something the workers wanted, to head off the workers from signing for a union. Henry told us about the tactics.

Once Stevens saw that we was really trying to organize, they tried all sorts of low-down actions. In order to make white workers scared of blacks, they put up pictures of whites who had been killed by some blacks in San Francisco, then went to whites and said, "You gonna trust some black man?" They sent spies to our meetings and even went into the parking lot and wrote down people's tag numbers. And they put turnstiles at the front gate so organizers couldn't get inside to pass out leaflets.

Before the campaign began, we parked on the street, and people's cars was being stolen, so the plant finally put in a parking lot. We'd also been asking for a place to eat. We had just a little bitty cafeteria the size of a small kitchen for all of us to eat in. It fit no more than four people, and you was on top of each other. So Stevens decided to build us a big cafeteria with machines, shelves, a dollar changer, a telephone, tables, and everything. They even got us a plant nurse, all to show us how good they could be without a union.

But they didn't care. They didn't even have no fire escapes, at least when I began. If there was a fire, we could only get out the front door on the street level or through one little entrance way around in back. That was even though the building was three floors and about a block long. Before the union we workers didn't know not having fire escapes was a violation. As soon as the union came, Henry asked us, "Where's the fire escape?"

"What fire escape?"

Henry said, "They supposed to have fire escapes in these buildings." But they didn't have them, and fires started in the plant lots of times. Those machines got too hot and caught afire, especially back in the card room. If they didn't get a card room fire out soon enough, we would've had to go all the way along the building, then down all those stairs, and a lot of people could've died. It was heartless. That's why so much solidarity developed between the blacks and whites.

One day after the campaign had started, we came to work and they was cutting outside doors up on the third floor where there wasn't no doors before. We said, "What y'all doing out there?"

"Putting in fire escapes."

The union brought OSHA in, who said the noise level was way too high, that it caused hearing loss in the workers, so they notified Stevens that they had to upgrade the equipment to cut down on the clamor. That was fine, but they also started requiring us workers to wear earplugs, so Stevens used that against us. See, earplugs was uncomfortable. We said, "I can't think with them in." It was like earplugs hindered your hand process, so we stumbled around with our clumsy hands for a while, then took them out.

So Stevens figured this was a way to discipline workers, to get them down on the union. They fired you if they caught you working without them three times. But people stuck with organizing, and the new equipment Stevens put in helped.

Stevens also took eleven workers at a time into a room with both the plant and personnel managers for captive-audience speeches. During my meeting, the manager sat at the head of the table, the personnel manager sat next to him, then I was next. To begin, they read all this written information to us about the disasters a union brought to workers, how workers went on strike and lost their homes, everything the workers valued. Stevens didn't say nothing about no benefits that'd come from unions.

So after they'd read this list, they said, "Has anybody got any questions?"

"I've got some questions," I said. "I want to know why is it that Stevens has always fought the union so hard?"

The manager looked at me, then barked, "'Cause we don't think the union has anything constructive to offer employees."

I said, real clear, "You don't think the union has anything constructive to offer employees, or is it that you don't think the union has anything constructive to offer the company?"

The manager got all flabbergasted; here's this black girl speaking up. "Look at the auto industry," I went on. "Y'all saying people in textiles can't have unions 'cause it's such a competitive field. What about the benefits to the auto workers? The steel workers? They be competitive."

He stammered, "People, people don't need textiles like they need cars."

"You seen anybody walking about naked lately?"

All them other workers sat there saying to theyself, "Oh, for God's sake, please shut up, girl, just please shut up." They never heard nobody stand up to the manager.

So I told him, "We come into the plant and work real hard for eight hours, then you take the product we done made and make towels, fine linens for beds, out of our creation. I ask you, 'How many of y'all has got a J. P. Stevens sheet?'" I paused. "All of you, I'm sure. But we workers don't. We can't afford to even buy our own products."

So one of the others breaks in, just when I'm getting my steam. "They make so much more money in autos and steel 'cause they live up north and the cost of living up there is higher. The cost of living is lower here."

"Uh-uh, that's not the answer. They got steel mills right up in Birmingham that pay good wages 'cause of the union."

"If that's the case," the plant manager snarled, "why don't you go work for them?"

I said, "'Cause I live here, and I can't see no use to run to another pasture when you could make your own grass just as green." Oh, boy, they was so mad with me! Oooh!

I remembered that speech he read to us, and later, when we filed charges in court against Stevens for unfair labor practices, they had to give a copy of it to the Labor Board and our attorneys. Then they had the hearing and asked me all sorts of questions. I saw the personnel manager sitting way in the back of the courtroom, and he looked like he be saying to hisself, "Please, please don't tell 'em about the meetings." But I did. They claimed that the speech they read us had been changed by then, but the judge didn't go along with it. They got discredited.

What really angered me the most was when they took one black guy who couldn't even read or write and decided to make him into a supervisor, to be a token designed to fail. They used him as an example that would fail. I went to the guy myself and pleaded with him, "You been in here all these years, and they ain't never offered you a good job. Can't you see that you ain't gonna be nothing but a damn token?"

But no, no, the black guy thought it was a opportunity to make more money.

I said, "If you take it, it's more demeaning than being poor." Stevens was using my own people then, which really made me mad.

Stevens was so stubborn all over. They was involved with twelve hundred law violations between 1963 and 1979. ACTWU started up a nationwide boycott of Stevens products in 1976, and all sorts of movie stars and important people came out in favor of it. Only real one against it was Dinah Shore; she advertised Stevens products. They even made a movie, *Norma Rae,* about trying to organize Stevens workers in North Carolina. It starred Sally Field.

Henry Mann, the organizer, really knowed how to network. If something happened today, I guarantee you by tomorrow knowledge would spread all the way down the vine. Stevens was violating OSHA's rules about the amount of cotton dust in the air. There was so much cotton flying around, we couldn't see just a few yards away. One day, my friend Marva bent over the water fountain to get a drink, and the water encountered so much cotton dust getting to her mouth that her lips was covered with lint. So Marva contacted Henry, and by the next day everybody up the organizing line knowed about it. Henry was darn good.

The union tried to help the workers who was fired. David Harris, a black man, had about twelve boys, so when he was fired, the union paid him a little to work in the union office. If a reporter or a church person came to find out about the union, David told how he'd been fired for refusing to dock somebody else's job. David was one of the first, but they fired a whole bunch of people, obviously for organizing. Doing that during a union campaign is against the law.

David and Henry, the ACTWU organizer, be followed. I wasn't, I guess 'cause I came to the union hall during the daytime. Then I left from there to go to work, and it was 6:00 in the morning when I got home. Maybe nobody had the gumption to follow a kooky woman like me around during that time of morning. They definitely tried to scare the pure daylights out of people, and many quit, but I don't scare easy. I always figure that any man is just like my daddy. That man puts his pants on the same way Daddy did, so he ain't so all-powerful.

Later, after we be organizing a lot, a photographer named Bob Masters came down from the ACTWU headquarters in New York and took photos of our activities. Also, we got some pictures of marches and scenes where workers was with Dr. King and Abernathy. They always had photographers at events. We used them for publicity. We got a photo of Rosa Parks too. There was pictures of me standing in a church looking at this big, big photo of Dr. King, just like I was talking to him and pointing out to him what we was going through. They was all at the union hall.

We knowed how much unions meant to Dr. King, and these pictures had so much history. Dr. King was up in Memphis, trying to organize the Sanitation Workers, when he be killed. He backed unions 100 percent, so workers wouldn't be treated like they was still under slavery. We also had organizing material in our union hall and sentimental things like posters that unions around the country gave us. Most of all, we had all the affidavits taken from the workers, which was locked in the bottom of a file cabinet.

One afternoon, when I opened the door to the union hall, everything was trashed! David was there, and he looked stunned. He was the first to find the mess. He called the police, and now they was gone. The vandals broke our equipment, threw papers around, ripped the posters, and poured chemicals on the photos that made them puff up, then stick together, ruined. So much history was destroyed.

Then I asked David, "What about the affidavits?"

"They be okay. They didn't break into the file cabinet." I was grateful. If the thugs had destroyed them, we'd of had a big problem. We probably would never have got a union 'cause a lot of workers was running scared by then. If we had to ask them again, they might not give us another statement.

"What the police say?"

"They said, 'We'll check it out.' "

"Right." But they never did.

⚜ thirteen ⚜

The Lord executeth righteousness and judgment for all that
are oppressed. He made known his ways unto Moses, his acts
unto the children of Israel.

—Psalm 103:6–7

Not only had we been taking so much abuse from Stevens all those years, but I took it at home because I was married to a man whose thoughts was always other than they should be. James couldn't believe I was involved with the union to try to improve our lives. He thought there had to be some other sinister reason I be attending those union meetings. And while I was out there trying to make a better world, he gave me hell. The union headquarters was in a motel, and James said, "I'm gonna get my mamma and daddy and bring 'em down in front of the motel and say, 'Look what kinda woman we got here!' I know what you be up to."

Henry Mann, our organizer, was such a good person and like a confidant to me. Some days, I'd be working hard, beating out my brains trying to get people to sign union cards, then Henry'd notice me at the end of the day and realize I looked down. Those days he came over and said, "Hey, you lookin' mighty sad about something. Want to talk?"

There was another guy, Harry Weintraub, the union attorney. He was Jewish, out of New York, and his daddy was a retired administrative judge. Harry helped me so much, especially when old Mr. James Robinson finally decided to file for divorce.

We've forgiven each other now, James and me. I can say now with a pure heart that we are really friends, but back then, when we was married, James and his family did so much to make me feel crazy. I started having problems with my menstrual cycle, then all of a sudden I had no desire for sex at all. Sex became just revolting to me. Now, I never believed in hoo-doo, in witchcraft. I'd always heard of it, but I said, "Ain't no way nobody can do nothing to you. It's just a bunch of bull." I never believed that somebody who wanted to hurt me could pour some powder down that I'd walk through then become all crazy and foolish. I believed there was no way that somebody could take a strand of hair outta my head and mix it up with menstrual blood and drive me crazy.

But one day as I changed furniture around in our old house, the one with no ceiling, I moved the chiffonnier and saw this little bag up on one of the rafters. It had a little bulge and was tied across the top. I said, "What on earth is this?" So I took it down and mashed it with my fingers. It felt really, really delicate, like flour. I untied the string, looked at it, and felt it directly. It felt smooth, like flour or the snuff Mama and them used to dip.

I smelled it, and it had a odd odor that I'd never smelled before. "What in the hell is this?" I said. And then it hit me. So I tied the string back around it and put it back up there, but all that day I was so angry. This terrible anger built up inside of me, but I didn't say anything to anybody. He came in later and I asked him, "James?" I looked right at him. "What is that in there behind that chiffonnier, up on that rafter?"

He started getting real defensive. "I don't know what you talkin' about."

"You no good son of a bitch. You caught yourself trying to hoo-doo me."

"I don't know what you talkin' about! I don't know what you talkin' about! I ain't puttin' nothing up there!"

I got so mad I called him a bunch of names that wasn't very ladylike. And I told him, "I'm just gonna show your damn ass that it didn't work. I'm taking my kids and I'm leaving." So I went down to my daddy's. Daddy didn't have nothing to say but, "Ummm." Sometimes I ached for Mama.

Later I went back home. I didn't believe in divorce and didn't know what else to do. Him and me went through some really bad times, partly connected with my work with the union, and one weekend I decided me and the kids had to get away. I told the kids, "We goin' up to Aunt Magnolia's and Uncle Clifton's on Friday, and we goin' to come back Sunday." They got all excited. Now Mama'd always taught us that when you left your house overnight, you cleaned it up 'cause you didn't know what you goin' to come back to. So that Friday I cleaned the house good, and I told the kids, "Y'all take a bath," then I took all their clothes, added my panties and bra, and I washed 'em. By then I had a washer and dryer. After I took a bath, I throwed the clean clothes in the dryer, and when we left the house, I left the dryer running. I also changed the linen on the beds, putting on yellow- and white-flowered sheets.

So we went on to Magnolia's, then came back that Sunday, and immediately the moment I walked into my house, I knowed somebody'd been there, and I knowed they wasn't friendly. I could just feel it. Even the kids said, "Mama, somebody been here, ain't they?"

"Yeah, probably your daddy." I kind of like passed it off. But I knowed whoever'd been there hadn't meant good.

I unpacked our clothes and went to wash the clothes we'd worn. Now when clothes are dried in a dryer, they're plump and fluffy. I went into the dryer, and the first thing I noticed was that the clothes was like flattened, like somebody went through 'em. I took them out of the dryer and realized my bra and my panties wasn't in there. They was missing. I thought to myself, "Now, that's strange."

I turned my house bottom up looking for them. I always kept my drawers arranged, but they wasn't nowhere. Finally, I'd looked through all my drawers, and I couldn't find 'em. I knowed somebody took them, but I didn't know why. Also, I noticed somebody had changed the sheets on my bed; now they was white. "What the hell is going on here?" I said.

Then the kids called, "Mama, here come Daddy, here come Daddy," and James come on in the house, and I knowed something was very, very wrong. I eventually realized that James and his family had set out to drive me crazy, maybe to give them more control. I followed James back into the bedroom. "I want to ask you something. Why is the sheets on my bed changed?"

He said, "What you talkin' about? Why would I change some sheets?"

"That's what I'm asking. Another thing. What happened to my underclothes that was in the dryer?"

Then he went into this big carrying-on fit. "You just crazy as hell! You just crazy! You losing your damn mind!" I knowed I wasn't crazy. I knowed that it was something very, very wrong.

Also, by this time sex was really, really yucky for me. I didn't even want him to touch me; I just could not stand for him to even think it. I had no interest in no sex at all. At one point James got mad and left and moved back there with his daddy and mama. Before long, his mama accused me of hoo-dooing him: "His shoulder hurt all the time. You done put a spell on him." I realized they was trying to justify all the things that they was doing to me.

In the meantime, when Tracy was about eight, she started talking about this teacher who wasn't hers but who was giving her presents. I mentioned it to one of James's sisters, and she acted like this river that had been dammed now was flowing. "I . . . I . . . I thought you knowed. That's the woman James go with." So she just started telling all of it, how the woman, Miss Roberts, was giving little ceramic presents to everybody in the family.

So I went over to the school and into Miss Roberts's classroom. She saw me and knowed me, but up 'til then, I didn't know her. Right in front of the kids, I told her, "Let me tell you one thing, and I don't want to have to repeat it. I don't give a damn what you do with James Robinson. You want him, you got him, but don't you ever come near my kids again."

She started, "Get outta my class."

"You don't tell me nowhere to go." I left and told James, "You do what you want to, but you tell her to stay away from my kids."

Finally one morning I came in from working nights, sent the kids to school, and went to bed. I thought James was working, but he wasn't. He was seeing his girlfriend. So that morning I was sleeping, and I heard the doorbell just ring and ring and ring.

"Who in the world is that?" Everybody knowed that I worked nights and slept days while the kids was in school. So I got up and pulled the curtains back, and there's the biggest, ugliest sheriff I have ever seen. I won't ever forget it because it was on our anniversary, the twelfth of August.

I opened the door and the sheriff said, "Is your name Mary Jimmie Robinson?"

"Yes."

"I got a summons for you to appear in court."

"What?" He just handed it to me. "What is it?"

"I don't know. I'm just supposed to deliver it."

So I closed the door, opened it up, and found out that James had filed for divorce. See, by this time he done got this woman pregnant, one of the teachers at my daughter Tracy's school. The woman should've known to take birth control pills!

Anyway, James came home, and we got fighting, and he hit me and knocked me around. I said to him, "I'm going down, and I'm issuing a warrant for your arrest." So I went on to town, and I issued a warrant on him for assault, and they picked him up. After he got out, he came back, got his clothes, and went over to live with his daddy and them.

While we was going through the separation, James jumped me, fixin' to beat me one more time, but Fitzgerald stood up to him and said, "If you ever put your hand on my mama again, I'll kill you." Believe me, James turned me loose and never laid another hand on me. Fitzgerald was about thirteen.

So we got divorced, and James and the woman got married, but the state of Alabama stinks as far as women getting any kind of consideration from the judges. James hired a lawyer who was the son of the judge, and so I only got $150 a month in total child support for four kids. The kids went to visit James every weekend, and James and the schoolteacher took them bowling, out to eat, spent all sorts of money on them. See, they had her money. Then the kids came home, and I didn't have nothing.

James and his new wife kept going on about how they wanted the kids. They might have even done some hoo-dooing on them. And it's devastating not to be able to do anything and watch your life fall apart. Finally I said, "Okay, if this is what you want, if you don't want to help me support the kids, then you take 'em."

By then the new woman realized that James didn't have no job. She was pregnant and already had another child, and it meant that she was gonna be taking care of six kids and herself and James on her school-teacher's salary. So they started doing all these nasty things to drive the kids away.

I tried to recover my life, but I didn't feel right about going out with other men. I still felt married, even though James was married to someone else. And I felt that if I did go out, I'd be being disloyal to the kids. Plus, I still had absolutely no sex drive. And I never really had anyone important in my life again. It was like all the men I knew came with baggage, and I didn't want them.

After a while I told Dean, James's brother's wife, about my lack of sexual feeling. "I don't have no interest at all in no sex. I just feel dead from the waist down. I don't know what it is."

Dean told her husband, Grady, what I said, and Grady told Dean that his daddy and James had gotten some hoo-doo something and had fed it to me without me knowing. I don't know if they used my bra and panties that time or not. But I didn't believe it then, I just couldn't. So I said to Dean, "Naw, ain't nobody done put a spell on me."

Then, a good while later, me and the kids went up to James's family's house, and we was sat around, talking. I looked at Grady and asked him, "Grady, Dean told me that your dad and James did something to me with hoo-doo."

He said, "I'm gonna tell you this, but if you ever say I said it, I'll deny it. But you need to go get yourself some help to counter the spell. I told Daddy and James that they shouldn't do that mess, but they went somewhere, and they got something, and they gave it to you. But you can get it off of you." Then he told me to go to this hoo-doo lady.

I just busted out, all angry. "Goddamnit! I ain't going nowhere. If their damn asses can live with what they've did, let them live with it. The evil will come back to them. I'm not going anywhere." I thought about Mama saying over and over, "If you dig a grave for someone else, you might as well dig one for yourself, 'cause you're gonna need it."

I also constantly had problems with my period. It would come on and then stay on for maybe two weeks. I thought maybe it was the stress or the change of life. Finally, when I moved to Montgomery, I told my friend Sarah about it, and Sarah said, "Your ass need to go to the doctor." I kept not listening to her and was bleeding and bleeding and bleeding, then finally she said, "You going to a doctor now." She called her doctor and told them what was happening, and they told her to bring me in. They found out that my hemoglobin was real low, and they put me in the hospital and did surgery. Then, soon as the surgery was over, I felt sensual and sexual again.

After that I knew beyond a shadow of a doubt that those people were evil at that time. They tried to hurt me and hurt me, so I would become this mindless person. They tried to destroy my mind, my body, my sexuality. It became like a battle of will. I had to prove to them that they didn't succeed at doing it. I'll never know exactly how they tried to do it, but they did.

At the same time I dealt with James, I worked and organized at the plant. When we first started organizing, we really worked to get people to sign their blue union cards. If we got the majority signed up, we didn't need no election. While I was signing them up, I realized a lot of the workers couldn't read or write. They be so vulnerable. After we got over a majority of workers signed in 1977, Stevens got a bargaining order. Stevens be supposed to deal with us, but they didn't. In fact, they used every little thing they could come up with to get people fired. They also harassed people so much, many couldn't stand the pressure of it and quit. All over the South, Stevens did the same thing. Courts ruled against them, they paid the fines or appealed, and they went on refusing to recognize the union.

It was easier to organize plants with lots of blacks in them. Many whites had been there so long that they felt like they had too much to lose to take risks, but the blacks usually said, "I ain't got nothing no way, and if they want my job, they going to get it anyway. I might as well go with the union." Many of the young white workers also joined right away, but lots of the older white workers walked by you and looked at you like you some kind of murderer.

Because Stevens was fighting against unions in so many different locations, the union had lots of tactics. The vice president of ACTWU came down to one of our meetings and told us that the only way that Stevens could be beat was to have a major contract with all of the Stevens plants. Then, if we needed to, we could pull a nationwide strike. Just a local strike wouldn't work 'cause they was just gonna shut down your plant and take the material somewhere else.

We also needed publicity. Henry and Harry always called me when they wanted dirty work did. One time I asked them, "How come me?"

"'Cause you're the only one crazy enough to do it, that's why."

At a meeting one night at the union hall, Henry and Harry, our lawyer, came in, motioned to me, and said, "Hey, kiddo, come here." I knowed any time Harry called me "kiddo," he wanted me to do something sneaky. So I walked over to him where he stood by a young woman. "This is Mary Thornton," Harry said. "She's a reporter from the *Boston Globe* and wants to get into the plant to get some pictures for a story. You think you can get her in there?"

I grinned at her. "Sure. Wear some old jeans and tennis shoes and a shirt tomorrow, then meet me at the plant. You and me'll go in the front door and walk into the back like you're working, then we'll split up. I'll draw you a diagram showing you where to go, and nobody'll pay no attention."

So about 9:00 p.m. the next evening we went into the plant. She turned to the right, and I turned to the left, and she took all these photos. The plant was really bad, with cotton dust hanging down like moss from the walls and machines. She also took pictures of the difficult conditions of the workers. But somebody went to the bosses: "I seen a lady in here taking pictures." Honey, you should've seen them running around trying to find her! I just cracked up, it be so funny, and I got her out the back door.

After that they tried to screen everybody that came into that plant, but she put the pictures in the *Boston Globe* and embarrassed Stevens. Oh, we had some hilarious times. They tried to show us a little bit, and we showed them a whole lot. All sorts of important people and organizations came out for the boycott, actors, the National Council of Churches.

I tell you one thing, when we workers woke up, we woke up with a vengeance. We fought back. My friend Johnny was a good example. He's a tall, blond white guy, with real curly hair. He don't take crap from nobody, and if you give him a inch, he'll take a mile. Also, Johnny's brilliant. After he left Stevens, he learned how to fix motorcycles, then he opened his own shop.

Together, Johnny and me gave Stevens problems. If they could have fired us and made us disappear, Stevens would have had it made. Before the campaign I saw Johnny around the plant, but I really come to know him when we started organizing. I was the union president, and Johnny and Alvin Pinker, a black guy, was the officers.

As a fixer, Johnny had one of the jobs where Stevens treated him better than most other workers, but he still fought for the union, which really pissed the bosses off. Johnny had access to every floor in the plant. So early on, I'd say, "Johnny, I need you to contact so-and-so on the second floor. Tell her Mary needs to see her." So we worked them just like they tried to work us. Everybody knowed that if anything happened in that plant that was absolutely chaos, me and Johnny was in it. We laughed so hard, sometimes we almost cracked up.

Our union finally had to take Stevens to court, to the National Labor Relations Board when they met in Montgomery, and for that we needed records. Now, Johnny was one of these kinds of peoples that keeps accounts. I'd say, "Oh, Johnny, did you know that such and such happened?"

"Yeah, I know."

"I wish I had some way of proving it."

"We have a way. I wrote it down on toilet paper." Then he carefully showed me what was in his pocket. He'd gone into the bathroom and wrote everything down, then kept it as a record, so at the right time he came into court carrying all this information on toilet paper. That made an impression.

Stevens always tried to find a legal way to get rid of Johnny and me, so when Johnny called in sick, he tape-recorded telling them. One time when he returned to work, they said, "You been absent for three days without permission."

"Are you sure you don't recall me telling you I was sick?" Johnny said. "You don't remember my phone call?"

"No, you didn't notify us." So Johnny told me he pulled out his tape recorder and played the tape. Oh, Johnny was good.

It was easy for me to get used to speaking in front of large groups or even on TV. I guess 'cause I always had a big mouth and 'cause Henry was so good at helping me get experience. He had three or four workers sit in front behind a table and run the union meetings. I started speaking in public by sitting up there, talking with the other workers, then after that it was easy. I never thought about a big crowd being any more difficult than the little crowd of my friends. As time went on, I became like a legend in Montgomery.

I went on the TV stations, raising hell, and I met some truly wonderful people. One time I went to the Central Labor Council, and the Central Labor councillor introduced me and several others. After the meeting this black woman, maybe in her early fifties, walked over to me and stuck her hand out: "I'm Fanny Neal."

"I'm Mary Robinson."

"I know who the hell you is." And just like that our relationship began. Fanny was light complected, a little taller than me, maybe a size fourteen, and she always kept her hair cut short. What I remembered the most was the determined look on her face. She had a big smile, and when she laughed, she laughed the way she talked, with one half of her mouth together, the other expressing her feelings vociferously. She was a warm, wonderful, very courageous black woman.

It always tickled me. Fanny never just said, "I'm Fanny"; it was always, "I'm Fanny Neal," like letting you know, "I'm proud of who I am, and I don't want you to be trying to guess about who the last part of me is." She was Fanny Neal, not Fanny. Fanny Neal's family was city people from Montgomery. Her maiden name was Fanny Allen. She had one daughter, but her husband'd been dead a long time when I met her. She lived with her sister and had two or three brothers. I know her family was close-knit.

I don't know much about her background except she worked in a shirt factory on Decatur Street and organized it. Then, after they closed the shirt factory, Fanny went out organizing. She worked with COPE (Coalition of Political Education) when I met her. COPE tried to get politicians in office that was favorable to labor. Fanny was the first one I heard say about the people she was fighting, "Damn 'em! Damn 'em! If they can't deal with me, by God, they'd better get the hell out of here!" That really made a impression on me. She was like my teacher. Fanny got me involved in politics. We worked on lots of campaigns together—for Walter Mondale when he was running for president and for state politicians—and I loved to do phone banks with Fanny. When we found somebody running for office that was favorable toward labor unions, we set phone banks up in the union hall. About nine of us usually worked the phones together, and me and Fanny tried to work in adjoining offices so we could see each other.

Fanny'd be so funny. We got all these printouts of names to call from different union locals, and the only people called was union people, so Fanny'd tell who labor was endorsing. Some people responded, "I want to vote my convictions," so we talked to them carefully. Fanny was very, very good. And sometimes the person who answered the phone would snarl, "It ain't anybody's damn business who I voting for," so Fanny'd hang up politely, get off the phone, say, "son of a bitch," and let out a string of obscenities which would go on for a minute. Then she'd pick the phone back up and be all sweet again, "Hello. This is Fanny Neal and I'm with COPE . . . ," just as nice as possible.

Fanny Neal also stood up. If she believed in something, she fought to the death for it. She wasn't soft-spoken like Rosa Parks, uh-uh, not Fanny Neal. When Fanny Neal talked, she demanded attention in her voice. She talked with *authority*, very straight, direct. She'd say, "I can be nice if I want to and then turn around and be a bitch." Fanny learned me a lot.

One of the reasons it was so much fun working with Fanny was her joking, especially about sex. In that way she was like my sister Luda Mae. We got talking about hysterectomies, and somebody said something about a hysterectomy making people lose their sex drives. Now, Fanny talked with her mouth kind of tucked together. "Yeah, I heard about all that shit about the operation, and I went around sick as a damn dog 'cause I needed one of them, but people be saying, 'If you have a hysterectomy, you won't have no more relations.' So, finally, I just had to have the damn hysterectomy, and after I healed up, hell, I could do it better than ever 'cause I didn't have to worry about getting pregnant!" I laughed so hard I thought I would roll.

I had so much fun with Fanny, and met many people. She introduced me to John Lewis, the congressman out of Georgia. He came out of the labor movement and was involved in civil rights. He was the first one beat on the march from Selma, and him and Fanny had worked together in the shirt factory that she organized.

Fanny was a warm, wonderful, very courageous woman, and people knowed it. The Southern Christian Leadership Conference gave different awards to different unions, and they created the Fanny Neal Award and gave it to the catfish workers organizing in Mississippi who had just won recognition. When they called out Fanny's name, she got a standing ovation.

Then one day I picked up the paper and turned to the obituaries. It said "Fanny Neal." I said, "Fanny Neal!" I read it, and it said she was dead. I didn't even know she was sick. I called over to the union hall and talked to Paul, the guy who worked there.

"Paul, did you know that Fanny was dead?"

"Yeah, I knowed it."

"Then why didn't you tell me?"

Paul said, "Oh, my God, Mary, you didn't know? I'm so sorry." She died fast, from cancer. Also, when I saw it in the paper, they had funeralized her, so I didn't even get a chance to say good-bye.

Paul had gone to the funeral. "Mary, it was so touching," he said. "There was so many people there, black and white, and they spoke so high of Fanny." She really did so much for labor; she was labor to the core. And I knew that labor was gonna suffer behind her death because she was very, very powerful.

I don't know what they put on her tombstone, but they should've said something that stood for strength 'cause she had it. Fanny didn't bite her tongue, and white people truly admired Fanny because she stood up. I learned a lot from Fanny. It was womens like Fanny that was the backbone of all these events.

⇒ fourteen ⇐

After 37 years of loyal and faithful service, I have a plaque,
$1,360 and brown lung.
—Thomas Malone, retired J. P. Stevens employee,
undated leaflet, 1970s

Stevens really treated their workers bad. Somebody could spend their whole life there, and when they retired, their pension was forty dollars a month, no insurance. If a woman worked there a year, they called her back in for some cookies and doughnuts, but she didn't get no sick leave. And textiles had such a monopoly in the South, people couldn't get other jobs.

Daddy always told me, "Anything not worth fighting for is not worth having." Before Stevens I walked around with my head down, but fighting for the union made me bring my head up, put my feets down, and say, "Okay, want to fight?" With Stevens I learned you will always have to fight for what is right. And I will always fight for the rights of the workers, in this country and around the world. Also, each time you stand up when somebody treats you wrong, it makes it easier the next time. When they know you know exactly what you're talking about, then they think to theyself, "Oh, this one'll be too much bother!"

I tried to keep the union informed about conditions in the plant. The card room workers was mostly black, and it be very dangerous in there. Cotton comes there first where it is picked out by what looks like mechanical fingers that are very, very sharp. The machines of the card room

168 Moisture of the Earth

also grind the cotton so it is just extremely fine, then the cotton comes out in a long sheet.

I went to work one afternoon, and one of the guys came up to me right away and said, "Mary, Richard just got his arm cut slam off. It's been forty-five minutes, and he is still just laying there. His arm is completely amputated and he's in shock." So I called our organizer and told him that we'd had a bad accident, and by the time I got off the phone, the ambulance got there and took Richard away. The card machine did not have a safety switch on it like it was supposed to. Richard put his arm in there 'cause the machine was supposed to stop.

The doctors experimented with Richard's arm and put it back on, but they said it'd be five years before they knowed whether it worked or not. In the meantime, last time I knowed, he was in daily pain and with six kids was living off of $116 a week.

There was accidents like that at other plants too, and what really made me mad was that OSHA is supposed to be inspecting the machines. But they wasn't, and if OSHA thought the managers was going to tell them that the machine didn't have a safety latch or switch on it, that's crazy.

By then Stevens was real well known throughout the country 'cause of its terrible labor conditions and its being unwilling to negotiate. The union had a majority in seventeen mills, but not one of 'em was under no contract. In March 1977, Stevens made the mistake of having their shareholders meeting in New York City at the Stevens Tower. Three thousand demonstrators circled the building to protest, and it made all the news. Stevens looked real bad. That's when Lucy Taylor and Louis Harrell testified. They had brown lung. Marva went from here, and we heard bits and pieces about what happened. Marva wasn't married, and she got fired early, so we used her as a spokesperson for the Montgomery workers.

I went to the shareholders meeting in March 1978 in Greenville, South Carolina. Stevens picked the town more carefully. It be like Stevens owned that town, so this time they thought they'd be in control. They didn't want no repeat of the 3,000 demonstrators they'd had the year before in New York. But about 250 of us workers met in a hotel in Greenville the night before to present our own human rights report. We traveled there from all over. Me and Myrtle Cauley went together. Myrtle was like Louise Bailey, very outspoken. Sol Stetin, a vice president of ACTWU, spoke. There was posters, and somebody said the union was like Moses, trying to lead the slaves to the promised land.

We went into what Stevens called Textile Hall the next morning. We had to get proxies from some of the stockholders to even be in the hall. They set up mikes all over this big auditorium, and the stockholders board sat up there in front with the president of Stevens. We sat as close to the microphones as we could 'cause there was going to come a time in the meeting when we'd be able to get up and ask questions. But Stevens didn't know that's what we was there for.

Now, Stevens had set up this so-called workers' group, called Stand Up for Stevens, to be in debates, to fly around with Stevens paying their expenses. It be just a sham. Stevens ran it and used it to say whatever they wanted said. So there was this one girl from them. She was wearing a Dolly Parton blond wig—that's what we called it—and she had real dark brown eyelashes. She fluttered her eyelashes and said, "I don't know why all the workers is coming up here talking about how bad Stevens be. I'm a fixer in a card room, and I don't have no problems."

Then I see she's missing a finger, and I think, "Mmm hmm, that accounts for you working in the card room. They figure you already missing one, you won't miss another."

Then this Miss Ramsey, the head of Stand Up for Stevens, gets up there. She's got on these tinted-lens glasses, and she goes on about how good Stevens is to her. James Finley was the president of Stevens, and she says that whenever Mr. Finley comes to visit her plant, he stands and talks to her for fifteen or twenty minutes!

I could take all that stuff, but here comes this black guy, one of my own kind, and he says that the union almost starved him and his family to death. "And," he says, "I feel like this. Any worker that works for J. P. Stevens that ain't satisfied, the same door that took him in will take him out." That just burnt me up. Me and a whole lot of other African Americans around the room. I guess he got nervous 'cause none of us ever saw him again.

We didn't have no clearance to talk during the meeting, but we disrupted it so they would have to address us. Sometimes they acknowledged us, but they also tried to ignore us, so we had to be real militant and just started talking. We stated our demands, like for safety and to keep the cotton dust down, and while we did it, they kept switching microphones on and off to stop our voices.

A woman from North Carolina sat with a oxygen tank on the back. She got up to go to the microphone, and people had to help her even make it up there. A big hush came over the whole auditorium while she was speaking 'cause she was nearly out of breath. She said, "I've worked for Stevens for such and such number of years, but now I can't work no more. I'm disabled 'cause I've got brown lung from working in the mills my whole life, and I got to walk with this oxygen on my back all the time." She coughed and struggled to breathe, and she looked so sick and tired. Then she told how she was trying to live on seventeen dollars a month retirement.

James Finley had a fixed face that didn't show no compassion, and when the woman finished, the damn president of Stevens came up there to the lectern on the stage and told her, "If you didn't have no better sense than to work in there until you got brown lung, I don't have no sympathy for you." She gave up her life for that damn company, and then he stood there and told her that! It even made the stockholders angry. I sat there, crying, and thought, "What kind of heart do you have?" Then I thought that he didn't have a heart; he got a pacemaker.

Also, while I was at the convention, I found out that another worker in a Stevens plant had his arm cut off in the same machine that Richard had his. After the machine cut the guy's arm off, they finally put safety switches on the machine. So when they started the question-and-answer period at the stockholders meeting, I got up to the microphone and began to question them.

"Mr. Finley, in the plant I work in at Montgomery, y'all are constantly talking about safety. But almost two years ago, one of our fellow workers in our company had his arm completely amputated, and he's been living on $116 a week with six kids. Now y'all talk about safety, but still you do nothing about the dangerous machinery in the plant. I understand that in another one of your plants here, in the Carolinas, you have had another worker have his arm amputated in the same kind of machine.

"You say how concerned you are, but I believe that the only time you are really concerned about health and safety is when y'all make a tour of your plants. That's the only time that our plant management considers it. When they know that y'all, the big mens, are coming into town, they have everything cleaned up. They sweep the floor; they get up all the oil; they cut the machines down so it's not so dusty in there. But by the time you walk out of that plant, they speed the machine up; they don't care if the oil is all over the floor; the guards are not kept up on the machines. I think that's bad."

Of course, the stockholders was surprised to hear somebody say those things. They all went, "Aaahhh."

"Are you telling me that when we be coming into the plant, the supervisors get the plant all cleaned up for us?" he said.

I says, "That's exactly what I'm telling you. And once you leave, they don't give a damn what kind of conditions that we have to work in."

Speaking up to those people affected me. After I got up there at the mike and asked a couple of questions, I got confidence. From then on I had plenty of confidence for confrontation. A lot of other workers came up, and they asked him questions, and a lot of the time Mr. Finley just refused to answer. He even shut the mikes off, so he wouldn't even hear them. That's the kind of man we worked for.

But I tell you, he messed up, he messed up, he messed up. The rest of the stockholders sitting up at that table got up and walked out. They sure did. And at that time Stevens had been on TV and in every newspaper across the country. So that next day the news media blasted Stevens's behind like they never been blasted before. Even some of them stockholders spoke to the media and said that they didn't want to be associated with a company with no more humanitarian feeling than he had. And they asked for his resignation. They made him step down.

Of course, by the time I got back to Montgomery, the plant knowed that I'd went up there and spilled the beans on them. Afterwards the company sent surprise inspectors down to our plant a couple of times and caught the managers with their pants down. So they started having safety classes involving the workers, so the workers could tell them if something was unsafe. But still, if it was gonna cost them money, they just ignored it. Later, I went to the national convention in Detroit in 1979, where I met the real Norma Rae, the one a movie starring Sally Field be based on. I didn't speak, but I did a lot of working with leaflets and workshops. Both conventions was inspiring.

Then ACTWU decided to send me to their national convention in California in August in 1978. I was real excited when I went to California, and life was so bad with James by then. So I asked my general foreman for a week's leave. He was a decent guy. He gave it to me. I went and had me a ball, a wonderful time.

It was so exciting, seven days with all these activities during the day from 8:00 a.m. to 4:00 p.m. and parties at night. They had different speakers from different unions at the general meeting, and Henry asked me to represent us and told me to speak my conviction, which I did.

I said, "I want to express the appreciation from all the workers at J. P. Stevens. We thank you for your help in organizing workers in bad need of unionizing. You know the plight of these workers—some dying of brown lung, some having their insides all shook out. We didn't even have no fire escapes before the union come. So we thank you." I got a standing ovation.

I met [singer and activist] Pete Seeger while I was there. He came up to me and gave me a big hug and said, "It's an honor to meet you."

The convention people taught us about unions with films. One was about the Haymarket Square riot, where police shot workers and hanged organizers.[1] They also encouraged us to read. They explained we needed to know about everything so when we was organizing, if someone asked us a question, we wouldn't just sputter around.

But I missed my plane when I was coming back from the first convention in California, so I called my friend Mildred and told her to tell my supervisor that I wouldn't be in that night. I'd be in the next night. That's the way it always was done if something happened.

Mildred met me at the airport when I got back. "You been fired," she said.

"Dog, you're joking. I can't believe they'd do it. I had permission to be gone, then let 'em know I'd missed the plane."

Mildred told me my supervisor said, "Tell Mary she's fired 'cause she's been out for three days without calling in."

"But I got permission."

"You got any witness?" I didn't have no witness. My supervisor was my friend. We sat and talked and laughed, and it never dawned on me that he would turn on me and claim I hadn't notified them.

Now, Stevens knowed full well that I was organizing for the union. I did television interviews, talks to church groups. I went to lots of rallies. There wasn't no question that they thought this was their chance to fire me for union activities.

I went out to the plant and walked right up to my general overseer. He started to stutter, so I talked to the personnel manager. He said they'd even try to keep me from getting unemployment. Still, they did not come right out and tell me that I was fired. So I went to the union organizing office and told Henry about it. He told me to go right back out there to the plant and demand that they tell me if I was fired. And, if they didn't, to go in that night and start to work.

So Mildred and I went back out, and my supervisor still wouldn't actually say the words. He just said that I could go to the office and apply for work there again. He knew I didn't want the second shift, which is what he offered. I needed to keep working the third shift so I could do the organizing during the day.

Finally, I called the NLRB (National Labor Relations Board) agents in New Orleans. By then every one of them board agents knowed my voice. I asked to speak to one of them especially. He was Jewish, not tall, with a big mop of hair, and boy could he cuss. He was my heart. I'd tell him something outrageous, and he'd go, "I can't believe them blankety, blankety blank, blank suckers did that to you."

So, when I call him this time, he says, "Mary, what's going on?"

"Stevens fired me."

"They *what?* Wait a minute!" He put the phone on speaker so everybody could hear. "Would you believe them folkses up in Montgomery done fired Mary Robinson?"

Then he said to me, "I'll be up there this evening by five o'clock."

They sent three board agents to Montgomery and said to Stevens, "You ain't fired this woman, as vocal as she is, for nothing but union activities." So I filed charges with the labor board, and they set a trial for October 1978.

When the other workers found out I was fired, they pitched a fit. One even called the union office and said, "If you and Henry will agree to it, we'll just walk out."

We tried hard to talk 'em out of that. I told Henry I thought the best thing I could do was go to the plant and pass out leaflets. "If I show up, maybe it'll calm them down."

So I caught the workers going into second shift and those coming out of the first. I told them, "Don't get so upset. If you do anything rash, it'll play into the company's hands. That's what the company's hoping for." It was. The company fired me because they thought that if they treated me bad enough, the workers would walk out, and then Stevens could just shut the doors up of this plant.

Instead, I said, "Go back in the plant, work just like you been working. I'll be back in there."

Sure enough, before too long Stevens started telling me, "You need to come back in. You ain't fired." But they wanted me as a new employee, with no seniority, after all those years of work. Finally, they called me and told me that they had an opening on the second shift, so I took it and told them I wanted a third shift when something opened up.

I was out eleven days, and I had a ball. Except for the time I was with my kids, I could leaflet and organize twenty-four hours a day. They'd really turned me loose. So they had to hurry up and get my ass back in there.

Also, Mildred decided to confront Robert, the supervisor, the one who turned on me. She'd known him since she was a kid. She went to his office and said, "Robert, you know you let Mary off, that she told you she was going to be gone that week."

"No, I didn't let her off."

"Yes, you did. Otherwise, she'd have never left this plant. She knowed not to jeopardize her job. She told me you okayed it the morning she let you know."

"But she didn't call in."

"But you don't have to call in every day when you get a week off."

Robert got to thinking about all that and called us to tell us he was coming over. We called Henry, and Henry said, "Just let him do the talking."

So we all sat around the table drinking coffee. Robert asked me, "Where were you when you were out?"

"Robert, you know I said I was going to the union convention in California."

He sat quiet, then said, "The union's never gonna win. Stevens is too big."

"We know it will; we'll never give up."

"Don't worry. I'll get you back in the plant." He knowed he'd better, that he was in trouble.

Two weeks before the trial for illegal firing, the company decided it didn't want to go to court against me after all; they was gonna give me my back pay. They was supposed to post a notice up on the wall that they had discriminated against me for union activities, but that requirement just hurt them so bad. The note they finally come up with just said, "Mary Robinson has been reinstated at her job," then they put it way up at the top of the bulletin board where nobody could read it. When the labor board came back in for other charges we'd filed against Stevens, they saw the notice way up there. They told Stevens to move it down so people could read it. That also made the bosses mad.

Stevens constantly watched me to see that I wasn't making no mistakes they could hold against me. When they responded to the labor board, they gave the board a backlog almost an inch thick that they'd kept on me. But the boss mens also got so they treated me with the greatest respect 'cause they knowed I'd bring up charges on anything they wasn't supposed to do.

In 1979 we also went up to Washington, D.C., to this *big* labor rally with people from all over the United States. And we had a ball. We took several buses from here, and the buses had microphones on them. So I went from bus to bus, leading people in singing labor songs, telling stories. I'd get one bus all laughing and militant, then I'd go to the next.

The rally was at the Labor Department. It tried to pressure Congress to give disability for workers with lung disease. I'll never forget it. It was so many coal miners with black lung and so many people that worked in the mills and had brown lung. I felt awed to see all those people wheeled in wheelchairs because they was cut or maimed or sick. I remember an old woman on oxygen whose face was as wrinkled as a dry field. Every year she worked etched itself in her face. She was used up, like nobody was there. She just gasped. And a man came who lost both his legs. Some of the sick workers wore big brown buttons that said "Cotton Dust Kills" and little yellow buttons that said "And It's Killing Me." Thousands and thousands of people had brown lung, byssinosis, at that time. We sang labor songs like

Come all of you good workers,
Good news to you I'll tell
Of how the good old Union
Has come in here to dwell
Which side are you on?
Which side are you on?

I looked up while we was singing, and all the workers in the Labor Department stood at the window watching us while we pushed peoples up there in wheelchairs. And we had told the sick people to bring all they empty medicine bottles and put them up there on the porch. It be like a truckload of medicine that people had to take to survive from diseases they got working in these industries. We dumped the empty medicine bottles on the labor steps. It be just heart wrenching.

Then they called the police on us. We was doing real good until then. The police ordered us to move back and told us to remove all the medicine bottles. The marchers got angry, hostile. And we started yelling and screaming, going on. The next thing we knowed, they took about forty people who was right in front down to jail!

But it was worth it because Congress passed a bill that said that brown lung was a disabling disease, and now anybody diagnosed with brown lung can get disability. We was dead and determined to make change for the peoples in *all* the textile plants, and we did.

I also went to Washington, D.C., for the Solidarity Day in 1981 'cause that was the time [President Ronald] Reagan done fired all the air-traffic controllers. This big sea of people marched up Pennsylvania Avenue and onto the grounds around the Washington Monument. It inspired us. Speakers came from all over. It was just absolutely wonderful.

Pete Seeger sang at the Solidarity Day in 1981, and he played lots of music. We sang "Solidarity Forever" and "Gonna Roll the Union On." Then I took people up from Montgomery again ten years later. The people had a ball.

There was so many good times. I always liked the militants. [chuckles] One time Henry called me and said, "Mary, they got this lockout up in Jasper with the teamsters." So Henry told me there had been a wildcat strike, and when the workers walked out, they locked 'em out. That's when the teamsters was in a big turmoil.

"We gonna help them out," Henry said, "and we need somebody to go up and walk picket line with them. You want to do it?"

"Yeah!"

So I made all the arrangements to go up there and stay for three days, me and some of the other peoples from Stevens. We got into Jasper on a morning in January, and oh Lord it was cold. These guys was already walking picket, but the supervisors went and got themselves some scabs, temporary workers who wasn't union. While the teamsters was locked out, they was gonna let the scabs in to work. That way they'd try to break the union.

I was out there walking with four big burly white guys. They wore overalls, was spitting tobacco all over. They looked like big old mountain men, and, little old me, I'm walking with them, carrying the picket sign. The plant was on the end of a dead-end street, closed in, and all at once here comes this pickup truck with scabs barreling down. And one of these big old guys jumps out, right in front of the truck. The truck squealed to a stop in front of him, and the big old guy starts clobbering the wheel of the truck. He yells, "If you carry your so-and-so ass into that damn company, you'd better stay in there 'cause if you come out again, we gonna beat the hell out of you!"

When you walking picket line, you have to keep walking. It's against the law to stop, and I twisted my neck, trying to see what's happening. The guy driving the truck just whirled that truck around and took off.

A supervisor came out of the gate to let the scabs in, and he saw what happened, and he was mad! He called the teamsters all kinds of names. And they was mad back. They yelled back and forth. This went on for about another week, then they called arbitration in, so finally it got it settled. But I tell you, those guys was my kind of guys! They did not take no shit. The teamsters do not play.

I came back to Montgomery and told Henry, "Henry, them guys is ruthless."

"Oh, you like them, do you?" he says back to me. [laughs]

We never did have a union vote in our plant in Montgomery. At that time if the majority of the people signed a union card, you was supposed to get recognition. But when we had the majority signed, Stevens refused to recognize us. That's when the union filed a unfair labor practice charge, and it ended up going to court.

The judge at the federal courthouse in Montgomery was really, really sympathetic. He looked like what any white kid would want for a grandpa—a sweet, gentle-faced man with hair that was practically gray. He acted just very kind to the workers when they was put on the stand, 'cause they be scared to be up against the corporate lawyers.

We wanted to dress all up in suits, like we was going to church, but our attorney, Harry Weintraub, told us to be clean and neat but just to wear working man's clothes. It was hard for the timid workers to go into a room filled with company officials and none of us could go with them. It took courage.

We organizers had filled out the union cards for the workers who couldn't read or write, and the company challenged that in court. The cards was filled out with one handwriting, then signed in another. So we put the peoples on the stand, and the judge asked them, "Did you sign those cards under any duress?"

"No, I signed it on my own free will."

We was proud of them. It was something for somebody like that to testify in formal court, but Harry, the attorney for us, was so good. He talked to those workers ahead of time and said, "Now, that you can't read or write is no reflection on you. It's not your fault." Then he put them on the stand and wouldn't let those company lawyers badger them. And we waited outside—none of us could be in the courtroom while each testified. That way we couldn't influence each other. But we'd be having a ball outside the room, trying to give each other courage.

Johnny Adams be so funny telling about the hearings. They just called Johnny up to testify, and when they asked if he had any records, he pulls out the toilet paper as proof! Johnny says we should have seen the looks on the faces of those fancy company lawyers! The reason the National Labor Relations Board came down so hard on Stevens was through the records Johnny kept, on toilet paper, everything.

Maybe a month after the hearing, we got a great settlement from the NLRB. Henry called me and said, "Are you sitting down?"

"Yes, what is it?"

"We got a ruling," he said. "It's in our favor. We won." I stood up and shouted and shouted. Then Henry told me, "When you go to the plant, you can't say anything to anybody. I'm gonna call a special meeting." But that be the hardest secret I ever kept.

So Henry sent fliers telling about the meeting, and he came to the plant. Everybody showed up. He told us, "We have a ruling," then he read it, and the place went wild. Wild! The back pay, everything was in the ruling. It was one joyous time. People cried. Louise Bailey just boo-hooed. Marva was so happy 'cause she had been fired a long time before, and she used her settlement to put herself up as a beautician. They was just happy. As part of the ruling, they had to recognize us as being the labor body for Stevens. We was the bargaining unit, and Stevens had to pay a fine for every day that they didn't comply with the settlement.

This was 1979. We had a big old humongous party with music, dancing, food. Sure did. Sometimes I wish I was back out there raising hell again.

I had to locate all the people who'd been fired and left the place. Half of them had moved way up north, and half did not leave no address. I had to get out and be Kojak, running them down. It felt wonderful to tell them.

We had an election right away, and they elected me president. Johnny vice president. I was kind of scared, 'cause it was something I had never did before, but with Henry helping me, I felt confident. Matter of fact, I got voted in twice.

But right after we got the contract, something happened. I called Henry's house. His wife said, "Henry's not here. He's in North Carolina," and she gave me his number. So I called North Carolina, and he answered. "Henry," I said, "what you doing in North Carolina?" He told me that they had just moved him out. The union hierarchy just up and called Henry and told him to be out of Montgomery right away, that our part of his job was over and he should report to such and such a place at such and such a time. He worked his butt off for us, and he didn't even have a chance to say good-bye! See, another organizer, Alice, just showed up, and she didn't tell us right then that she came to take Henry's place. It broke my heart. His wife moved too, and I never saw Henry again.

It really made us angry. Some union higher-up did it without consulting us. I can sort of understand. Henry was a brilliant organizer, so they thought they should send him to a new assignment, but we still needed him. And Henry had such a bond with the people. It was devastating to us. We didn't even get a chance to say good-bye. Not even good-bye. He doesn't work for Amalgamated no more, so we don't know how to find him.

Alice, the new organizer, was okay, but not as good as Henry. Still, we learned so much from organizing. Johnny called the organizing "our boot camp for life."

So I kept being president and helped the workers deal with the company however I could. It be a constant battle of wills. After we got representation, we was supposed to have a steward on each shift. When the workers was taken to the office, the steward was supposed to go with them to make sure they was treated fairly. But a couple of times when workers asked their bosses, "Can I go get my shop steward as a witness?" the boss said no. That was a labor violation. I was in charge of twenty-seven stewards at three different shifts. If a problem couldn't be worked out between the supervisor and the steward, then I'd be brought in.

One time I went down to Tallassee with Alice and a couple of other women to do some organizing in a real old textile plant there. The plant was right at a river with a road that went beside it. You could just stand there and watch the workers come out and look at the people's faces who come along in their cars, and you could tell who worked in that plant and who was just traveling through. The mill workers' faces look so tired and strained, like life was worked out of them. The dust levels was so high. You said, "My God, what have they did to them in there?"

Alice and I split up, and I be passing out leaflets when the company men came out like a big swarm of bees to complain about where I was standing. You could sure feel the hostility. Then a patrol car came along, and I said, "Uh oh, I'm fixin' to go to jail." But instead, the patrol officer helped direct traffic where Alice was working. Finally I saw two guys go by and park and then come back. I thought, "Oh no, somebody done hired someone to come out here and get me."

The men came up and said, "Would you give us a whole stack of those leaflets?"

"You're not gonna throw them in the trash can, are you?"

"No, we've been looking for somebody to come down here and help us for a long time. It's awful in there." And so they started trying to organize!

Stevens was so hard on me at times that friends sometimes said, "Why don't you go look for another job?" Well, I could do that, but I feel that you should never be satisfied with just working in the place and letting it stay the same. It's like a house; if you don't constantly try to keep fixin' the house up, it'll fall apart. That's the way it be with a job. A union is not an organization that's bent on destroying a company; it's the workers banding together to better they ownself.

A few years later we went up to Roanoke Rapids to renegotiate our contract, and the company informed us that they was closing down some plants, but Montgomery wasn't one of them. They had started exporting companies overseas, where the labor costs was cheaper. Then they told us they was closing our plant 'cause it was the furtherest south and the transportation costs was highest.

Workers didn't get no severance pay with the other plants that closed, but because we had a court order, we went to the NLRB to convince them that the real reason Stevens was closing us down was 'cause we'd given them so much grief. That gave us some power to negotiate.

So they couldn't just shut us down; it cost them money to close our plant, the same as three years of salaries. We tried to negotiate the best conditions we could for our workers as they was let go. This was one of the times when I be really, really proud of myself. When we learned for sure the plant would be closed, I called Henry, and he told me, "Sit down and just think and think about what would be most fair to the workers. Think about what you can do to ensure that everybody will be treated decently."

By that time the blacks and whites had a good relationship there, and we wanted to keep that. I called one of the women attorneys in New York City, and she said, "We need to work it out so no one will feel discriminated against." So when we got the whole plan together, we went to the workers. When they learned how hard we'd tried to be fair, they wasn't too upset. Some people came out with some pretty good money. The union came through for them. We also worked it so the workers could buy their insurance for a year and so that they were let go according to seniority.

I remember being very, very scared myself 'cause I knowed that with as much hell as I done raised, that the companies might blackball me, keep me from getting another job. But when I applied for a job in an axle-manufacturing plant, I said I'd worked at J. P. Stevens, and they told me, "That company gives you a high recommendation." I was shocked. I figured that if anybody was gonna get it, it'd be me. That's when I learned that if you fight for something that's right, they respect you for standing up.

I kept up on my organizing and was hoping to do it full-time someday, and the same year the plant finally closed at Stevens, the union called me up and told me they was doing an organizing job at a textile plant in Columbus, Georgia, and would I go there to work.

It was summer, and they told me, "You can come up here and bring your kids and stay in the Chamomile Hotel. We need you to do some card signing." The kids loved it up there 'cause it had a swimming pool.

Columbus was a company town, just textile, nothing much else. The houses be small bungalows with maybe three or four generations of textile workers that had come out of that house. Sometimes you found a house with a grandfather, grandmother, son, and his son, all of them had done worked in that textile plant.

We went from house to house, trying to get them peoples to sign up, but a lot of them'd had some kind of falling out with the union before. See, it's much easier to get people to sign up for the first time. All you have to do is say, "Look, I know you don't like whatever's going on here, no overtime, no sick leave, whatever. Together workers can change this."

But people have a tendency to think that unions is supposed to protect them, whether they is right or wrong, and when the union won't do it, they'll jump out of the union. Like if a worker stays out of work for ten days without calling nobody, then gets mad at you 'cause you can't do nothing about them getting they behind wrote up! [laughs] So they say, "You ain't no good. I'm getting out of the union." Union representatives have got to be fair.

And when we went to do the drive, Amalgamated didn't mess around. I bet they sent twenty-five of us up there working together. We hit them hard and heavy in a short amount of time. We was at the gates every day, three shifts, and we had access to the plant break area, where we sat and talked to the workers. The union had that in their initial contract, which made it a lot easier. The leaders gave us organizers addresses to use to go from house to house, talking about the importance of signing the cards again.

A lot of days was disappointing if you hadn't signed anybody up, and the companies was smart. They knowed what issues in the plant the workers didn't like, so as soon as we was there, they started improving things.

One of our local organizers worked in the third shift; he's African

American. One day he didn't show up, and we said, "I wonder what happened to Macey?" We called his house and got no answer. The next evening, when I joined our group for strategy, I heard the peoples talking, "Oh, that's just awful. He shouldn't have did that."

"What happened?" I asked.

"The company offered Macey a supervisor position, and he took it and dropped us."

We'd tried to talk: "Macey, they just using you, 'cause they know you so strong." That's what they did. The company just went after the strongest person they knowed, a person that had a lot of influence on others. The company'd said to people like Macey, "You have to look out for your ownself. You got a wife and three kids, and we'll help you. Those union people is outsiders."

Within six months after our drive ended and we was out of there, I got a call, and they said, "The plant in Columbus fired Macey. We knowed they would." But it was a wake-up call for Macey, 'cause after they fired him, the union picked him up and hired him, and Macey ended up being the executive director over that region. He was mad then, and he gave their asses pure hell. He was their worst nightmare. Eventually, we got enough cards signed in Columbus so they kept the union.

I tell you, I was a nice, little old black girl from the country when I started, but Stevens made me into a woman.

❖ fifteen ❖

But so deeply concerned were we with the health and safe delivery of Pecola's baby we could think of nothing but our own magic: if we planted the seeds, and said the right words over them, they would blossom, and everything would be all right.
—Toni Morrison, *The Bluest Eye*

After Stevens ended, I had surgery and couldn't take the job in the axle factory. Then I needed work, and my friend Sarah got me a job where she was working as a school bus driver, part of the school support personnel. The bus drivers are womens, probably 95 percent, and the maintenance workers, the janitors, all black, are mens, but the mens earn much more. All the maintenance workers make more than all the school bus drivers.

The pay is terrible. In 1993 I was earning less money than I made at Stevens ten years before, and it's hard, responsible work, to have the lives of all these kids in your hands. And our bodies catch pure hell. If you got short arms, you got to stretch, so it's hard on your back. And breathing that air all day isn't good for your lungs.

The state of Alabama does not recognize public-employee unions as a bargaining unit for workers, so everything has to go through the legislature. Montgomery County looks for the uneducated to drive the school bus or be maintenance workers. I get really frustrated when I see people taking advantage of a person because they don't know how to defend themselves or because they don't feel they can.

But I drive kids to a special school for juveniles in trouble with the law and really enjoy working with them kids. They talk, talk, talk to me, just like I'm their friend. I get real involved with the kids' lives. That's probably why I've stayed at the job so long. The kids mind me. I don't get on that bus in the morning unlessen I pray and ask God to take care of these kids and help me keep them safe. Anytime I can, I give encouragement to one of them kids.

A lot of these kids have never had no kind of guidance. They been bounced from one place to another, put in foster care as little bitty kids. Most of the kids is from low-income families, out of the housing projects. They don't see a lot of hope in their lives. When a child's got one parent locked up and the other dead and they's being raised by a grandmother that's past the years when she really wants to try to raise another child, that child's just there, on its own. And lots of the girls. I wouldn't take a million dollars for any of those kids.

When I started working for the school, I started organizing the bus drivers and janitors, but it's much harder to pull together than at Stevens because the school bus drivers are spreaded out so bad into different schools. I worked and worked on organizing, and finally we got representation by AFSCME (American Federation of State, County, and Municipal Employees), a union that tries to represent all sorts of government workers—people like clerical staff, bus drivers, librarians, food workers. Still, I feel alone in my work, unlessen I go to one of the national conventions, and then it's just a one meeting thing. They don't network like we did at Stevens.

The unions need the militancy of thirty, forty, or fifty years ago, when we had womens who went out there and just said, "Okay, I done just had it with this treatment, we goin' to strike." Then other people from other unions came in and joined them. We also need to deal with big issues. Like while I was at Stevens, we was dead and determined that we was going to make changes for people in *all* the textile plants, so that if they contracted brown lung, that they would all be compensated.

I try to teach the support personnel what I learned in the Amalgamated Clothing and Textile Workers Union: that your labor is the only thing that you got to sell to the employer, and you can either sell it cheap or you can sell it high. But some of those people be so vulnerable. There's people who can't even read or write, and young ones, not just the old. They're so ashamed, and they ain't gonna challenge anybody.

It reminds me of when I started going down to the archives and courthouses and started looking back through the old records to find my family, and it broke my heart when I saw that some of my people couldn't read and write. When I saw where they made their little X on the papers, that was just so hard. I just rubbed my fingers over it. Oh Lord, I thought, knowing nothing more than that X made them so vulnerable. Vulnerable like some of the people I organize for.

I'm sure the reason the school board started me working with the juveniles was 'cause of my union organizing. I had started to cause a lot of flack by then, so I guess the supervisors figured, "We'll send her over to drive those delinquents for the summer, and they'll either kill her or make her quit." But it didn't work that way. It made me more committed to the job. If it wasn't for my feelings toward those kids, I probably wouldn't be working here now.

I feel so sorry for these kids now. What I hate the worse is that they don't have no memories of no childhood, no memories of flowers, just these projects. The projects remind me of concentration camps, with a bunch of people together with all these different opinions and attitudes, and it can't help but be a whole bunch of confusion all the time.

When I was a child, we might not have been free in the sense of not having to work, and Mama and Daddy didn't own no land, but as kids we was free in the sense that when we walked out, we could walk as far as we could see. That was our escape. We could always walk through the woods and collect hickory nuts, different kinds of leaves.

But kids now, they don't have no outlet. Each way they turn, there's a fence up that tells them, "This is as far as you can go, as far as you dare to venture. 'Cause if you go across the street, you in somebody's else's territory. If you go too far to the left, you on somebody else's property. Two feet to the right is too far." So they be housed in. They don't have no chance.

In the neighborhood where I used to live, my grandkids was so free, and our backyards joined each other so we sat out there in the evening time, under the pecan tree, and talked. Miss Gert and Mr. Doo lived behind me. She be tall and skinny, and he be tall and skinny too. On Saturday mornings me and Miss Gert met out there with a cup of coffee. They was both elderly, and they was real good to the neighborhood kids. Mr. Doo was such a dear person. Every month on the first, Mr. Doo took about four or five old womens to the store, or he took them to town, or he'd pay their bills. Miss Gert worked a miracle with flowers, and she could grow the biggest ferns. And whenever she got anything to eat, she called me. Her voice sounded sort of like music. "Mary, I got hot chickens' feet, pigs' ears, pigs' feet. You want some?" She fixed all the old-time foods.

There was three little kids in one family that didn't have much concern or supervision, so when they was outside, it was like everybody's job in the neighborhood to watch them, to take care of them. They ran around all day, and nobody worried about them 'cause everybody knowed they was at one of those houses. Childrens need the kind of care that they had in that neighborhood. It takes a village to raise a child.

I'm so lucky. All my kids turned out real good. They may not all be doctors and rocket scientists, but they work steady, and I couldn't love them any more. They could've been kids that caused me to have all kinds of gray hair, but they didn't. They're kind and respectful, and you can count on them. So, I'm blessed. I'm truly blessed.

I stayed close to my brothers until their deaths and close to my sisters. Luda Mae, my oldest sister, lives in New York, but if she comes back here, she stays with me. We call her Sister, and she looks just like Mama. Luda Mae be crazy, she so funny. [laughs] She loves to get around my kids and tease them. Fitzgerald's real quiet, so she especially loves to make him laugh.

Fitzgerald came in the room one time when he was young, and she said, "How's it going, young man?"

"It's alright."

She says, "Aunt Ludie been having a little problem here lately." She pats her hip on the back. She's talking about arthritis but calls it Arthur. "This old Arthur been trying to jump on me."

Fitzgerald stops moving, and he gives her his full attention. She goes on, "The other morning I went to get up, and Arthur was right there in that hip. And, all of a sudden, Arthur runs around here." She points to her front. "So I say, 'Hold it, hold it, Arthur, now wait a minute. You done went too far. I may not be using it, but it's still mine.'" Fitzgerald just fell down on the floor laughing, and everybody in the room was just howling.

Shane still stays in Albany, New York, and has three boys. She's got all her spirit, but life's not been everything she hoped for. I've so wanted her to come home to stay, but oh she hated that cotton, and she could never put it out of her mind. Magnolia's still married, and her son's in the armed forces. She's quiet, like she always was, and Ann Lois, who's as sweet as anything on God's earth, has got rheumatoid arthritis real bad.

But one by one we lost our brothers. J. W. was a diabetic and died in a coma. Jack died of cancer. Tom, my oldest brother, stayed with me while he died. He also had cancer. But I didn't cry. God has been so, so good to me, as far as my peoples is concerned. I grieve, but I don't grieve in the sense of crying. Up until this day I've never cried for my mama, although I've cried for my daddy, I've never cried for Jack, and I've never cried for Tom or J. W., either one of them. I grieved for them, but I didn't cry.

And I look at it this way. If death had not been something good, God would have never created it. A lot of people think you're crazy when you say that, but God never created nothing that wasn't positive, and death has goodness to it. That's the reason why the Bible says that you should cry when a person comes into the world and you should rejoice when they leave. Because death is something good that is eternal, and you know that when you come into the world, that's not eternal.

After Stevens closed down, I still had the three minor kids—Fitzgerald, Tracy, and Ron Deron—and when I went to work for the school system, driving the bus, I wanted to have some life insurance. Every year when school starts up, we get this multitude of people running around selling insurance. So, me and Sarah, my friend, was sitting on the bus, and this woman said she was selling insurance. She said she was selling us whole life, but she actually gave us term life insurance. We talked about the premiums, and she told me that they would be eight dollars a month. And I said okay, and she told me, "The premiums won't go up, but as your childrens get older, at 18, they will automatically come off."

"Then what about the premiums?"

"Oh, they'll stay the same." She never mentioned nothing about it being term insurance and that at a certain age it would end and that the payments would double. Later, when I filed a lawsuit, I found out that this company has a history of doing this with other groups of people. The way they had it set up, your premiums didn't go up until ten years later—but then they doubled them.

So it went on fine, but in 1993 I got my check, and I noticed that my net had dropped. So I looked back through the itemized things, and I noticed that the insurance had went up from eight dollars to sixteen dollars. So I kept calling place to place, further and further up the insurance ladder, and the peoples got real nasty. Finally one said, "You didn't read your policy?"

"No, I didn't. Because I believed what the woman be telling me."

"She's no longer with us, but we're sorry that she misrepresented the company."

"You're not as sorry as I am." And I hung up the phone. For the next two or three weeks I thought, "Ten damn years. They have just used the hell out of me." So the more I thought about it, the madder I got. I knowed this lawyer and told him what happened.

He said, "Mary, did they do this to more than just you?"

"Yeah, Frank, to a whole bunch of people." I knowed they had a group of people because my friend Sarah was one of them.

So he went down to the board of education and talked to one of the people I'd talked with on the phone. She just opened the books to him, but then somebody came in and told her she shouldn't do it. But by then Frank had already wrote down numbers of people's names.

He called me back. "Mary, you're absolutely right. I'm gonna file a lawsuit, but now I can just file it on your behalf or do it with a lot of other people."

"File it in a way so that everybody that they wronged will be made right from it."

So he subpoenaed the board of education insurance records, and then he sent out letters to everybody, and we put a sign up telling them about it. But, 'cause I've been doing the union, I'm not the favorite person of some people. When they heard about it, they said, "I ain't foolin' with this business. This ain't nothing but some of that old union shit." So these peoples throwed it in the trash can, but peoples I had never seen before did it with me.

I told Frank, "This is not about money, it's about the fact that these low-down-ass companies is constantly ripping off poor people 'cause they feel like we haven't got sense enough to stand up and fight for what's right."

So, on the weekend before we went to court, Frank called me and gave me a figure for settlement and said, "I think I can do this."

I said, "I'm leaving it totally up to you. You do what you think is fair."

He said, "I have to tell you that the amount is sealed. You can't tell nobody how much it is." I agreed to that, but now I wish I hadn't. Because this way nobody can say publicly that the company is crooked, so crooked they had to pay out X amount of dollars to us because what they did is against the law. I get mad every time I see them advertise. They wasn't no fly-by-night company.

But I did tell Frank, "You also make them agree that they will write a new policy that will spell out, 'This is whole life insurance,' and that the premiums for these particular people will never go up. Lessen they agree to it, we not dealing with them at all. We'll go to court, and the world'll know it."

See, when Frank and them started to investigate, it turned out that this insurance company had just paid out a whole bunch of money for the same identical thing! They had been doing this down through the years. And while they was doing it, the company done collected millions and millions of dollars from people in the ten-year period before they upped the premium. So the company didn't give a damn about you dropping your policy when the premium went up, 'cause they had done got ten years out of you already.

When Frank called to tell me we'd won, I just felt like I had been vindicated. I knowed that I was smart enough to know what they did was wrong, but so many other people didn't know they'd been taken. A lot of the people I work with don't understand how these things work. Many dropped out of school, and the corporations, they be ruthless, ruthless.

The money I got hasn't really changed my life a bit. I feel like the same person I was. I don't see life in a materialistic way, no way. 'Cause everything we look at here on earth, it's gonna be done away with. It's gonna be gone. So it don't even faze me.

A lot of people benefited from that lawsuit. I didn't even know many of them. I went to one of these schools doing some organizing one day, and I walked into the school lunchroom. This cafeteria worker was there.

I walked up to her and stuck my hand out. "Hey, how you doing? I'm Mary Robinson, and I'm with AFSCME."

She looked at me. She was probably in her early fifties, kind of a stout woman, darker than I am, and she started to smile. She said, "Are you the Mary Robinson that filed the lawsuit against that insurance company?"

"Yeah."

Her face just began to glow, and she said, "I want to thank you. I want to thank you that you was smart enough to know that this was wrong. How did you figure it out?"

I said, "I know what I was told. And I would have never bought insurance that didn't last. I intend to live as long as God intends for me to live. Insurance companies do not tell me when to die."

Oh Lord, there has been so many, many poor people who've been cheated bad. These insurance companies that wrote black people up thirty years ago, they was ripping people off. They knowed that the most important thing to a black person was that when they died, they didn't want nobody to worry about having to bury them. So folkses took out all these little insurances and paid on them for fifty years—and then they died, and their family found out that they had a two-hundred-dollar damn burial plan, after all those years.

The companies made billions of dollars doing it. People'd sell eggs, anything. They'd struggle to get fifty cents or a dollar or seventy-five cents for a little old insurance that wouldn't even bury you in the first place. And the companies be not regulated right. Any time the government starts talking about regulations on them, they go and pile a whole bunch of money on those lobbies up there in Washington, saying, "We don't need no more government control into this." So the government backs off, and they continue to rip people off.

I used to hear people say that God brought them here on earth with a purpose, that God knowed what your life was gonna be like before you was conceived in your mama's womb, but a lot of people go through life without ever finding out what they were here for. But I know what I'm here for. I done figured that out. I was put on earth for the underdog, for the people that can't fight for themselves. I just raise all kinds of hell and cause all kinds of problems. Taking advantage of vulnerable people, it's uncalled for.

God gives me the ability, he gives me the strength and guides me, and we do it. That's it.

✥ sixteen ✥

*And I saw a new heaven and a new earth; for the first heaven
and the first earth were passed away; and there was no more
sea. . . . And God shall wipe away all tears from their eyes;
and there shall be no more death, neither sorrow, nor crying.
. . . I will give unto him that is athirst of the fountain of the
water of life freely.*

—Revelation 21:1, 4, 6

One day I was driving the kids home on the school bus, and the students was very quiet. Two lived out close to the airport, and it was near evening. I was going over an open part of the highway, and I always like to look at the sky, especially when there is different formations of clouds, like mountains and valleys, and that day I was looking.

I suddenly saw something. I said, "Wow," and blinked, and I thought, "When I look at it again, it's goin' to be gone." But I looked at it again, and it was still there. The sky was filled with buildings, ancient-looking buildings, like they came out of the clouds and then extended up into the blue in the sky. It was just as plain as me looking at you. There was so many windows, so many. It was a city in the sky. The city stayed there and stayed there. Then I thought of the Bible verse, "In my father's house, there are many rooms."

I didn't mention it to the kids on the bus, because I knowed God didn't want me to. He let me see it, nobody else. And he did it in a way in which there would be no doubt in my mind what I was looking at. Like he said, "I'm actually goin' to let you see this," and he did.

The buildings had such a peacefulness about them. I don't know how to describe it, but they was like no other buildings that I have ever seen in my life. Not fabulous buildings, just grayish looking, like they had been there for years and years, but they wasn't decayed. They was ancient, just beautiful. The buildings was perfectly shaped, straight, like temples you read about in the Bible, but with all these windows. I guess just every window represents a room, and the rooms was for God's people, and there was a multitude of them.

Then the words came so clear. God's words: "I go to prepare a place for you, and in my house, there are many mansions, and if it was not so, I wouldn't have told you." And God hasn't told me why he showed it to me. I don't know what God wants me to do other than tell people about it. The only thing I can figure is that he is letting me know, "You've got a lot of faith, and I'm goin' to show you something that will increase your faith even more, to let you know that I am God. No man, nobody, can do what I'm showing you." God was saying, "I am God." God let me know that "I am who I am, and I can do what I said I can do. I will do what I promise you."

It never crossed my mind that I might be dying, but if I had had a choice of dying, it would be then. And I would not trade it. Now there is nothing no man on the face of the earth can do to hurt me 'cause I know where there's a building not made by human hands, and it's been there ever since the beginning of time, and age hasn't done anything to it.

I came in home that night, after I dropped the kids off the school bus, and I went to the couch and sat down and said, "Why? I don't know why God showed me that." I know I'm not supposed to question why he did it, but I said, "Why, God, why?" Then God just answered, he just answered, "Tell my people I am on my way." That's what happened.

One morning, about a week or so after I saw the city, I knowed the minute I got out of the bed that God had came in that night where I was sleeping. I went to bed the night before, and when I got up the next morning, when I put my feet on the floor, I knew that he had came in. When I stepped down off the step to my bed, I felt totally different. I did not even feel like the person that had gone to bed that night. And I said, "Something happened to me."

I had a peace I don't understand, and it got more and more that day, and I knowed that something was going on with me. When I encountered things that would normally upset me, they didn't in the same way. At first I thought, "When I tell people about this, they gonna say, 'She's crazy.'" But nobody doubted. Nobody said, "It was just your imagination."

I told my cousin Lizzie Mae, she's a Seventh Day Adventist, and she said, "It's the New Jerusalem in Revelations." She gave me a book that referred to Revelation. Several other people told me about the New Jerusalem in Revelation too. When I first started reading Revelation, I could not make any sense, but I think God is leaving the meaning a mystery.

The other night I was laying in bed, and my thought was, "I want to see your face."

God answered, "You want to see my face?"

"Yes." There was no light, 'cause I don't like a light in the room at night, and I was laying there, and all of a sudden these whole bunch of images came, they was faces, but no faces you could identify. It was truly awesome. Sometimes it's like he takes me up, and I can fly.

I can feel God's emotions. I'll be sitting in the church, listening, and I will touch my face with my hands, and there'll be tears that I couldn't even feel come out. I can sense his joy. I can feel when he's happy or sad, and when I see little childrens, God makes me just reach out and touch them.

Mostly, I see God as a compassionate father, but I also see God in some female ways. You know when you be growing up, you had a friend you felt you could tell anything in the world to, and that you didn't have to worry about that friend telling anybody else, and when you felt like you just needed somebody, a closeness, I see God like that. I see him in every aspect of my life. I see him in the morning. Every day brings new joy.

And God's like a loving mother. When you was sick and your mother held you or when one of your kids was sick, when the baby cannot even talk, when you held that baby, you gave the baby comfort. That is what God's like. Like the Virgin Mary, she birthed God into the earth the way we birthed our babies.

I thought one morning, "If I could get on the top of a mountain and I could gather every human on this earth, I'd tell them that God is a living God, and he has a piece of hisself in every one of us. Every single one of us. We are all precious to him."

And now I've made a transformation. And I don't make a distinction anymore between my child or your child. I love them each. Black or white, gay or lesbian or straight. Everybody is a child of God.

What makes the person is the heart. It is the heart that controls the soul. It's the heart that makes you who you be, and if you have a heart that has no compassion in it and no love in it, it protrudes outside of your body, but if you have a heart that loves and is compassionate, that's what God knows as you.

There are still times when I question God. I ask, "Why does a lot of things happen on earth? Why did you do this? Why did you do that?" We struggle with why there is suffering. Sometimes it doesn't make sense. Why are children born with deformities? Why are people cruel?

When I was a child, I used to watch whites. Every Sunday they would get dressed, and they would go to church, and I even thought some way or another that there was two gods, that God was two. I couldn't believe that they was going to the same god that I was. I think part of me was angry that my god was a black god and he had no power and the white god was still superior. I thought we went to church and this black god that we was going to serve, he was just a figment of my imagination, that they was going to see a white god that was somebody for real, that had power, because come that Monday, we would be the ones that would go back there in the fields, in the hot sun, and their god wasn't allowing them to go.

Even now when I know God is one, I wonder why evil happens. Then I think, some things he won't let you know why he does it, but he speaks of evil and forces, like Satan, we can't see. Still God constantly tells us through the Bible about his goodness, about his mercy, how we should treat each other, how we should love each other. And I think when I get impatient, trying to understand evil, it may be that just over that next hill are the answers that we always looked for. I know that one day everything will be made known. He will show why he had to let it happen.

But the peacefulness that came to me with God, I cannot describe it. There be times when I would go to bed at night with a problem, and I'd lay there and worry about it, but now God'll say, "I won't let you worry," and God puts me to sleep in a heartbeat.

But I think God is angry about his earth. I do. I think he's angry because we haven't taken care of it. We have eroded his soil, we have taken the beaches and made them into sewers, we have taken oceans and polluted them and cut down his forests.

I get my greatest joy outside because I know that what's outside is God's creation. Everything. This is a creation he left us millions of years ago, and when I'm out there working in my yard, working in my garden with plants, I know this is something he left here for us, but he is not happy with some of the ways we've used it. See, the devils have angels too, and they have made us believe that we was helping the earth with some of the things we have did to it, but we aren't. And now we are reaping the results.

There is no doubt in my mind that a lot of the diseases have to do with our environment, the pesticides and what is in the water. God created the earth, but we couldn't be satisfied with the way he created it, and now we have created a monster, and it's only a matter of time to where we is goin' to have a disaster.

For years and years people lived with the water out of the earth. God put that water there, and he taught man how to get it out, then all of a sudden we filled it full of chemicals. And the vegetables we grow now are with chemical fertilizers, not the fertilizer Mama and Daddy used from the cow which had grazed on natural grass. And now we inject a chicken with additives, then we eat it. So God's not satisfied.

Alabama is beautiful in the fall of the year as all the leaves are turning color and fallin' off the trees. Then spring comes, with all the lively green colors. So I say to my friends, "This is God's way of replenishing himself. He says to us, 'If I can change each year, why can't you?' I believe the seasons is God's way to try to send us a message."

Somebody said, "Maybe God wants you to preach."

And I said, "No, he don't. Not now. He don't want me to do nothing right now but just what he told me to do. He said, 'Tell my people I'm on my way.' And if there's anything else that he wants me to do, it will happen." But God takes you through transformations. Every day you can feel something that you know that you haven't felt before.

I think about the city in the sky. I know that the vulnerable, the illiterate, belong in that city. They ain't going to be throwed out of there. Nope, no doubt about it. All the wrong that was did here is going to be made right up there. And that's where Mama is at.

I see everything now in a total different light than I seen it before. I know I've always been a compassionate person and a caring person, and I always felt that I would never have nothing 'cause I would give it all away, and that don't worry me, that don't bother me, 'cause I know what I need to survive. You got to get contentment, and you got to let love in your heart. If you don't have that, all the other things don't amount to nothing. But something happened the day I saw the vision, something that was very, very good.

I know that God can fix what's wrong with the world, and when he fixes it, ain't nothing nobody can say about it. I know that even though he says, "The poor will be with you always," he's not going to let the little people suffer. He's not going to let somebody keep making you poor because of they power. He's not going to do that.

We have to keep working with him. We have to keep chipping away, and we may not make but a half inch of gain in a whole year, but we have made that half inch. And we keep on, keep on, keep going. We keep letting them know that we may not be a mountain—maybe just a little bitty hill—but they have to climb that to get over us.

I used to get frustrated when I couldn't get things better. I'd get just really, really frustrated, but I don't do that no more. Slowly it came to me: Let God do it, let him. He's the only one that can do it anyway, although he uses me as the person to do it. And when the time is really right, he will let me make it happen.

It's a long story from Adam and Eve, Noah and Moses, and I believe people like Fannie Lou Hamer and Dr. King are part of it. I believe that there are good people that have died and left this earth, like Abraham, Isaac, and Jacob, but they are also part of this earth right now. Because God's about goodness. I think there are people here now that we don't see. Like I can always feel the presence of my mom around me. So she is part of the same story that Abraham is.

When I went to bed last night, I was laying there, and I was thinking about Mr. Paul's house up there and all the sheds, the little buildings that was out there, the big barn he had. Now somebody bought that farm, and they told me that some strangers bought that barn and they used the wood to decorate a den in their house.

And I think about it now, whoever bought that, they don't know what they took inside that house with them. They took some memories in there of a white man and of some black people that had worked there, that had touched that wood. And the people that live where we used to, when they walk outside, they don't realize that there once was black feets that walked through this yard. Their bodies was tired, and then they went out in the morning time all rested and did a hard day's work again and came in through the same path and was tired, tired.

Everything up there represented my mama and daddy, and that's all I have of them. A lot of people would look back at them and say, "What did J. D. or Sarah accomplish in they life?"

"Well," I'd answer, "my mama and daddy accomplished more in the years that they lived on this earth than a lot of peoples will achieve in two hundred years, because they gave us something that nobody can ever take away from us. They gave us pride. They gave us a sense of belonging. They gave us the ability to work hard. They gave us the base that God wanted us to have, that he wanted us to be and live from."

By me staying down here in Alabama to live, I can go back in my mind and remember it all, and my brothers and sisters who left down here don't have that. I guess Shane felt like her lot down here had been so hard, she wanted to forget. 'Cause when she comes home, and we be sitting around sometimes talking, I'll say, "Do you remember such and such a thing?"

And she'll say, "I don't. You have to remember 'cause you stayed here, but I left, I put it behind me." I guess Shane wanted to forget things, but there be lots of things that you can lose in life that are really important to you, but you don't realize that.

Yes, the most hurting part of my life now is connected with where we was born and raised. I say they took my childhood, and they destroyed it. Now it's this huge old mansion that sits where we used to live at. And everything that was visible there that would remind us of our childhood is gone. The person who bought our land destroyed eight kids' memories of when they was young, that's what he did. We can't go up there and say, "This is the ditch that we jumped off of." Shane got a scar where she jumped off that little ditch one day and onto a piece of glass. And we lost the little chinaberry tree that had a lot of cuts carved in it. We would sit there with somebody and take a piece of glass and make our initials on the tree.

We used to watch whirlwinds when we was kids, and we'd think it was absolutely amazing that when a whirlwind came and it moved across the earth, it left this clean path. And that's what it feels like to me, that when the new owners came in up there, they took a whirlwind, and they cleaned the top of the earth, but it still couldn't erase the things that was underneath that soil, that was still a part of us. See, still, in some way God gives you a claim to the land you love.

If I had a choice today of the way I live right this minute or being back with my mama and my daddy at the side of the road with a yard that we swept with a broom, a fruit jar full of wild flowers, and my sisters and brothers running around that yard—even with my mama out there washing on a rub board—I'd change it in a heartbeat.

The love God gave us was good.

⊰ Epilogue ⊱

Untold Stories of African American Resistance

*It is in vain to dream of a wildness
distant from ourselves. There is none such.
It is the bog in our brains and bowels, the
primitive vigor of Nature in us, that inspires
that dream.*

—Henry David Thoreau,
Journal, 1856

While working on this project, Mary and I learned countless details of her family's history and uncovered new information about African American resistance in the vicinity of Mary's community. In Washington, D.C., in 1997 I examined old files from the 1930s about Elmore County in the NAACP collection in the Library of Congress. I found newspaper stories about a shoot-out in neighboring Tallapoosa County between a white posse and black sharecroppers who were trying to form a Share Croppers Union. As mentioned in the introduction and in Mary's story, organizer Ralph Gray was shot and killed and activist Ned Cobb was sent to prison for twelve years for his role in the incident.

On the first day of my final working visit with Mary, in July 2000, I handed her the articles from the Library of Congress. She put on her glasses, and as she read, she clicked the roof of her mouth with her tongue, closely studying the *Montgomery Advertiser* of December 20, 1932:

"Death Estimates Vary As Alabama Deputies Battle Armed Negro Communists: Blacks Flee To Woods After Ambushing, Wounding Four Officers, Reviving Share Croppers' Union Trouble of Last Year: One Dead Is Identified; 300 White Men in Posses Hunting For Fugitives." An *Alabama Journal* article declared on December 30, 1932: "POSSE CLOSES IN ON NEGRO REDS IN SWAMP: Tallapoosans Throw Cordons Around Refuge of Radicals Hunted in Bloody Gun Play; Tallapoosa Sheriff Bars Newspapermen From Search as 20 Automobiles Loaded With Armed Men Quit Tallassee."[1]

I watched Mary as she read and then asked, "Do you think people knew about it and kept the information from the young?"

"They probably was afraid to tell us." Mary ran her finger down the *Montgomery Advertiser*, shaking her head. "The newspaper talks about 'four or five dead negroes laying about in the fields,' like they was cows." Suddenly, she said, "They refer to the Greathouse boys of Liberty Hill. Maybe they be talking about Rev. Greathouse's kin? He be from up there by Camp Hill. We'll ask him."

We then made phone calls for directions, left Montgomery, drove past Wetumpka, and began to wind our way through the Piedmont uplands of Tallapoosa County, with its green wooded hills and bluffs. We eventually crossed the Tallapoosa River to Tallassee, the community out of which the posse rode.

Finally, about thirty miles from Mary's childhood home, we arrived at a yard filled with flowers. We walked up to the front door of the blue frame house and knocked. No one answered. We rounded the corner, stepped beneath an arch of pink flowers, and rapped at the door. A balding man, maybe in his late sixties, answered the door.

"Yes?" he said hesitantly, and then he recognized Mary.

"Hey, Rev. Greathouse, Mrs. Greathouse," Mary said enthusiastically.

Mary introduced me and then took out the newspaper article. "Mr. Greathouse, Fran brought this from the NAACP Collection at the Library of Congress. It said something about a big revolt, a riot, they had about 1932, and it talked about the Greathouse boys. I wondered if they was kin to you?"

Rev. Greathouse skimmed the article as his wife read it over his shoulder. "Yes, they are," he said. "They're some of my brothers and my father, too, Tomas Gray. He was one of the leaders. The posse shot my uncle, Ralph Gray. Through the mouth. See, I was born in 1928, the youngest in a family of nineteen kids, so I'm too young to be involved, but I knowed about it. You should talk to my oldest brother. He's ninety-three and can remember everything."

Mary said, "It happened not far from where we growed up, but us kids never heard nothing about it. Fran was asking me why we didn't know. I told her I think 'cause adults wouldn't let no childrens be around when they was talking grown-up talk. It be too dangerous. They might tell something they heard to a white kid."

"That's right," Rev. Greathouse said. His wife nodded her head with vigor. "I knowed about the revolt 'cause it was my family," he continued, "but there was other things I didn't know. They couldn't take a chance. Plus, so many peoples couldn't read, they couldn't spread news that way. But the shoot-out was a big event." His wife nodded again.

They gave us directions to his half brother's house. We thanked them and left and then drove down a curved country road. Thick trees lined the path on both sides. I pictured people trying to outrun a posse in those woods. We finally came to a brick house, set back from the road, and were met at the door by Grady Canada's polite sixty-two-year-old daughter.

Mr. Canada was a tall, very dark, strong-appearing man of ninety-three, with large ears and hands, deep blue eyes, and prominent cheekbones. He was African American but also part Crow and Comanche Indian. An oxygen tank sat next to him. Mary chatted politely and then explained our purpose.

Mr. Canada said he knew a great deal about the Share Croppers Union, although he had not actually joined. Instead, he had worked in the local textile mill for thirty-two years, two months, and seventeen days. As an illegitimate child of Tomas Gray, he had been raised by his grandfather, who had taught him to be a blacksmith, so he had not been as deeply influenced as much as his siblings by his father's and uncle's radical ideas. He knew Ned Cobb, was friends with his children, and had witnessed how hard it was on the family during Cobb's twelve-year imprisonment. The conversation then turned to religion, and he and Mary talked warmly about their religious experiences.

Following our meeting, I telephoned Mr. Canada and tape-recorded our conversation.[2] "Did you ever attend any of the Share Croppers Union meetings, Mr. Canada?" I asked.

"Yeah, just once," he answered. "It was in an abandoned house. Me and a couple of boys got there just about good sundown, between sundown and dark. There were about six men standing out there with high-power rifles. They said, 'Go in.' We did, and there wasn't hardly any room to sit down. A man was up making a speech, but there was so much smoke in there from cigarettes and kerosene lamps that you could just see the top of the men's heads. We sit there about five minutes, and I told the boys, 'I'm leaving.' [They said,] 'We too, we too.'

"We hightailed it back home. We didn't go back no more. I was scared when I seen them men standing out there with them rifles. I knowed they expecting trouble, that something was going to happen. I got eight kids depending on me."

"Why were they forming the union?" I asked.

"See, the whites they worked for wasn't giving them nothing. They'd work them and cheat them out of what they made, so they made a union out of it."

"Did people say it was Communist?"

"Yeah, they said it was, but it *was not*. I don't know if it was a branch off of it, but they called it a union. A Share Croppers Union, that was the name it was. Black, colored people, weren't the only ones who wanted it. Poor white people did too. They all joined in together."

"Were the people religious?" I asked.

"Yeah, some of them was. And some of the meetings was in churches. I would say that they, the union, was in the right, but I just don't like rioting." He laughed, "Not me."

"That meeting that you went to, was that before your Uncle Ralph was killed?"

"Yeah, it was eight or ten months after that that Ralph was killed in front of his family. They stuck a gun down his mouth and pulled the trigger, but his daughter fought them like a lion."

"You said there were white people in the union also."[3]

"Yep. The Ku Klux was trying to get my father, he was Tommy Gray, one of the leaders, and he was at our house one night. He said he was goin' to head off walking to home, and I told him, 'It's too late in the evening. It's dangerous for you to walk. They after you too much.'

"He said, 'Oh, no, nobody's goin' to bother me,' and he left.

"When he got nearby his home, this big old car drove up with two strange white men inside. He thought about what I'd told him, but they ordered him, 'Get inside,' and he didn't have no choice.

"Then they said, 'We been looking for you all day. You're in danger. Put your head down, we taking you out of here.'

"He said, 'I got to tell my kids.' He didn't trust them.

"They said, 'We'll tell them.' My daddy didn't really know what was gonna happen; he thought maybe he was going to get lynched, but they kept driving all night and took him first to Tennessee, then up to New York. They was union people, and they helped him escape. He said he never had such a good time in his life. Everything he wanted to eat, they gave him, and everywhere he wanted to go, they took him."

I had read about a young woman named Eula Gray, a daughter of Tommy, and I asked Mr. Canada if he knew her. "Sure did," he said. "She was my half sister. She was secretary of the Share Croppers Union. So, anyway, when it was too dangerous for my daddy to run the union, Eula took over."

"She was young when she did it, wasn't she?" I asked.

"About eighteen or nineteen."[4] Canada continued: "Eula was one in a thousand. She stood her ground. From the time she was a little girl, she was strong. See, I was born out of wedlock, and so she was my half sister, but I was the oldest of all the kids, and she was the third. I was four months older than my younger half sister, and Eula was two years younger, and we played together.

"She was always into something. Our daddy raised peanuts. He'd have two or three or five bushels of peanuts, and he'd hang them up in a room, and Eula'd take her finger and run it around in the sack and get them so that the peanuts would sift through holes, and she could get them out. Anything Daddy put out—peanuts, peppermint candy—she'd get in and take some out. She wasn't mean, just mischievous. She loved to get into things. The only way to keep her out of a cookie jar was to hide it."

I told him that I had read "that women were really involved with the unions, that they had what they called 'sewing meetings,' where they'd organize and study."

"Yep, Eula organized the whole thing, the union. She was the head of it for a while, but womens had separate little meetings of their own. If it was too dangerous to leave literature around, they stuffed it into the stomachs of dolls they made at the sewing meetings where they would organize.

"The sheriff and them knowed about Eula, but they couldn't hurt her too bad. My brothers was too close by. The sheriff said they didn't want to have to kill them all. They knowed they'd bother one, they'd have to kill them. They didn't want to do that, but they was cruel. They was rough."

Mary and I spoke with many people, several of whom were over age ninety. Two of them still lived in Mary's home community—Mr. Canada and a woman who lived midway between Mr. Canada and Mary's childhood home. All knew about the Share Croppers Union. Except for the families directly involved, however, none of the eight rural people of Mary's age or younger whom we interviewed had heard of the events. We wondered why. I felt that Mary's generation of African Americans and the generations that followed had been robbed of role models. People in her community had risked their lives in the struggle of justice—a struggle so dangerous that they intentionally hid their actions and dared not share their knowledge with their children. That subsequent silence proved to be another loss.

Mary and I talked to other people about violence in this community. Mary herself recalled being haunted during her childhood by the shadow of Sheriff Lester Holley. She asked different African Americans about their experiences with him. An older black man named Willie Townsend, who was a retired deputy sheriff, told us, "Earl Varner's mother is still alive. You should talk to her," he said. "Supposedly, Holley killed Earl."

Townsend gave us directions to Mrs. Daisy Varner's house, and we drove through Wetumpka's African American neighborhood, down side streets lined with trees and broken sidewalks. Finally we came to a small, white frame house with a front porch. It was late evening, and insects hummed. A graceful wooden rocking chair and potted plants sat on the front porch. We knocked on the front and side doors, but no one answered. Mary looked in a window. Finally the side porch light turned on, and an old woman opened the screen door. She was large boned but not heavy; her face was broad and strong.

"Miss Varner, don't be frightened. My name is Mary Robinson, and this is Fran Buss. I grew up here, and Willie Townsend gave us your name. We've been trying to figure out some things that happened when I was a child, and we'd like to ask you about your son Earl."

"Come on in. I've been sick," she said and motioned us inside.

I looked around the room. A bust of a cement angel with delicate hair and wings was centered on a chest on the wall to the left, and photos of young people in military uniforms were arranged around the angel. Mary established connections with Mrs. Varner. Mary had been in Mrs. Varner's daughter's class in school; her dad's girlfriend lived a few blocks over.

"If you've been sick, we don't want to make you feel bad," Mary offered, "but we wondered if you could tell us what happened to Earl."

The old woman started to silently cry, spoke a few sentences, and then sniffed and wiped her hands across her face. She repeated this as long as we spoke. "He was my oldest boy, and he was so sweet. He kept saying, 'Mama, you work so hard. I'm gonna take care of you.' But the law enforcement people in Wetumpka was upset with Earl because he be dating a girl who was half white and looked white. Then Earl be coming home one evening from work in Montgomery, and he was stopped by Sheriff Holley. Holley accused him of drinking. Earl said he didn't have but one, and according to the story, Holley bashed him 'cross the head. He crushed my Earl's skull." Sheriff Holley then transported Earl to jail, charged him with resisting arrest, and gave him no medical care. Earl died in jail that night, and Mrs. Varner knew nothing about the arrest until someone came to inform her that Earl was dead.

As we spoke, the dark enveloped the rest of the world until it seemed only we existed—the still grieving mother, Mary, the cement angel, the circling moths, and me. When Mrs. Varner's other adult son came home, he confirmed the story. He was only fourteen when it happened, so he does not remember the details clearly, but after Earl's death civil rights groups attempted to prosecute Sheriff Holley, with limited results. Holley and his supporters continued in power.

In our search for information about African American resistance to discrimination in Elmore County, Mary and I heard another story. This one concerns an African American Vietnam casualty who had been refused burial in Wetumpka's main cemetery. We had asked around for more information without success. But by my last visit with Mary, she had found some additional information.

"That Vietnam veteran that had to be sent away for burial, well, his mom is one of my newfound cousins! She's all twisted up with rheumatoid arthritis and in a nursing home, but her mind is alert. Let's go see her."

We drove through the countryside to the nursing home. It was a pleasant structure with flowers, fountains, and rocking chairs outside, but the facility was smelly and cluttered inside. Mrs. Annie Mae Brodie, previously Annie Mae Williams, sat nearly alone in the dining room, struggling to feed herself. Her twisted body had deteriorated so rapidly that at first Mary did not recognize her. But when Mary introduced me and explained our mission, Mrs. Brodie's face responded with enthusiasm.

"We've been trying to find out information about your son Jimmy,"

Mary explained, "but we haven't gotten nowhere. Can you tell us where to look?"

The disease and the steroids given for it affected Mrs. Brodie's speech, and we listened carefully to the seventy-two-year-old woman. "He was killed on May 16 or 17, 1966," she whispered. "He was nineteen, with the Green Berets. He was killed by a grenade. The soldiers that was his friends told me how much he loved his hometown, so we wanted to bury him here."

She continued: "He was the first death in Wetumpka, but the city wouldn't bury him in their fancy white cemetery. They offered me a pauper's grave. I refused to go along with them, but it didn't work. My boy was unburied for over a week! We even brought in the Southern Christian Leadership Conference and organized a protest march in Wetumpka, but it didn't change their minds! Then the government said they'd bury him in Arlington National Cemetery or the National Cemetery in Anderson, Georgia. I chose Anderson, Georgia, 'cause it be closer."

Her voice cracked and broke with bitterness: "I signed for him to go into the service. He was underage, but I signed. And look what happened. And the *Wetumpka Herald,* not a word about his death, not a word about his sacrifice or the controversy." Mary reached out and held her hand and tried to help her with her food.

After we left Mrs. Brodie, I went to the Alabama Department of Archives and History and looked up newspaper coverage of the death and burial of Jimmy L. Williams. The May 19, 1966, "Veteran Corner" and "Men in Service" segment of the *Wetumpka Herald* contained nothing about Private Williams. The May 26, 1966, two-inch segment titled "Negro News" was likewise silent, even though the dispute was at its height. But a short United Press International (UPI) story in the *Birmingham World* from Wednesday, June 1, 1966, page 1, referred to the controversy: "[Demp] Thrash [the mayor] said he was getting calls 'from all over the U.S.' and charges that someone is trying to smear this town's name. 'We have never had any racial trouble. White and colored people live next door in harmony,' he said."[5]

Mary and I visited Mrs. Brodie once again before I left. Mary brought her a feast of home-cooked food, cleaned out Mrs. Brodie's little refrigerator, and straightened her room as we talked. Mrs. Brodie was not surprised, of course, by how little we had found in the newspapers about her son's burial arrangements. She told us that everything she had owned had been stolen, including the mementos she had cherished from her son, so I promised to send her any material I found.

Then we talked about other racial events that had occurred in Wetumpka over the years. Three of Mrs. Brodie's children had been among
those who integrated the Wetumpka schools in 1965. Most of the children suffered harassment, and white segregationists firebombed two
houses. She described attending the first integrated PTA meeting, when
she forced herself to sit in front. Mary and I bent close to Mrs. Brodie's
lips to listen to her disclose additional details of her life. She whispered
to us that she suffered more than that portrayed in Alice Walker's book
The Color Purple.

After I returned home to Tucson, Arizona, from that final research trip,
I found a column by Jack Anderson in the *Los Angeles Times* for May 27,
1966, "HOMECOMING FOR HERO: Color Line Drawn on Green
Beret's Coffin." It stated that funeral services for Jimmy L. Williams were
postponed because the city cemetery reported it had plots only for white
persons, and Williams was a Negro. It quoted Mrs. Brodie: "It really hurts
to not have him recognized as a first-class American citizen in death. . . .
In all his life in Wetumpka, the white people never recognized him as
one."[6] I sent the material to Jimmy's mother.

Later Mary was able to put me in touch with Debra Bracy, one of the
eighteen students who had integrated the high school in the summer of
1965.[7] In a letter to me Debra described the constant harassment the
black students faced in high school as they were called racist names,
pushed, and stung with slingshots made from rubber bands linked together and pulled back three to five feet. These stings left welts on the
black students' backs, necks, and arms. Finally Debra chased down one
of her attackers and retaliated by jabbing him in the shoulder with her
pencil.

She recalled: "I was whisked off to jail without anyone knowing where
I was. I was arrested for stabbing this student in the back. I stayed
overnight in jail without anyone in Wetumpka being eligible to get me
out. Not my parents, not any of the ministers or civic leaders, could get
the sheriff, Lester Holley at the time, to release me from jail." After her
release she was also suspended from school for the rest of the semester.

Debra described potentially more deadly violence: "This particular
New Year's Eve night, my sister and I attended the Emancipation Procla-
mation program held annually. We arrived back home from the program
after twelve that night. It was January 1, 1966, [and] the entire family
had turned in for sleep. . . . I noticed the dogs were barking, but I did not
get back up. I figured the dogs heard hunters. . . . [Then] I heard the

crashing of glass in the dining room, which was located in the middle of the house. Upon entering the dining room, which was one room away from where I was in bed, I discovered the window curtains in flames, burning rapidly. We are very thankful that three family members were not asleep at that time. It was a very close call getting everyone up and out by the time this block house burned to the ground. Believe me it burned very fast."

The family saw vehicles leaving, her father rushed to his truck to try to follow, and he discovered one of the "homemade firebombs" in the back of his truck. She continued: "It was still burning as he pitched it to the ground. It is felt that this firebomb was intended to go into the window on the front side of the house. It is a good thing it missed, because it would have gone right into my parents' bedroom and possibly shattered into their face. . . . These turn[s] of events caused total devastation for this family. We had no place to live."[8]

The Bracy family split up until her parents obtained a two-room shack, where they all moved in together. Eventually her parents purchased land and built a home for the family. No one was ever apprehended for the firebombing. Many people were afraid to associate with the Bracys. The family lost everything. Despite their suffering, Debra and her siblings listed their names on the March 30, 1968, NAACP Youth Program application for a charter.[9] Debra has worked giving legal assistance to low-income people during much of her adulthood.

Mary's story and the episodic history of resistance in her home community that she and I uncovered raise significant questions. The shoot-outs associated with the Share Croppers Union took place just a decade before Mary was born, within twenty or thirty miles of her parents' home, and seriously disrupted traditional racial patterns of African American submission. Why did she not know about these dramatic events? Why had they not entered the strong, local storytelling tradition? Why had the very existence of the Share Croppers Union been so efficiently and effectively purged from local memory?

Part of the answer, we believe, is that powerful forces tried to eliminate the union from local social knowledge. Although the silencing involved came primarily from the dominant white culture, it also came from African American parents. Many tried desperately to raise children who were self-assured enough to survive the constant attacks on their spirit yet suitably humble in the presence of whites, as the parents felt the times required. The lynching of fourteen-year-old Emmett Till in 1955 served as a horrific example of the consequences that might occur without such "training."[10] Throughout her experiences Mary has repeatedly said that in some ways God kept people safe. If the mistreatment that was considered normal in those days was inflicted on young African Americans today, Mary feels their response would be violent and would probably be met by violent repression. But back then parents did not dare to tell their children the whole truth about acts of resistance, because they feared children might inadvertently give dangerous information to whites.

In the Jim Crow South, as documented in Mary's story, whites desperately tried to create an illusion of black inferiority, a standard of fairness (defined by whites, of course), and racial harmony. They attempted to reinforce that illusion either by denying any event that indicated otherwise or by blaming it on outside agitation. The most obvious part of this attempt is the silencing of a written record. For example, when the three-hundred-man posse was closing in on the members of the Share Croppers Union taking shelter in a swamp, the sheriff forbade reporters and photographers from following and recording their violent actions. The town newspaper said nothing about the Vietnam veteran burial controversy. And, according to Debra Bracy, her hometown newspaper reported that the explosion at her family's home was the result of a gas tank (rather than a firebomb) and then claimed the community never had racial problems.[11]

Another efficient technique for silencing participants in such organizations as the Share Croppers Union was by labeling its supporters "Reds," or Communists under the control of Moscow. Although it is true that the sharecroppers wanted dramatic changes in land policy and some of the union's administrators from Birmingham were Communists, the African American sharecroppers came from vastly different perspectives than European and Asian Marxists. Most of the sharecroppers were part of an African American population that was profoundly religious and acted on perceptions based on their own lived experience. Attempts by outside party officials to influence them were thus frequently ignored.[12] Grady Canada just laughs when he hears charges of Communist control of the rank and file. Yet a call for drastic economic change and an attitude that conceived of sharecroppers as responsible historical agents spoke deeply to the sharecroppers' visions. These beliefs called forth a commitment so intense they were willing to die for it. The Communist charge was used again in the 1950s, during the struggle for integration of the schools, when the White Citizens Council argued that the actions were the result of Communist agitators.

Both the dominant white power structure and the African American resistance movement itself silenced black women's roles in these events. Over and over, the crusade was portrayed as a "struggle for manhood." This was articulated dramatically following the murder of Ralph Gray in 1931, when he became a symbol of martyred black manhood. The poet Ruby Weens portrayed Gray as representing "hosts of dark, strong men, The vast army of rebellion!"—a vision of resistance with little room for the female.[13]

Even when nineteen-year-old Eula Gray stepped up to direct the movement and enlarged its following after her uncle's death, district bureau member Harry Wicks stated that the sharecroppers "are holding meeting regularly without any direction from us, except what this *little girl* can impart to them."[14] He thus diminished her stature. Despite her achievements, the union replaced Eula Gray as soon as possible with a young man. Even her admiring brother, Grady Canada, furthered this notion when he declared that women in the Share Croppers Union had their own *little* meetings.[15]

Likewise, historian Robin Kelley has characterized some white women who undoubtedly risked their families and their community standing for the union as "*restless housewives*."[16] Also, because so much female resistance has been articulated as a crusade by mothers for the needs of their children, female leaders like Eula Gray are not often recognized for their simple human competency.[17] Similarly, with the Montgomery bus boycott in 1955, most of the actual, behind-the-scenes organizing was undertaken by women, but the male public leaders received the credit.[18]

People hear a wide range of subversive stories at different stages of their lives, and their responses derive from complex interactions, many determined by society's defined gender roles. Mary participated, but was not intensely involved, in the resistance of Alabama's African American community during the integration efforts of the mid-1960s. At that time she was earning a living and caring for four babies and struggling to control her abusive husband. A few years later, when her children were a little older and the resistance was directly tied to her work, Mary responded to the multiple oppressions of gender and race with great passion. Her participation at this time suggests to me that if a movement can gain initial momentum, people who have not appeared overtly political in the past may respond to it with deep hunger down the line.

Similarly, politically conscious people without the support of a larger group effort might eventually shut down. Mary worked for twenty years in the hope that the labor union movement would rise again, organizing school bus drivers by herself and repeatedly attempting to inspire her reluctant, frightened coworkers and to maintain regional contacts. Eventually, her enthusiasm died, however, and she turned her attention to other forms of helping people. But if similar passions flame again, I hope that other people like Mary would be ready to respond.

Finally, the control of knowledge by society's dominant powers is almost never total. Alternative versions of the past continue, and stories do circulate. Even though Mary's generation did not hear the stories of the Share Croppers Union in their youth, many of the children did know about a local lynching. Mary herself suspected that her father was a member of the NAACP. The author Theodore Rosengarten had heard rumors that a survivor of the Share Croppers Union still lived near Camp Hill. He ultimately made connections with Ned Cobb and recorded his story, publishing the account in 1974. Information about the book circulated; Mary knew such a book existed, although she did not know about the Share Croppers Union. When I came to Alabama looking for more details from Mary, she learned how to search public archives. She interviewed many of her surviving elders and collected their stories and then passed these stories on to me as well as to many others—her family, coworkers, and community. Thus a more modern version of storytelling continues today.

The dominant groups in control do make mistakes, however, and such mistakes can have ironic results. Even in the nearly totalitarian regime in which Mary grew to adulthood, someone left boxes of used clothes, books, and magazines along the side of the road for needy blacks. In one such box the teenage Mary found a copy of a romance novel set on a slave plantation. The story depicted the lives of slaves and even hinted at interracial sexual activity. Any writing about slavery, even highly distorted work like that novel, evoked a voracious curiosity in Mary. As she devoured the book, she became enraged by the racial caste system of the South. This finding sparked in Mary a great desire to learn more about slavery and uncover the "mysteries" of the historical African American experience.

Mary, as a young person, tried to conceive of an alternative world to that of her segregated community, a world she could describe as just, a world with meaning outside legal property. She looked around at both the kindnesses and cruelties that surrounded her; she listened to the visions articulated by the preachers she heard each Sunday. She saw a spirit world populated with Bible characters, the soul of the earth, and her developing image of a Christian god. She saw a world in which African American teachers, preachers, parents, and community people loved each other. She found strength in her vision of a compassionate creation.

The histories that Mary tells and investigates throughout this work suggest that those on the bottom of a spatial hierarchy enforced by deadly violence must often speak of their knowledge only through metaphor, as those on the top try to claim language itself. Yet the perspectives of the oppressed reveal the flaws in the networks the powerful rely on to enforce their will. When they tell their tales of resistance, they claim a space in what we perceive as truth itself. The sheriff will die, they avow, surrounded by those who know the reality of his circumstances, and one day that truth will be told and the crimes he has committed will be as obvious as the walls that crumble in his jail.

On one of my final days in Alabama, Mary and I drove back to Wetumpka and walked through the cemetery that had refused to bury Jimmy L. Williams. In newspaper stories Wetumpka's mayor at the time described the cemetery as a resting place for slaves on one side, whites in the middle, and blacks on the other side. But we never located the segment for slaves, and the small segment for blacks was down a short hill—invisible and segregated from the white cemetery and its monuments to Civil War heroes and landed families.

Mary and I walked among the tombstones, thinking about the past and the story we had put together about her life and her community. "The land, it belongs to God and the people that loves it," she declared. "Those people whose bodies be lying over there with the Confederates, what do they own now?" As we left the cemetery, Mary called me over to a grave, fenced somewhat separately by a black wrought-iron fence. A tree had twisted up and through a fence rail, so that it grew beyond. Now the tree was gone, but the remaining wood stayed intertwined.

"Look," Mary said. "It was like this tree just determined that it wasn't gonna let death take it away and it lived."

Notes

PREFACE

1. For more understanding of oral history as a shared construction, see Personal Narratives Group, editors, *Interpreting Women's Lives: Feminist Theory and Personal Narratives* (Bloomington: Indiana University Press, 1989), and Michael Frisch, editor, *A Shared Authority: Essays on the Craft and Meaning of Oral and Public History* (Albany: SUNY Press, 1990).

2. Anne McClintock, *Imperial Leather: Race, Gender, and Sexuality in the Colonial Context* (New York: Routledge, 1995), 317.

3. Toni Morrison, *Beloved* (New York: Penguin, 1987), 162.

4. Theophus H. Smith, professor of religion, *Conjuring Culture: Biblical Formations of Black America* (New York: Oxford University Press, 1994), 71, quotes James W. McClendon Jr., who talks about "biography as theology." McClendon says, "the focal point for the project is the exemplary character of persons (not only canonically recognized saints but also ordinary persons) whose lives embody and display the theology of their community of references" (James W. McClendon Jr., *Biography as Theology: How Life Stories Can Penetrate Today's Theology* [Nashville, Tenn.: Abingdon Press, 1974], 90). Mary's life suits such a purpose.

PROLOGUE

Epigraph: Bayley Wyat is quoted in Eric Foner, *Nothing but Freedom: Emancipation and Its Legacy* (Baton Rouge: Louisiana State University Press, 1983), 106.

INTRODUCTION

Epigraphs throughout the introduction are from the following sources: W. E. B. Du Bois, *The Souls of Black Folk* (1903), in *W. E. B. Du Bois: Writings* (New York: Library of America, 1986), 545, quoted in Elizabeth Hale, *Making Whiteness: The Culture of Segregation in the South, 1890–1940* (New York: Vintage Books, 1998), 13. Nate

Shaw [Ned Cobb], as quoted in *All God's Dangers: The Life of Nate Shaw,* edited by Theodore Rosengarten (New York: Knopf, 1974), 33. Alice Walker, *In Search of Our Mothers' Gardens* (San Diego, Calif.: Harcourt Brace Jovanovich, 1983), 233. Nate Shaw [Ned Cobb], as quoted in *All God's Dangers,* 303. Psalm 12:5; all Bible verses cited in this book are from the King James version, the translation from Mary's childhood. Governor James Folsom, Administrative File, Pardon and Parole Board, January–September 1955, 13852, Folder 13, Alabama Department of Archives and History, Montgomery; Governor James Folsom, Administrative File, Pardon and Parole Board, SG 13853. Fran Buss interviews with Mary Robinson, 1999. Fran Buss private collection, Tucson, Arizona.

1. See Geneva Smitherman's discussion of African American vernacular English in her *Talkin That Talk: Language, Culture, and Education in African America* (London: Routledge, 1999), especially 64–65.

2. I define *resistance* as the struggle against repressive social structures. That struggle might be experienced by an individual or a group, who might be either unaware or very conscious of the struggle. The civil rights movement itself, efforts undertaken by a mass population over many years, or an individual act undertaken by a parent to coerce a school to improve conditions for his or her child—I would label both as acts of resistance. Resistance can also include ideas or cultural creations such as songs or poetry. For a more complete discussion of these possibilities, see *Forged under the Sun / Forjada bajo el sol: The Life of Maria Elena Lucas,* compiled and with an introduction by Fran Leeper Buss (Ann Arbor: University of Michigan Press, 1993), 26–31.

3. Sojourner Truth, born about 1821, was a deeply religious ex-slave abolitionist and feminist. She believed that "the force that brought her from the soul murder of slavery into the authority of public advocacy was the power of the Holy Spirit" (from Nell Irvin Painter, *Sojourner Truth: A Life, a Symbol* [New York: W. W. Norton, 1996], 4). According to religion professor Charles Marsh, Fannie Lou Hamer, a sharecropper from Mississippi who became a leader of the Mississippi Freedom Democratic Party in 1964, combined "a liberating, reconciling faith, shaped by a skillful blending of African American hymnody and spirituality, prophetic religion, and an indefatigable belief in Jesus as friend and deliverer of the poor" (see Marsh, *God's Long Summer: Stories of Faith and Civil Rights* [Princeton, N.J.: Princeton University Press, 1997], 5).

4. For a description of this image as a metaphor of resistance, see Vincent Harding, *There Is a River: The Black Struggle for Freedom in America* (New York: Vintage Books, 1981), introduction, xi–xxvi.

5. See Kathryn Nasstrom, "Beginnings and Endings: Life Stories and the Periodization of the Civil Rights Movement," *Journal of American History* (September 1999): 700–711.

6. When I use the term *white* throughout this book, as, for example, in comparison to *African American,* I do so in a similar manner to that of the American studies professor Ruth Frankenberg in her work *White Women, Race Matters: The Social Construction of Whiteness* (Minneapolis: University of Minnesota Press, 1993). Frankenberg begins by stating that "both white people *and* people of color live racially structured lives. . . . any system of differentiation shapes those

on whom it bestows privilege as well as those it oppresses. White people are 'raced,' just as men are 'gendered.' To be white therefore is not to be 'racially neutral' but is to be part of a 'location of structural advantage, of race privilege'" (1).

7. Hale, in *Making Whiteness*, talks about segregation as an attempt to "erase the visibility of middle-class blacks" (21).

8. See Charles S. Aiken, *The Cotton Plantation South since the Civil War* (Baltimore, Md.: Johns Hopkins University Press, 1998), 134.

9. Ibid., 28.

10. Peggy Blackburn, "Wetumpka," *Historic Elmore County Magazine* (*The Wetumpka* [Alabama] *Herald*, 1996–97), 1.

11. Early work on reproductive labor in capitalism was done by Joan Kelly, "The Doubled Vision of Feminist Theory: A Postscript to the 'Women and Power' Conference," *Feminist Studies* 5 (spring 1979): 216–27, and Heidi Hartmann, "Capitalism, Patriarchy, and Job Segregation by Sex," in *Capitalist Patriarchy and the Case of Socialist Feminism*, edited by Zillah R. Eisenstein (New York: Monthly Review Press, 1979).

12. According to the *Arizona Daily Star*, December 2, 2001, A1 and A9: "The AP—in an investigation that included interviews with more than 1,000 people and the examination of tens of thousands of public records—documented 107 land-takings in 13 Southern and border states."

13. See Jacqueline Jones, *Labor of Love, Labor of Sorrow: Black Women, Work, and the Family, from Slavery to the Present* (New York: Vintage Books, 1985), 61, for a discussion of that compromise process.

14. Dolores E. Janiewski, *Sisterhood Denied: Race, Gender, and Class in a New South Community* (Philadelphia, Pa.: Temple University Press, 1985), 16.

15. See Karen Anderson, *Changing Woman: A History of Racial Ethnic Women in Modern America* (Oxford: Oxford University Press, 1996), 167, for a discussion of black women's roles in the extended family.

16. See Janiewski, *Sisterhood Denied*, 27–54. During the 1950s desperate Alabama women wrote Governor James E. Folsom for help with their family members who found themselves in prison. Several of these letters for mercy indicate that the legal infraction that landed a family member in prison was actually the result of an unfortunate step over a racial border, often made when the person was intoxicated. For example, one letter tells of a sixteen-year-old (apparently African American) boy who, after drinking alcohol, entered a skating rink that was off-limits to blacks and was then arrested and sent to an adult prison. His mother wrote to the governor: "I went to see him he is a nurvas reck. I fell of so much I am afraid he loose his mind. He said he be a good Boy if he get out. Seeing him looking so bad I is a nurvas rech him a yong boy just all most driving me crazy. . . . He hide takes spells all most kill him. Been that way for three year." (Governor Folsom, Administrative File, Request for Pardon, January–September 1955, 13852, Folder 13, Alabama Department of Archives and History, Montgomery). The childish innocence that led to the lynching of fourteen-year-old Emmett Till is attributed in many sources to his inadequate socialization; Till, a resident of Chicago, was visiting Mississippi and was thus unfamiliar with the

strict racial customs of the segregated Jim Crow South. For the complex issues involved here, see Stephen J. Whitfield, *A Death in the Delta: The Story of Emmett Till* (New York: Free Press, 1988), especially p. 40 and the final chapter.

17. Author interview with Cynthia Williams, May 28, 1980, Part 2, Tape 282B, 10–12 and 21, Fran Buss Oral History Collection, Schlesinger Library, Cambridge, Mass. See also Anderson, *Changing Woman*, 167.

18. Edgar T. Thompson, foreword to Jay R. Mandle, *The Roots of Black Poverty: The Southern Plantation Economy after the Civil War* (Durham, N.C.: Duke University Press, 1978), xiii.

19. Mandle, *Roots of Black Poverty*, 83.

20. According to the *Sixteenth Census of the United States, 1940: Volume 11, Characteristics of the Population* (Washington, D.C.: Government Printing Office, 1943), African Americans were slowly moving away from Elmore County. During the 1940 census 13,616 blacks lived in Elmore County, a decrease by 566 from those counted in the 1930 census. However, the number of whites in Elmore County increased over this period, from 20,081 in 1930 to 20,916 in 1940.

21. Daniel Kryder, *Divided Arsenal: Race and the American State during World War II* (Cambridge: Cambridge University Press, 2000), 2–3, 209.

22. Ibid., 210. Kryder states that "in some parts of the South where black migration threatened the labor supply, blacks were unable to purchase railroad tickets. To conceal their actual destination, migrants bought tickets to the next station on the road and then left the train and repeated the process until they escaped the state" (215).

23. Hale, *Making Whiteness*, states that after the Civil War "it was racial identity that became the paramount spatial mediation of modernity within the newly reunited nation. Not self-evidently more meaningful, not more real or natural than other markings, race nevertheless became the crucial means of ordering the newly enlarged meaning of America" (7).

24. Author interview with Cynthia Williams, May 28, 1980, Part 3, Tape 283A, 38, Fran Buss Oral History Collection, Schlesinger Library.

25. Whitfield, *Death in the Delta*, 109.

26. Aiken, *Cotton Plantation South*, 140.

27. Smith, in *Conjuring Culture*, 132–33, talks about the black North American tradition as represented by the work of W. E. B. Du Bois. This work uses the idea of "ritual ground" and "symbolic space" to narrate black experience. People talk about freedom "up north" or oppression "down south," about depictions of the South's "crimson soil," as bricks "red with the blood and dust of toil."

28. Jacquelyn Dowd Hall, "'The Mind That Burns Each Body': Women, Rape, and Racial Violence," in *Powers of Desire: The Politics of Sexuality*, edited by Ann Snitow, Christine Stansell, and Sharon Thompson (New York: Monthly Review Press, 1983), 329.

29. Howard Zinn, *A People's History of the United States* (New York: Harper and Row, 1980), 340–41, 203–4.

30. "How Did Black Women in the NAACP Promote the Dyer Anti-Lynching Bill, 1918–1923?" Internet documents selected and interpreted by Angelica Mungarro, under the supervision of Karen Anderson, May 2002, reviewed and edited by Marian Horan, Kathryn Kish Sklar, and Thomas Dublin at the Center

for Historical Study of Women and Gender, Department of History, State University of New York at Binghamton.

31. Hamer, as quoted in Marsh, *God's Long Summer,* 12.

32. Author interview with Annie Mae Brodie, formerly Annie Mae Williams, August 17 and 24, 2000, Fran Buss private collection. Debra Bracy letter to Fran Buss, September 10, 2000, Fran Buss private collection.

33. According to the author interviews with Annie Mae Brodie, Mrs. Daisy Varner, August 15, 2000, and the Debra Bracy letter.

34. Kathleen M. Blee, *Women of the Klan: Racism and Gender in the 1920s* (Berkeley: University of California Press, 1991), 176.

35. See Hall, "'Mind That Burns Each Body,'" 328–49.

36. See Jones, *Labor of Love, Labor of Sorrow,* 37–38.

37. Governor James E. Folsom, Administrative File, Pardon and Parole Board, SG 13436, Folder 5.

38. Hall, "'Mind That Burns Each Body,'" 332.

39. Annie Mae Meriwether, NAACP, Library of Congress, Part 11, C-348, Montgomery, 1927–36, 2.

40. "Josephine's Story," in *Dignity: Lower Income Women Tell of Their Lives and Struggles,* edited by Fran Buss (Ann Arbor: University of Michigan Press, 1985), 35.

41. See Evelyn Brooks Higginbotham, *Righteous Discontent: The Women's Movement in the Black Baptist Church, 1880–1920* (Cambridge, Mass.: Harvard University Press, 1993).

42. For more on the specifics of the economic arrangements for sharecroppers and tenant farmers, see Aiken, *Cotton Plantation South,* 29–35.

43. Ibid., 353.

44. Ibid., 350. Mimi Conway, *Rise Gonna Rise: A Portrait of Southern Textile Workers* (New York: Anchor Books, 1979), 12.

45. Sara Douglas, *Labor's New Unions and the Mass Media* (Norwood, N.J.: Ablex, 1986), 205.

46. For more on this racial, social, and class dynamic, see Aiken, *Cotton Plantation South.* He states: "In 1940, blacks accounted for only 2.1 percent of the employees in the United States textile mill industry and only 4.5 percent in 1960" (351).

47. An attempt to neutralize such empowerment is evidenced by a "Catechism for Slaves," from "Frederick Douglass' Paper," June 2, 1854, in *The Southern Episcopalian* (Charleston, S.C.), April 1854.

48. "Old Testament warrior" is from Lawrence W. Levine, *Black Culture and Black Consciousness: Afro-American Folk Thought from Slavery to Freedom* (Oxford: Oxford University Press, 1977), 43.

49. Ibid., 36, 39.

50. From Marsh, *God's Long Summer,* 47.

51. Levine, *Black Culture and Black Consciousness,* 158.

52. Ibid., 175.

53. Higginbotham, *Righteous Discontent,* 2.

54. Ibid., 131–32.

55. Ibid., 8.

56. Ibid., 3.

57. Hamer, as quoted in Marsh, *God's Long Summer,* 23.

58. Robin D. G. Kelley, *Hammer and Hoe: Alabama Communists During the Great Depression* (Chapel Hill and London: University of North Carolina Press, 1990), has traced this movement in Alabama starting in 1929. Mary and I found Alabama records from 1932. By 1939 the Southern Tenant Farmers Union included thirty-five thousand members. Other segments of this radical activist movement began in Arkansas in 1934 and spread to Alabama, Mississippi, Oklahoma, and Tennessee. For more on this movement, see Aiken, *Cotton Plantation South,* 126.

59. Nat Shaw [Ned Cobb], who spent twelve years in prison for his part in the Share Croppers Union, described his religion in this way: "Now to me, a Christian person is but a Christian person, I don't care who it is and I don't care what denomination. If he been newly generated and born by the holy spirit of God, which is the high power, who is the man that rules the heaven and earth, and what He don't rule, it don't exist—that's the mercy man of the world" (as quoted in Rosengarten, *All God's Dangers,* 454).

60. Jeannie M. Whayne, *A New Plantation South: Land, Labor, and Federal Favor in Twentieth-Century Arkansas* (Charlottesville: University of Virginia Press, 1996), 193.

61. Kelley, *Hammer and Hoe,* xi, quoting Joseph North, *No Men Are Strangers* (New York: International Publishers, 1958), xi.

62. Kelley, *Hammer and Hoe,* 39.

63. Ibid., 41–42. These confrontations occurred nearly simultaneously with the arrest in northern Alabama on March 25, 1931, of the so-called Scottsboro Boys, the nine black young men charged with an alleged rape of two young white women. An all-white jury sentenced eight of the young men to death, and the case was argued internationally in a racially charged atmosphere. The international Communist movement, among other groups, ultimately came to their defense. See James A. Miller, Susan D. Pennybacker, and Eve Rosenhaft, "Mother Ada Write and the International Campaign to Free the Scottsboro Boys, 1931–1934," *American Historical Review* 106, no. 2 (April 2001): 387–430.

64. NAACP, Library of Congress, Part 11, C-348, Montgomery, 1927–36.

65. This date and place are found in Kelley, *Hammer and Hoe,* 165–66.

66. Author interview with Grady Canada, September 22, 2000, Fran Buss private collection.

67. Paula Giddings, *When and Where I Enter: The Impact of Black Women on Race and Sex in America* (New York: Bantam Books, 1984), gives vivid details of the risks involved with Rosa Parks's decision, the workings of the Women's Political Council, and the fears about getting involved and the hesitations by the ministers, including Dr. Martin Luther King. See also Stewart Burns, editor, *Daybreak of Freedom: The Montgomery Bus Boycott* (Chapel Hill: University of North Carolina Press, 1997), 11.

68. Burns, *Daybreak of Freedom,* 11.

69. It was in this county that Viola Liuzzo, a white civil rights worker from Detroit, was killed during the march from Selma in 1963. Churches were being

burned during the voter registration drive, and the KKK threatened those like McGowen who worked on the drive. Finally, what became known as the Black Panthers was formed in Lowndes County in 1966. For a detailed account of these events, see Aiken, *Cotton Plantation South*, 220.

70. See the account of that mass meeting in Burns, *Daybreak of Freedom*, 10.

71. Author interview with Catherine McGowen, June 1993, Fran Buss private collection.

72. Burns, *Daybreak of Freedom*, 11.

73. Smith, *Conjuring Culture*, 90.

74. King, as quoted in ibid., 24–25; italics mine.

75. Ibid.

76. For more on this point see Sara Evans, *Personal Politics: The Roots of Women's Liberation in the Civil Rights Movement and the New Left* (New York: Vintage Books, 1979).

77. Baker is quoted in Giddings, *When and Where I Enter*, 284.

78. See Nancy Maclean, *Freedom Is Not Enough: The Opening of the American Workplace* (Cambridge, Mass.: Harvard University Press, 2006).

79. Douglas, *Labor's New Unions*, 206.

80. Aiken, *Cotton Plantation South*, 352.

81. *Wetumpka Herald*, January 2, 1964, 8.

82. "Stevens vs. Justice," reprinted from "Here Come a Wind . . . Labor on the Move," *Southern Exposure* (summer 1976), various issues, Box 230, Chapel Hill, N.C., 27514, Georgia State University Special Collections, Southern Labor Archives Pamphlet Collection, Box 32.

83. Douglas, *Labor's New Unions*, 204.

84. "Further Harm Is Done," a Report of J. P. Stevens and Company from Stevens Workers and the Amalgamated Clothing and Textile Workers Union, Georgia State University Special Collections, J. P. Stevens Folder, Box 32.

85. See Elisabeth Schüssler Fiorenza, *The Book of Revelation: Justice and Judgment*, 2d edition (Minneapolis, Minn.: Fortress Press, 1998), 1. She reports that the Babylon/Rome that is presented as the oppressor in Revelation is interpreted to be Western imperialism by Base Christian Communities in the contemporary third world (see p. 233). These are activist Christian groups based on the ideas of liberation theology, a form of theology that emphasizes social and political liberation as the anticipation of ultimate salvation.

86. Ibid., 8.

87. Smith, in *Conjuring Culture*, states: "A troubling aspect of Christian apocalyptic tradition in general can also be found in black American apocalyptics. In each case one finds a theological irony: the irony of a religion that espouses forgiveness and reconciliation on the one hand, and yet harbors a vigorous hope for divine wrath and retribution on the other" (223).

CHAPTER 1

Epigraph: James Baldwin, "Sonny's Blues," quoted in Gerald Early, *Tuxedo Junction: Essays in American Culture* (New York: Ecco Press, 1989), 307, quoted in Hale, *Making Whiteness*, 13.

CHAPTER 2

Epigraph: Alice Walker, *The Color Purple* (New York: Pocket Books, 1982), 3.

CHAPTER 3

Epigraph: Nat Shaw [Ned Cobb], quoted in *All God's Dangers,* 27.

CHAPTER 4

Epigraph: Nat Shaw [Ned Cobb], quoted in *All God's Dangers,* 9.

CHAPTER 6

Epigraph: Lillian Smith, *The Winner Names the Age,* edited by Michelle Cliff (New York: W. W. Norton, 1978), quoted in Minnie Bruce Pratt, *Rebellion: Essays 1980–1991* (Ithaca, N.Y.: Firebrand Books, 1991), 25.

CHAPTER 7

Epigraph: Fran L. Buss, 1988.

CHAPTER 8

Epigraph: Alice Walker, *In Search of Our Mothers' Gardens: Womanist Prose* (New York: Harcourt Brace Jovanovich, 1983), 143.

CHAPTER 9

Epigraph: Zora Neale Huston, *Their Eyes Were Watching God* (1937; reprint, Urbana: University of Illinois Press, 1978), quoted in Anderson, *Changing Woman,* 174.

CHAPTER 10

Epigraph: Bernice Johnson Reagon, "African-American Women: A Continuing Tradition in American Radicalism," paper presented at the Berkshire Conference on the History of Women, Douglass College, June 8, 1990, quoted in Anderson, *Changing Woman,* 211.

CHAPTER 12

Epigraph: Lillian Smith, "Buying a New World with Old Confederate Bills," *South Today* 7 (winter 1942–43): 11, quoted in Hale, *Making Whiteness,* 241.

CHAPTER 14

Epigraph: Thomas Malone, quoted in two-page pamphlet, "There's a Hole in

Willie Brice's Christmas Stocking," Georgia State Archive, Special Collections, Southern Labor Archives, Box 32, J. P. Stevens, 2.

1. On May 3, 1886, police fired into a crowd of strikers in Chicago, killing four. Workers demonstrated the next day. A bomb exploded at the demonstration, killing seven policemen, but there was no evidence about who planted the bomb. Four organizers were hanged as punishment, resulting in protests around the world. For more details from the perspective of the workers, see Howard Zinn, *A People's History of the United States: 1492–Present* (New York: HarperPerennial, 1980), 271–72.

CHAPTER 15

Epigraph: Toni Morrison, *The Bluest Eye* (New York: Pocket Books, 1970), 9.

EPILOGUE

Epigraph: Henry David Thoreau, *Journal,* August 30, 1856, quoted at the beginning of Simon Schama, *Landscape and Memory* (New York: Vintage Books, 1995).

1. Even the *Wetumpka Herald,* which rarely discussed African American news, stated, "One Negro Known to Have Been Killed and Score or More Wounded: Sheriff Golden Answers Call for Help As Well As Sheriffs in Other Counties," December 22, 1932, 36130–0100, Alabama Department of Archives and History, Montgomery.

2. Phone interview with Grady Canada, August 11, 2000, tape recording, Fran Buss private collection.

3. Robin Kelley has written that "once in a while sympathetic poor white tenant farmers, especially women, attended SCU meetings . . . , but racial divisions in the black belt were drawn so sharply that black organizers felt it was too dangerous to even discuss the union with whites." Whites could pay a heavy price. "In 1934, white Tallapoosa tenant farmer J. W. Davis was kidnapped and lynched by vigilantes because of his support for the SCU." Poor whites also showed support by leaving food and supplies for the sharecroppers. See Kelley, *Hammer and Hoe,* 47–48.

4. According to Kelley, when Eula Gray was replaced by a man because of her gender, "the SCU in Tallaapoosa County had grown to 591 members organized in twenty-eight locals, ten youth groups, and twelve women's auxiliaries" (*Hammer and Hoe,* 44).

5. The *Montgomery Advertiser* for Friday, May 27, 1966, had a much shorter article on p. 2, stating, "War Victim's Burial Set in U.S. Plot." It stated that "when the family discovered the family operated cemetery was full, Mayor Demp Thrash offered the family another lot but they did not like the location and turned the mayor's offer down."

6. Jack Anderson, "Homecoming for Hero: Color Line Drawn on Green Beret's Coffin," *Los Angeles Times,* May 27, 1966, part 1, p. 5.

7. Debra Bracy's older sister Sophia was also among those who integrated the high school. The two girls were the oldest in a family of eight children who lived on a farm in an area called Redland in the southern tip of Elmore County.

8. Letter from Debra Bracy to Fran Buss, October 13, 2000, Fran Buss private collection.

9. NAACP activities had been banned for the entire state of Alabama from June 1, 1956, until 1964, eight years later. Taylor Branch, *Parting the Waters: America in the King Years, 1954–63* (New York: Simon and Schuster, 1988), 186–87.

10. Fourteen-year-old Emmett Till was visiting in Mississippi from Chicago; he did not follow the local customs and bragged about a white girl as "his girl." He was subsequently murdered by three white men who ultimately escaped punishment. Juan Williams, *Eyes on the Prize: America's Civil Rights Years, 1954–1965* (New York: Penguin Books, 1987), 39–57.

11. Letter from Debra Bracy to Fran Buss, October 13, 2000, Fran Buss private collection.

12. For example, in May 1932 twenty-five-year-old Al Murphy was appointed Share Croppers Union secretary. He stopped calling on local blacks to "demonstrate in front of landlords' homes [and demand] that the food advances be continued until the crop is taken in." Quoted in Kelley, *Hammer and Hoe*, 44. Kelley also states that local blacks "had never taken these suicidal directives seriously."

13. Ruby Weens, as quoted in Kelley, *Hammer and Hoe*, 46.

14. Ibid., 44.

15. Telephone interview with Grady Canada, September 15, 2000, Fran Buss private collection.

16. Kelley, *Hammer and Hoe*, xi; italics mine.

17. Ibid., 47.

18. Giddings, *When and Where I Enter*, 284.